CRITICAL CONCERNS
IN MORAL THEOLOGY

Other Books by Charles E. Curran

American Catholic Social Ethics:
  Twentieth Century Approaches
Christian Morality Today
Contemporary Problems in Moral Theology
Catholic Moral Theology in Dialogue
The Crisis in Priestly Ministry
Politics: Medicine and Christian Ethics:
  A Dialogue with Paul Ramsey
New Perspectives in Moral Theology
Ongoing Revision in Moral Theology
Themes in Fundamental Moral Theology
Issues in Sexual and Medical Ethics
Transition and Tradition in Moral Theology
Moral Theology: A Continuing Journey
Dissent in and for the Church (Charles E. Curran *et al.*)
The Responsibility of Dissent: The Church and
  Academic Freedom (John F. Hunt and Terrence R.
  Connelly with Charles E. Curran *et al.*)
Absolutes in Moral Theology? (editor)
Contraception: Authority and Dissent (editor)

Critical Concerns
in Moral Theology

CHARLES E. CURRAN

UNIVERSITY OF NOTRE DAME PRESS
NOTRE DAME, IN

Library of Congress Cataloging in Publication Data

Curran, Charles E.
  Critical concerns in moral theology.

  Includes index.
  1. Christian ethics — Catholic authors — Addresses,
essays, lectures.   2. Social ethics — Addresses, essays,
lectures.   3. Pastoral theology — Catholic Church —
Addresses, essays, lectures.   4. Catholic Church —
Doctrines — Addresses, essays, lectures.   I. Title.
BJ1249.C814   1984   241'.042   83-40593
ISBN 0-268-00747-0

To those friends
Some going back more than thirty years
Who gather each summer "in the woods"
To relax and share

Contents

PART FOUR: PASTORAL PRACTICE

Acknowledgments

It is always a pleasant task to thank those who have helped me in my research and writing. Cindi Vian typed the greater part of the manuscript. Daphne Burt-Schantz also helped with the typing. I am also grateful to John T. Ford, C.S.C., who has served six years as chair of the Department of Theology at The Catholic University of America, and to Johann Klodzen, the administrative assistant of our department. The library staff of Mullen Library at The Catholic University of America have continued to be most helpful — Bruce Miller, David Gilson, Alan Flood, F.S.C., and Mary Liu, as well as Carolyn Lee. John Ehmann, my gently prodding editor at the University of Notre Dame Press, has assisted me in many ways. Mark O'Keefe, O.S.B., prepared the index.

I gratefully acknowledge the permission of the following publishers and periodicals to republish materials which first appeared in their publications: *Studia Moralia*, for "An Evaluation of Häring's *Free and Faithful in Christ*; *Horizons*, for "An Evaluation of Recent Works in Fundamental Moral Theology"; The Thomas More Press, for "Moral Theology and Homosexuality,' which originally appeared in *Homosexuality and the Catholic Church*, ed. Jeannine Gramick; Lexington Books and D. C. Heath and Company, for "Biomedical Science, Morality, and the Human Future," which originally appeared in *Science and Morality: New Directions in Bioethics*, ed. Doris Teichler-Zallen and Colleen D. Clements; *Le Supplément*, for "An Analysis of the American Bishops' Pastoral Letter on Peace and War"; *Journal of*

Religious Ethics, for "Roman Catholic Teaching on Peace and War in a Broader Theological Context"; *Linacre Quarterly,* for "Theory and Practice; Faith and Reason: A Case Study of John R. Cavanagh"; *Clergy Review* for "The Pastoral Minister, the Moral Demands of Discipleship, and the Conscience of the Believer."

Introduction

The articles presented here have been written for different occasions and purposes over the past few years. No attempt has been made to give an artificial unity to these collected essays as they appear in this volume. However, the articles themselves do reflect the critical concerns in contemporary moral theology. With this in mind, the essays have been grouped together under the following critical concerns — fundamental moral theology, sexual and biomedical ethics, social ethics, and pastoral practice.

An important critical concern in moral theology today is the area of fundamental moral theology. The changes that have occurred in moral theology in the last twenty-five years have been enormous. Prior to the Second Vatican Council, manuals of moral theology were the standard textbooks not only in Catholic seminaries but also in colleges. The *aggiornamento* in Catholic life and theology in general has had great repercussions in the area of moral theology. The aim of the older manuals was to train confessors as judges for the sacrament of penance; today the aim of moral theology is life-centered. The manuals relied on a Neo-Scholastic philosophical underpinning, whereas today a pluralism of philosophies undergirds the various approaches to moral theology. Scripture and theological themes have become more integrated into many contemporary approaches to moral theology, while other emphases have also emerged. So great have the changes been that only recently have there been attempts to publish what might be called contemporary manuals or textbooks in moral theology. The first two chapters attempt to evaluate some of the significant new approaches to systematic fundamental moral theology developed by Bernard Häring, Timothy O'Connell, Daniel Maguire, Enda McDonagh, and Franz Böckle.

A second critical concern for moral theology involves the area of sexual and medical ethics. There can be no doubt that sexual ethics has furnished the primary area of tension and disagreement in Catholic life and theology in the last two decades. Precisely in this area a tension exists at times between official church teaching and the experience of a good number of people. Some moral theologians in response to this tension and to other changes affecting the discipline have re-evaluated and criticized the methodology involved in the approach to sexual morality of the former manuals. The area of sexual ethics is always going to be very volatile, but questions in sexual ethics today also involve fundamental issues in methodology as well as the proper response that Catholics owe to official church teaching. In the light of all these realities, sexual ethics will continue to be a critical concern in the immediate future of moral theology Chapter three will discuss and evaluate different contemporary approaches to the issue of homosexuality.

In addition to sexual ethics Catholic moral theology has traditionally been interested in medical ethics. Some of the original motivation for involvement in medical ethics came from its relationship to sexual ethics. Questions involving marriage, sterility, and impotency as well as human reproduction are intimately connected with sexual ethics. Interestingly enough, until two decades ago Roman Catholics were practically the only ethicists interested in and writing about medical ethics. The increased interest in medical ethics in the last few years has been brought about by the advances that have occurred in biomedical science and technology. Today we have much more power over health, and even over human life and death, than we have ever had before. The important moral question facing the entire society today is how we are going to use that power. Chapter four addresses the moral directions that we should take with regard to the developing biomedical and genetic technologies that exist now and will become even more sophisticated in the near future.

A third concern in moral theology is the area of social ethics. To its great credit Catholic moral theology and official Catholic teaching have always been interested in the area of social ethics and social morality. However, there have been important recent developments which have given even greater importance to this area. Contemporary theology and hierarchical church teaching have tried to see social morality more intimately connected with faith itself. The Second Vatican Council lamented the dichotomy that exists between faith and daily life. The International Synod of Bishops in 1971 emphasized that action on behalf of justice and the transformation of the world is a constitutive dimension of the gospel and of the mission of the church. In general significant contributions to social ethics have emerged in some parts of the world — especially the liberation theologies developed in South America and in other third-world countries.

Today also more interest in social ethics exists on the American scene itself. Without a doubt the most significant development has been the pastoral letter of the American bishops on peace and war issued in May 1983. Chapter five gives an analysis of the document itself, while the following chapter tries to relate the Catholic teaching on peace and war to the broader theological context — ethical methodology, eschatology, and ecclesiology. Chapter seven also considers a peculiarly American phenomenon — the community organization approach used by Saul D. Alinsky. Such an approach no doubt marks the most innovative development in Catholic social action in the last few decades. Unfortunately, Catholic social ethics has failed to reflect on this practice. Obviously Alinsky's approach is not the total solution to social action and social justice, but it has been a significant reality on the American scene and deserves critical theological reflection.

A fourth critical concern is pastoral practice. Catholic

moral theology has always been intimately connected with pastoral practice. Moral theology exists primarily in and for the church and serves the life of the community of believers. This close relationship to pastoral practice and the life of the community is a very significant characteristic of religious ethics and distinguishes such ethics from other philosophical approaches.

The entire history of moral theology has been very much influenced by pastoral practice. The manuals of moral theology came into existence in the seventeenth century as a means of preparing confessors for the sacrament of penance. St. Alphonsus, the patron of moral theology, admitted that under actual pastoral experience his theoretical outlook retreated from a rigoristic approach to moral theology. In the light of the very direct and significant relationship of moral theology to pastoral practice, the practical aspect of moral theology has at times too much predominated at the expense of the speculative and the theoretical. However, on the other side of the coin, such a relationship has always influenced moral theology to deal primarily with the real problems of real people and not with artificial problems which appeal primarily to academics.

Recent developments in moral theology have intensified its relationship with pastoral practice. More emphasis has been given to the experience of the life of the community. Theology reflects on this experience in the light of the Scriptures and of the whole Christian tradition. Praxis has become central in a number of contemporary theological approaches with a corresponding importance given to the reality of orthopraxis for the life of the believing community.

Some of the topics treated in other sections show the importance of pastoral practice. The discussion of Alinsky's approach to community organization well illustrates the method of theology reflecting on the life and experience of the community. The tensions existing in sexual ethics in the Catholic community arise from some apparent differences between official teaching and the experience of a significant part of the community on particular issues. Chapter eight involves a case study of how John R. Cavanagh as a believer and a psychiatrist dealt with the tension existing between practice and theory in the life of the church. The final chapter proposes two approaches which can help the contemporary pastoral minister in dealing with the tensions that arise between official church teaching on moral questions and the experience and conscience of the believer.

Contemporary moral theology is experiencing changes in two very significant areas. On the level of content or substantive issues new questions arise in the light of such contemporary developments as nuclear weapons or biomedical technologies. In addition there is also dissatisfaction with past approaches to traditional areas, especially that of sexuality. On the level of methodology and of the theological and philosophical underpinnings of moral theology, we are faced with a pluralism of approaches vying for acceptance rather than the monolithic methodology of the era of the manuals of moral theology. In the midst of these continuing changes and tensions this book addresses four areas of critical concern in contemporary moral theology.

PART ONE

Fundamental Moral Theology

1: An Evaluation of Häring's
Free and Faithful in Christ

In 1954 Bernard Häring published *Das Gesetz Christi*, a 1446-page moral theology textbook for priests and laity.[1] For many Häring's work stands as the most creative and important accomplishment in moral theology in this century, the most original and significant contribution in the recent history of the discipline of moral theology. Perhaps a greater historical perspective is needed to sustain the latter judgment, but all can agree that no book of moral theology has been translated into more languages and used by more people than Häring's *Law of Christ*.[2]

Since 1954 Häring has written more and lectured more extensively than any other Catholic moral theologian. The festschrift published in honor of his sixty-fifth birthday in 1977 lists sixty-seven separately published volumes but makes no attempt to mention his many articles.[3] In 1981 Häring published the third and final volume of *Free and Faithful in Christ: Moral Theology for Clergy and Laity*.[4] This new three-volume moral theology is not merely an update or a revision of *The Law of Christ*; it stands rather as the culmination of Häring's work in moral theology.

The discipline of moral theology and its practitioners owe much to Bernard Häring. As dialogue and responsibility are two important characteristics of Häring's moral theology, so other moral theologians are invited by Häring's own methods to enter into critical dialogue with him. This chapter will attempt such a critical dialogue and evaluation of Häring's new treatise.

The first section will indicate the general approach taken

3

by Häring and point out its strong and positive features. The second section will raise questions about possible deficiencies and weaknesses. The third will consider some important aspects in Häring's approach to moral theology, while a fourth will then briefly consider certain content areas treated by Häring.

I. Overall Approach

The cornerstone of Häring's moral theology is the recognition that for the Christian, religion and morality are intimately connected. Beginning with his doctoral dissertation, *Das Heilige und das Gute*, Häring has insisted that ethics for the Christian is a religious ethics.[5] Our moral lives and our religious lives are intrinsically and intimately connected. Religion for the Christian involves the response to the free gift of God manifest especially in Jesus (I, 62-67). Such an understanding stresses the responsorial, dialogical structure of the Christian moral life and is opposed to an ethics of self-perfection or an ethics of duty. God, Christ, and faith do not merely supply the grace which enables Christians to live out a morality based on natural law. The gift of grace itself obliges us to respond.

Häring does not propose to develop a rigid system based on a single concept, for the Christian moral life is centered on discipleship in Christ Jesus and not on an abstract concept or idea. However, he proposes a leitmotif and key concepts for moral theology. Responsibility as an expression of creative freedom and fidelity is the leitmotif of his moral theology. Häring claims that the choice of a leitmotif can be made only after carefully studying the biblical pattern and after discerning the special signs of God's present action in history (I, 59).

In an earlier section on biblical perspectives (I, 7-27) our author explains the biblical material in such a way that the leitmotif of responsibility is clearly highlighted. The Bible, especially the Old Testament, presents God in the context of his creative word and call to fellowship. Throughout this brief treatment the concept of God's call is emphasized. Häring discusses the New Testament perspectives from a Christological basis beginning with Christ as the new covenant and including Christ as prophet, as eternal Word, as God with us, and as the one who calls us to discipleship.

Häring's moral theology is Christocentric. Christ is the unifying symbol and the reality of the Christian moral life of responsibility and the expression of creative freedom and fidelity. The Redemptorist agrees with Dietrich Bonhoeffer that the point of departure for Christian ethics is not the self or standards of value but the reality of God as he has revealed himself in Jesus Christ. Häring proposes a Christology from above, or a descending Christology, as the basis for moral theology. Christ is revealed as the Word incarnate through whom the Father speaks his love. Jesus is both the Word who calls and the one who is called and sent. Jesus of Nazareth is anointed by the power of the Holy Spirit for his twofold response to the Father who has sent him and to those to whom he is sent. Christ thus is the most striking symbol of the call of God and of the human response. We too are called in Christ and respond in and through Christ and his Spirit (I, 60-62).

We are in the words of the title of chapter four "Created and Recreated by Freedom and for Freedom in Christ." Creation is an event of freedom and for freedom. It is God's solemn, joyous, and free decision to share with creation, in and through the Word, his own love and freedom. Christ is the Word of freedom par excellence, for he is the free gift of the Father for self-giving love even unto death on a cross. As a free gift of the Father, he is free to give himself to us, a creative freedom which is manifested in his total availability to sinners, the poor, the oppressed, and the marginal. Christ has freed humanity from a multifaceted bondage in sin and has called humanity to the freedom of covenant liberty and service of others (I, 104-163).

Christ is the symbol reminding us that a Christian ethics of responsibility entails as much creative fidelity as creative

freedom. Häring opposes an existentialism which is characterized by arbitrariness, discontinuity, and individualism.
In particular our author frequently objects to the ethics of
Joseph Fletcher precisely because of its one-sided emphasis
on an individualistic freedom (I, 42, 83, 341, 349, 358, 364).
Christ is the faithful one. Commitment to him requires commitment to the covenant and to the goal commandments,
especially that of love.

Throughout his work Häring is true to his Christocentric
perspective. The basis of the distinctively Christian anthropology is Christology (I, 120). Christology and anthropology cannot be separated, for only in Christ do we
know the full truth about humanity (II, 14). His detailed
discussions of economic life (III, 244ff), political life (III,
327ff), and peace (III, 391ff) all begin with Christological
considerations. The important discussion of truth which is
the synthesizing theme of volume two begins with Christ
himself, the saving truth (II, 7ff).

The German Redemptorist thus employs the symbol of
Christ to flesh out the meaning of responsibility as the expression of creative freedom and fidelity. The development
of his leitmotif clearly involves a commitment to salvation
truth and does not give primacy to abstract philosophy (I,
85). In developing his ethics of responsibility Häring rightly
recognizes the many dimensions and aspects of the moral
life — personal, communal, social, historical, and cosmic.
Häring's personalism is evident in practically every page of
the three volumes. One expects that a heavy emphasis on
freedom and responsibility would necessarily stress the personalistic understanding of morality. The person is the very
basis of his moral theology with its emphasis on fundamental
option, basic attitudes and dispositions of the person,
character, and conscience. For Häring moral theology is not
primarily a study of acts, for acts are ultimately rooted in the
person (I, 85-96). Häring's personalism colors his entire
approach.

Unlike some who stress personalism, Häring is very
aware of the dangers of a narrow personalism which sees

things only in terms of I-Thou relationships. Christ's fidelity to the mission entrusted to him by his Father creates a community of disciples. We commit ourselves to be disciples of Jesus who was "the man for others" (I, 76-82). The communal solidarity and social dimension of morality are not forgotten. The responsible and creative Christian lives in solidarity with all other human beings because of the covenant commitment. Also, a distinctively Christian ethic of responsibility never forgets that historicity is an essential dimension of human existence (I, 90-101).

The commitment of the Christian to the world is well exemplified in volume three with its subtitle *Light to the World: Salt for the Earth*. The Christian sees the world in total interdependence with human history—a world to be shaped and transformed, not just to be contemplated. Häring, as would be expected, includes chapters on social, economic, and political ethics. *Free and Faithful in Christ* criticizes an individualism which has too often characterized the Christian approach (III, 249, 333). Our author denies that Jesus' mission was nonpolitical, spiritual, and eschatological. On the other hand, he warns against a false reductionism that would equate the mission of Jesus and of the church merely with the political order. He asks if Dorothy Sölle does not make prayer primarily a political activity. The political is an all-pervasive aspect of human existence, but not the only dimension of the Christian life. One can neither deny nor absolutize the political (III, 326-351). In addition, Häring includes the cosmic dimension of morality and devotes an entire chapter to ecology. The present ecological crisis calls Christians to a conversion and renewal in regard to the attitude toward the environment (III, 167-208).

Häring's moral theology puts heavy stress on the personal without forgetting the other dimensions of morality. Freedom, fidelity, and responsibility all point to the very heart of the human person. The basic response of the person is understood in the light of the theory of the fundamental option. This fundamental option coming from the heart of the human person involves the basic freedom of the individual.

Contemporary psychology, especially the work of Erikson, Maslow, and Frankl, contribute much to our understanding of the fundamental option. The development of the fundamental option and its continuing deepening in the human person depend upon continuing conversion. More than any other contemporary moral theologian, Häring has insisted on the centrality and importance of continuing conversion in the life of the Christian.[6]

The fundamental option is embodied in the basic attitudes or virtues which characterize the Christian person. Häring refers especially to the eschatological virtues and gives special attention to gratitude, humility, hope, vigilance, serenity, and joy (I, 201-208). One can readily see how the emphasis on these embodiments of fundamental option stems from the basic dialogical character of the Christian life. The Christian perceives all of life as God's gracious gift; hence Christians are a eucharistic people who give gratitude and thanks for the gracious gift received in and through Christ and the church. The importance of gratitude, adoration, and worship permeate all of Häring's work. We are primarily worshipers in spirit and truth and ever grateful for the gifts of divine life and love. In fact, the first volume of *Free and Faithful* ends with a chapter entitled simply "Synthesis" which develops the point that adoration is not just something added to the moral life, but rather it is the heart and source of that life (I, 471-485). Christ has revealed himself as the perfect adorer in spirit and truth and calls us to that same spirit of adoration. With Christ and the church we glorify God by integrating worship and witness of living faith, hope, and love. Within such a perspective the sacraments are privileged signs of adoration. The priority of the sacred and of adoration does not deny the importance of our moral commitment to others and to the world, but rather religious conversion engenders moral conversion. Emphasis on the human person as adorer also comes to the fore in the second and third volumes when Häring attacks manipulation and technological approaches which fail to understand an anthropology which sees the human person as more than a maker or a doer (II, 136, 145, 165, 180-187, 256; III, 190-197, 235).

Intimately connected with the eschatological virtues of gratitude and adoration is the virtue of vigilance. Since the Christian moral life is not one of self-perfection but of response to the gift of God, the Christian must always be vigilant to the call of God in the historical reality as mediated through the signs of the times. Just as gratitude gratefully recalls the past and vigilance keeps one alert to the present, hope opens horizons to the future. Hope makes one eager for growth and ongoing conversion. However, in all of this we Christians also know and experience the dispositions of serenity and joy which come from the fact that the joy of the Lord is our strength (I, 201-208).

All Christians are called to holiness. The gospel call to perfect discipleship cannot be reduced to a mere counsel for a few. Häring's dynamic personalism results from his emphasis on continual conversion, growth in the moral life, and a call to deepen the fundamental option as well as the eschatological virtues which characterize Christian existence. The goal-commandments or normative patterns (*Zielgebot*) play an important part in our author's insistence on growth and development in the Christian life. An older moral theology stressed commands and laws that were static and prohibitive and accepted a split between a static moral theology and a lofty ascetical and mystical theology. The goal-commandments are found in the gospel vision with its emphasis on love, justice, peace, and reconciliation and are illustrated in the beatitudes. These constitute the normative ideal for all Christians. In the light of the goal-commandments the Christian can never be satisfied with the status quo. These goal-commandments are an essential part of the Christian life as a normative ideal and cannot be dismissed merely as counsels or *parenesis* (I, 249-253).

Instead of making a fundamental option for God and the good and striving to deepen that option, the Christian can unfortunately turn away from God and the good through a fundamental option. Chapter eight of volume one discusses the matter of sin and conversion. Sin in the light of the fundamental option must be seen as the breaking of this intimate relationship of love with God which also embraces a relationship with neighbor and the entire world. In this context the author echoes many contemporary moral theologians in showing that mortal sin involves more than the external act and must be a fundamental option. Often he reports that young children are unable to make such a fundamental option against God. The chapter ends with a discussion of conversion in the light of Christ himself who constitutes the living gospel and the sacrament of conversion. The sinner is called to a change of heart and to be reconciled with the life-giving Father through Christ and the Christian community of the church which celebrates the reality of conversion and penance. Continual conversion should be a part of every Christian life as one strives to grow in union with God and neighbor (I, 378-470).

Within this much broader context Häring discusses the morality of actions themselves in chapter six on conscience and in chapter seven on traditions, laws, norms, and context. He proposes a holistic theory of conscience as opposed to incomplete notions which identify conscience with a particular faculty of intellect or will, or reductionist tendencies which reduce conscience to either sociological or psychological factors. A holistic theory of conscience is built on the innate yearning for wholeness and openness; on the firmness and clarity of fundamental option; on the strength of the dispositions of the person, especially the eschatological virtues; on the mutuality and reciprocity of consciences (note the antidote against a false individualism); and on actual fidelity, creativity, and generosity in the search for truth in a readiness to act on the word (I, 224-301).

In the discussion on tradition, laws, norms, and context Häring spells out the implications of responsibility as expressed in creative freedom and fidelity and made manifest in Jesus. The danger always exists that like the Pharisees we will substitute human-made traditions for divine tradition. The Christian must be ever vigilant and critical in trying to discern the divine tradition in the midst of so many traditions. Our author objects to an understanding of natural law which is not integrated into the law of Christ, not holistic in its approach to the human, and which fails to recognize the importance of historicity. In normative ethics *Free and Faithful in Christ* underscores the need for both teleological and deontological aspects and proposes an authentic contextual ethics which recognizes conflicts and compromise (I, 302-377).

Up to now this review has systematically presented Häring's general approach to — and overall methodology of — moral theology. In my judgment, such an overall view and approach deserve the highest critical acclaim and acceptance. Häring has a holistic vision which brings together and tries to develop harmoniously the different aspects and elements of moral theology. The leitmotif of responsibility furnishes a much better model for moral theology than a deontological model of obedience to law or a teleological model with emphasis on self-perfection. By joining creative fidelity to freedom our author is able to recognize the basic reality of freedom but to guard against the dangers of one-sided individualistic and existentialistic freedom. Häring's moral theology is centered on the person who responds from the heart in creative freedom and fidelity, but his ethics also recognizes the communal, social, historical, and cosmic dimensions. Too often moral theology has been limited to the discussion of the morality of the act — is this act right or wrong? Häring rightly sees acts as related to the person as the tree from which the fruit comes and in the whole framework of covenantal existence. The broad vision of *Free and Faithful* relates the moral life of the Christian to all aspects of the Christian life, especially worship, sacraments, and spirituality as well as to the significant realities of both beauty and the arts.

II. Weaknesses

The basic outline and fundamental approach to moral theology in *Free and Faithful in Christ* presents a very good basis on which to erect a moral theology, but there are some deficiencies in Häring's development of his theological ethics. Specifically, the weaknesses of his approach to general moral theology, especially as found in the first volume of *Free and Faithful in Christ*, include a lack of integration, a failure to develop a philosophical basis for much of his structure of responsibility, an inadequate development of some of the individual parts, a tendency at times to over-react in terms of criticism of what has gone before, and some problems created by the literary style. All of these criticisms will emerge in the following comments.

One must put these criticisms in the proper context. The weaknesses in my judgment are secondary because they affect not the basic approach and vision of the author but only the development and explanation of some of the aspects of moral theology. In addition, all must recognize the almost impossible task of trying to write a systematic treatise in moral theology today. Despite the criticisms to be developed here, I believe that Häring's work stands as the best existing treatise in moral theology.

Philosophical Grounding and Integration

Throughout the three volumes there is no consistent philosophical grounding of Häring's thought. He rightly recognizes that theological ethics is not the same as philosophical ethics. However, it seems that theological ethics needs more philosophical grounding than the professor at the Academia Alfonsiana is willing to admit and use.

Our author very early in the first volume accepts the three different approaches to truth as proposed by Max Scheler: *Heilswissen*, the knowledge of salvation; *Seinswissen*, the knowledge of being; and *Herrschraftwissen*, the knowledge of dominion or control (I, 29). *Heilswissen* is searching for truth and witnessing to truth that is concerned primarily with salvation coming from God and with human relationships in the light of salvation. *Seinswissen* refers to the knowledge of truths in themselves and to speculation about being. *Herrschraftwissen* is concerned with the structure of society, but it can frequently become a knowledge of dominion and control. Although recognizing that there is an existential philosophy that gives more attention to the ultimate meaning of life and the dignity and freedom of the human person living in community, our author speaks negatively of "all philosophical speculation primarily concerned with the metaphysical categories of being and beings" (I, 30). The disparaging of the philosophical and the metaphysical is found throughout the book (e.g., I, 82-85). There can be no doubt that an older Catholic moral theology gave too much attention to the philosophical and the metaphysical and stressed a static and objectivistic understanding. Yet Häring in these theoretical considerations seems too easily to dismiss what is not immediately and directly connected with the knowledge of salvation, although he does recognize the need for some philosophical and metaphysical considerations. He agrees with Berdyaev in making freedom rather than being the basis of his philosophy (I, 68). Unfortunately there is no sustained development of this freedom-based anthropology.

Häring's limited theoretical acceptance of the role of metaphysics and philosophy is consistently evident throughout the work. The leitmotif of responsibility could use a more in-depth philosophical grounding. Häring himself does not entirely neglect this aspect, for there are frequent references to what might be called a personalist value theory. In this and in previous works he shows his dependence on the ethics of value of the phenomenological school, especially Husserl, Scheler, and von Hildebrand. In discussing the leitmotif of responsibility Häring does mention this theory. The fundamental attitude (*Gesinnung*) is the person's overall disposition to respond to the aspects of value in the consistent and committed way. The particular attitudes are dispositions to respond to certain sets or spheres of values (I, 90-96). Moral knowledge must be seen not as conceptual knowledge of ethical norms but as value experiences (I, III). Häring could have developed more explicitly and in greater depth his personalist value theory as a way of explaining and grounding his leitmotif of responsibility.

A well-developed personalist value theory could then readily serve as the integrating factor in the further discussion of fundamental option, conscience, moral norms, and natural law. In the elaboration of fundamental option Häring makes some reference to personalist value theory, but this theory does not ultimately ground his understanding of fundamental option. Our author points out that there are three kinds of value blindness corresponding to the main objects of moral knowledge — basic value, type of value, particular value (I, 183-184). However, there is no systematic explanation of fundamental option in light of this value theory. It would be quite logical to develop some of Häring's basic themes in accord with this threefold type of value. Fundamental option corresponds to the commitment to basic value which is ultimately the relationship of covenant love with God as revealed through Christ by the power of the Holy Spirit. Virtues and dispositions correspond to the type of value, whereas conscience and norms deal with particular values. As it stands, Häring's chapter on fundamental option is not really grounded in any philosophical understanding. In contemporary Roman Catholic thought, fundamental option is often grounded in a transcendental Thomism as exemplified in Josef Fuchs,[7] but this chapter again illustrates Häring's wariness of any philosophical grounding or backing for his position.

There are other problems of integration in the chapter on fundamental option. The first short section (I, 215-218) deals with conversion in the light of the fundamental option. Chapter eight, however, discusses sin and conversion at length but does not mention fundamental option. There could be an integration of the fundamental option with conversion which would then also show the deepening and development of the fundamental option in terms of continual conversion.

In the chapter on fundamental option and in the chapter on conversion Häring brings in significant data from psychology. In the second section of the chapter on fundamental option, "Contribution of the Behavioral Sciences and Philosophy," our author spends quite some time on Erikson and then refers briefly to Kierkegaard's stages on life's way, to Maslow's description of peak experience, and to Frankl's search for meaning. The book summarizes Erikson's eight steps of human development with their specific crises and decisions that have to be worked out. These important moments or crises obviously call for a deepening of the fundamental option. Note that, despite the title, little or no attention is given to the philosphical (I, 168-181). Häring deserves great credit for his breadth of knowledge and his ability to bring into his moral considerations these other important aspects, but there is a further step of integration which needs to take place. The chapter on conversion with its appeal to developmental psychology and the stages of conscience as developed by Lawrence Kohlberg illustrates the same problem. Häring again indicates the breadth of his knowledge and insight, but there is neither an integration nor an explicit critique of Kohlberg except for a comment in the footnote (I, 234-246). However, there are deficiencies in Kohlberg's stages especially from the viewpoint of Häring's moral theology which emphasizes the character and disposition of the person as well as the content aspect of morality as contrasted with the formal Kantian approach of Kohlberg.

The weakest part of Häring's first volume is the discussion of the human act and moral norms. In a sense there is no treatment of the human act and its morality as such. In the whole matter of norms one would expect to see a discussion based on a personalist value theory, but such is not the case. Häring develops a section on natural law which properly insists on integrating human reason and natural law into his Christocentric ethics. His approach avoids the two extremes of an autonomous reason and the renouncing of reason. Our author insists on the historicity of human nature and the distinction between nature as givenness and nature as source. The question of normative ethics is covered in thirty pages, but about ten pages are given to Luther's concept of the law (I, 338-367). Häring asserts that his ethic of responsibility combines features of both deontological and teleological models. We need deontological criteria that help us to evaluate the foreseeable consequences. This section of *Free and Faithful in Christ* calls for an authentic contextual ethic which avoids the extremes of legalism and of subjectivistic individualism. Our author recognizes that one of the most important tasks of moral theology is to elaborate carefully an ethics of conflict and compromise, but unfortunately he contributes little to the endeavor. The German Redemptorist does not even dialogue with many of his contemporaries who are discussing the approach of proportionalism. This section is disappointing. Häring does not really develop an approach to the morality of human acts, nor is the relationship between the act and the person considered. He offers a cursory treatment of norms which unfortunately does not appeal in any way to personalist value theory.

However, a word can and should be uttered in defense of Häring. Too often other approaches seek to reduce all of moral theology to the human act and spend undue time on the question of norms. Recall too that Häring is writing, not primarily for philosophers, but for the community of believers trying to live the Christian life. Nevertheless, even recognizing what Häring is trying to do and the sterile rationalism he is trying to avoid, his own discussion of human acts and norms is not sufficient.

The discussion of conscience in chapter six also suffers somewhat from the lack of a strong overall philosophical grounding and the failure to develop any real theory explaining the judgment of conscience. The strengths of Häring's discussion on conscience have already been mentioned — a holistic approach seen in the context of the person who exists in multiple relationships. The German Redemptorist recognizes the contribution of psychology and the importance of the reciprocity and mutuality of consciences to prevent the danger of a narrow individualism. However, the reader is disappointed to find no precise theory or explanation of how conscience works and the criteria for judging whether or not the decisions of conscience are correct. Here, again, our author could appropriately use his personalist value approach to construct a theory of conscience. One other deficiency in the chapter is the discussion on church authority and the place of dissent within the believing community. Häring mentions the prophetic ministry of dissent within the church and frequently rails against "the dominion and knowledge of control" too often excercized by an overly authoritarian church in the past. However, there is no extensive discussion of the positive role of the church as a moral teacher nor a satisfying explanation of the possibility of dissent.

The first volume ends with a "Synthesis" built around the notion of adoration. However, this small chapter does not really involve a synthesis or integration of what has gone before, nor does it serve as a basis for what will follow in the remaining volumes on special moral theology.

Further Questions of Integration

The question of integration in a manual of moral theology involves how all the material fits together. In the past most manuals of moral theology — expecially in the Jesuit and Redemptorist traditions — followed the outline of the ten commandments. The Thomistic school generally used the outline of the virtues. In the later editions of the *Law of Christ* Häring divides the material of special moral theology on the basis of our relationships with God, neighbor, and the world. There can be no doubt that any attempt to order all the material of moral theology is bound to be somewhat artificial. There is probably no systematic way in which the material can be perfectly organized. The second volume of *Free*

and Faithful in Christ is subtitled *The Truth Will Set You Free.*
The metaphor or symbol of truth is the basic organizing
principle. This volume begins with a long section on truth
and then follow chapters on beauty, communication, four
chapters on faith, and chapters on hope, truth, and the
liberating truth in sexual language. The German Redemptorist warns that the second volume should not be considered
as individual moral theology, while the third is held to be
social ethics. Häring rightly wants to insure that the social
dimension is not relegated to only one part of moral theology
but rather permeates all of moral theology. Throughout this
volume the professor at the Academia Alfonsiana tries to
relate the material to truth and to the leitmotif of responsibility as expressed in creative freedom and fidelity.
However, the relationship of beauty, the theological virtues,
and sexuality to truth is somewhat artificial. One can speak,
for example, of sexuality in terms of language and truth, but
the over-all connection is rather tenuous.

Volume three bears the subtitle *Light to the World: Salt for
the Earth.* In this volume Häring discusses bioethics in the
opening chapters and then considers responsibility in and
for the world, ecology, culture, socioeconomic life, politics,
and peace. To justify the inclusion of these questions of
social ethics in one volume Häring tries to employ the
metaphor of healing. The whole of redemption is a work of
healing; therefore, theology — especially moral theology —
has a therapeutic dimension. The therapeutic metaphor
logically can cover both medical ethics and the mission to the
world because Christians have an obligation to heal themselves, each other, and to join hands to create a healthier
world (III, 111). The last four chapters — culture, socioeconomic life, politics, and peace — follow the order found in the
second part of the Pastoral Constitution on the Church in
the Modern World, although our author does not explicitly
refer to this basis for his ordering. Once again the metaphor
of healing tying the whole volume together appears forced.
There is also the problem of integrating the metaphor of
healing with the subtitle of light to the world and salt for the

earth and with the leitmotif of responsibility in creative freedom and fidelity.

Another aspect of integration concerns the relationship between the first volume of general moral theology and the subsequent two volumes dealing with specific questions. The Häring trademark is definitely found in the volumes on special moral theology. The Christocentric and biblical approaches are consistently employed. However, the lack of a developed ethical theory of value grounding the moral evaluation of human acts in the first volume means there is no consistent ethical theory of moral evaluation of acts in the consideration of individual and social ethics.

The question of complete integration in a work covering all of moral theology is probably unsolvable. Häring himself is well aware of the difficulty and even of the danger in trying to erect a rigid system of moral theology (I, 59). All have to recognize that there will always be some artificiality in trying to combine all the aspects of the moral life in one integrated and somewhat systematic vision. The use of either the ten commandments or the theological and moral virtues presents many difficulties. Häring cannot be criticized too negatively, for there is no perfect solution. Ironically, it might be that Häring attempts too much of an overall synthesis in the second and third volumes and arrives at the somewhat artificial organizing principles of truth and healing.

Sitz im Leben *and Style*

The *Sitz im Leben*, or life-setting and context, of Häring's book is at one and the same time a strength and a weakness. Moral theology, like all theology, is related both to the church and to the academy. Perhaps more than other branches of theology, moral theology is heavily tilted toward the life of the church. The history of moral theology shows that the discipline has been intimately connected with the life of believers in the church community. There can be no doubt that Häring is a dedicated church person doing ethics in and for the church. Some of the writing in contemporary moral theology is much more directed to academe — to the aspect of moral theology as second-order discourse. There is a legitimate tension in all theology between the academic and the ecclesial aspects, for both are necessary. Häring clearly and, in my judgment, correctly gives precedence to the ecclesial aspect. His book is a moral theology for clergy and laity. The whole focus of the volumes is on the Christian moral life as such and embraces much more than a consideration of the morality of acts and of the distinctions between sin and no sin and between mortal sin and venial sin. One should not expect to find within such an approach an overly detailed philosophical discussion of particular problems and questions. Too often in the past and in the present books on general moral theology are primarily act centered or spend an inordinate amount of time on problems and questions that are more a matter of interest for professional speculation than for practical living. However, within this framework I still think there is room for a more in-depth philosophical support for Häring's understanding of responsibility and a need for a more developed and coherent theory about the judgment of conscience and the morality of acts which then can be applied to the areas of individual and social ethics.

Within the ecclesial context Häring is reacting to the type of moral theology which went before him — the manualist approach with its concentration on acts and sins and its failure to pay attention to the spiritual, Christological, and eschatological dimensions of the fullness of the Christian life to which all are called. Häring rightly points out that one of the most uncreative approaches in the church is to stress fidelity to certain negative commandments to such an extent that fidelity to Christ and to his goal commandments of justice, love, mercy, and forgiveness is neglected. Our author is strongly opposed to the legalism and contract mentality of the older approaches together with a philosophical stance that was not integrated into the saving truth made known in Christ Jesus. At times the Redemptorist moral theologian appears to give too much attention to this dialogue with former approaches, so that it might have too great an effect on his own work. An older Catholic moral theology, for example, can rightly be criticized for being uncreative, but Häring perhaps goes too far in his incessant call for a prophetic moral theology. Christian moral theology must be prophetic, but at the very minimum there is always need for discernment between the true prophets and the false prophets. Prophetic is always a good word in Häring's vocabulary, whereas priestly almost always has negative connotations. Häring would be the first to admit that every change is not necessarily for the good and that there are false prophets, but his rhetoric does not always show the necessary nuances precisely because he seems to be overreacting to the conformity and lack of creativity in previous times.

The style and rhetoric of these volumes borders occasionally on the homiletic—more so in the first and general part of the work than in the specific considerations in the second part. Since Häring above all stresses truth as saving truth, one can readily understand the proclivity to a more homiletic style; but sometimes this style seems to detract from what the author is trying to relate. This style plus the lack of integration and systematic rigor occasionally gives the impression of needless repetition. However, in general the treatise is clear and easily readable. One can only admire how the author of *Das Gesetz Christi* could twenty years later write an entirely new three-volume work of moral theology in English, a language which he never really used before 1963. Obviously, credit is due to Mrs. Josephine Ryan, who prepared the manuscript for him, but Häring himself communicates exceptionally well in both spoken and written English.

III. Further Theological and Ethical Considerations

Christology and Eschatology

After a consideration of Häring's overall approach to moral theology with its strengths and possible weaknesses, our critique will now examine in greater depth three of the basic theological and ethical considerations in Häring's thought — his Christology and eschatology, optimism, and ecclesiology. As has been pointed out, Häring's moral theology is Christological with a heavy emphasis on a descending Christology. This fits in very well with his basic understanding of the Christian life as involving God's gift and human response. Christ is the Word incarnate, Truth incarnate, Love incarnate. In Christ we also see the perfect response to the Father's gift.

The Christological emphasis means that Häring sees Christian ethics as a distinctive kind of ethics. Christians should be distinguished by their true humanity and cohumanity, for at the center of faith is the dogma of the incarnation of the Word of God. God incarnates himself in full humanity and in cohumanity in Jesus Christ, true God and true man (I, 247). Häring thus disagrees with the autonomous moral theology now prevalent in Germany and with those who would reduce the beatitudes, the goal-commandments, and the harvest of the Spirit to mere ideals, or *parenesis*, which have no role in normative Christian ethics. On the other hand, Häring recognizes that such a position does not deny that generous people not professing the Christian faith might be guided by the same dynamics, for we believe that Christ is Redeemer and Lord of all, and his Spirit works in all and through all and for all (I, 246-259, 23-35). Our author, in agreement with the Second Vatican Council, recognizes that not everyone who calls oneself an atheist is truly such. People who because of their good will do what is right will be saved. Häring contrasts the hidden atheist and the open unbeliever to attack those who hide their godlessness under a cloak of religiosity (II, 357-364). Thus a specific and distinctive Christian ethic does not claim to have an absolutely unique ethical content.

The fear has been expressed that a descending Christology, defined as one which takes its starting point in dogmatic affirmations about the divinity and messianic election of Jesus and moves from these affirmations to the consideration of his earthly historical existence and its meaning for us, too readily tends to accept the status quo and does not involve a critique and a call for change.[8] There can be no doubt that many Christologies today are ascending Christologies, and this is especially true in contemporary critical social theology such as liberation theology. These ascending Christologies begin with the historical testimony concerning the man Jesus and our ability to sympathize and empathize with him and then move to a consideration of the messianic and divinity claims made by the followers of Jesus. However, Häring is proof that a descending Christology does not have to maintain the status quo but can call for change. It is true that Häring does not call for radical change, but he certainly insists on real change and growth.

An ascending Christology is more ready to recognize the struggles, conflicts, and opposition in the Christian life than a descending Christology. Häring does not deny such aspects of struggle, opposition, conflict, and discontinuity, but he does not give sufficient importance and depth to these aspects. The power and strength of sin and the sinful structures which become incarnate in our social and political ethos should receive more emphasis. We are here dealing with Häring's generally optimistic worldview. Häring's Christian optimism — which is never a naive optimism — is related not only to his Christology but also to his eschatology.

Eschatology deals with the relationship of the present world and reality to the fullness of the kingdom. In a true sense we are living between the two comings of Jesus. Häring consistently holds for a heavy emphasis on realized eschatology being brought about by the redemptive activity of Jesus. The emphasis on the final coming and the fact that the fullness of the kingdom will come only at the end of time is comparatively less. Phrased in another way, our author emphasizes the redemptive work of Jesus and fails to give enough importance to the discontinuity between the present and the fullness of the Kingdom. Häring often implicitly refers to the Redemptorist motto *copiosa apud cum redemptio* with his emphasis on the superabundance of redemption (e.g., III, 210, 406). Intimately connected with such an eschatology is a failure to emphasize enough the continuing power and depth of sin and evil in the world.

Optimistic Worldview

The German Redemptorist is consistent in his Christology, eschatology, and hamartiology. His Christology emphasizes the importance of incarnation and redemption. Corresponding to this is an eschatology which stresses the superabundance of redemption already given in Christ. No one can accuse Bernard Häring of denying the existence of sin, but he seems to give the impression that the redemption means that the power of sin can be overcome and the struggle against sin is not as difficult as it would be in the theology of one who would stress more that the fullness of redemption will only come at the end of time. Not only is Häring consistent in his basic theological positions, but also in the light of this theology he logically tends to an optimistic worldview.

The aspects of the tragic, of suffering, and of conflict do not receive enough attention from Häring. The section on hope, as would be expected, does recognize the realities of suffering and struggle, but these aspects are not given enough importance and significance, especially in the other sections of the work. For example, in his short discussion of a world political community based on the federal principle of a world authority, our author fails to recognize the many obstacles which stand in the way of such a plan (III, 381-385). Our author's frequent references to Teilhard de Chardin are consistent with his own optimistic worldview. There are more than ten citations of the renowned French Jesuit within a sixty-page segment dealing with faith and hope. The German Redemptorist strongly agrees with Teilhard's emphasis on the incarnation as the great event that should guide all our responsible hope for the transformation of the world (II, 347-404).

Häring's emphasis on growth, creativity, and historicity also contributes to his evolutionary and optimistic worldview. An older Catholic moral theology can correctly be described as static. The legal model emphasized obedience to law, often the minimal law that marked the boundary line between mortal sin and venial sin. This act-centered and minimalistic moral theology gave no consideration to growth in the moral life. One of Häring's major contributions to moral theology has been his insistence on the need for growth and continual conversion in the Christian life. Perhaps in so stressing the need for growth in the moral life, Häring too easily leaves the impression of an evolutionary growth and development in all of human existence which does not appreciate enough the tragic and suffering dimensions of our pilgrim existence.

Creativity is a very important reality for Häring. However, as mentioned above, while Häring rightly stresses creativity in the Christian life and in Christian theology, he tends to forget some of the limits on such creativity. Historicity is likewise a very important concept for Häring which he employs in three different contexts. The older Catholic natural-law theory stressed the eternal, essential, and immutable aspects of human existence, whereas Häring recognizes the historical character of all human existence (I, 319-323). Throughout his life the German Redemptorist has been calling for a change, even a radical change, in the understanding of Catholic moral theology. An older manual approach can no longer be accepted in our time. Too often the church has been bogged down by holding on to antiquated traditions and laws (I, 302); too often in the past the church has imposed a particular thought form and culture on others. The contemporary church and modern theology must avoid this type of imperialism. Häring's historicity — especially in the light of his emphasis on growth, creativity, and evolutionary development — often gives the impression that every historical change is a part of the evolutionary development and something better than what went before.

Häring's theoretical optimism coheres with what he has practiced throughout his life. Häring served as a medic in the German army, on the Russian front, during World War

II. He experienced first hand the cruelty and savagery of war, and in 1977 he wrote *Embattled Witness*, his reflections on his wartime experiences.[9] Our author's chief reason for writing about this experience is "to show that, even in the midst of all the crime and inhumanity of the war, there was so much goodness in people on all sides" (Introduction, p. vii). Häring has frequently been opposed by more conservative groups within the church and has been suspected of doctrinal and moral deviation by various sectors of the Roman Curia. However, even in the midst of harassment and suspicion, Häring has always retained his composure, his patience, and his basic optimism. I would temper Häring's optimism and its theological and ethical grounding. However, Häring's optimism is thoroughly consistent with his theology, his ethical emphases, his personality, and his religious conviction about the superabundance of redemption.

Ecclesiology

Häring's ecclesiology well exemplifies a contemporary Roman Catholic approach. Bernard Häring accepts the hierarchical office in the church but still insists on the church as the people of God — a *koinonia*, or fellowship, in the Holy Spirit. Unfortunately, the structures of the church today are still too often affected by a self-understanding of the church as a perfect society. Harmful tensions too often result when authoritarian tendencies, conformity, and control characterize the church and thereby contradict the divinely revealed symbol of Christ the prophet who embodied freedom, creativity, and fidelity (I, 80).

Häring, like the Second Vatican Council and long before it, insists on the universal vocation of all Christians to perfection. By reason of baptism all are called to the fullness of the Christian life. This universal call to perfection receives great emphasis throughout Häring's moral theology. Our author strongly accentuates the charismatic and prophetic function in the church. The prophetic aspect in the church is not necessarily identified with the hierarchical office, although the hierarchical church is also called to be prophetic and to be open to the voices of prophets in the church (I, 345-349). As mentioned above, Häring's stress on the prophetic aspect at times seems to need some nuancing.

Free and Faithful also stresses the pilgrim aspect of the church (I, 80). The church is called to freedom but is composed of people whose freedom is frequently controlled and blocked by the bondage of power and falsehood. The effects of distorted authority structures and the unfaithfulness of members and officeholders have added to the sinfulness of the church. Recalling these realities is the first step toward repentance (I, 159). The church itself is in constant need of ongoing conversion. The very loftiness of the vocation of the church constitutes the strongest call to ecclesial conversion and renewal on all levels (I, 426-429).

The understanding of the church which Häring most insists on and consistently incorporates in a very creative way into his entire moral theology is the sacramental model (I, 80, 429). In fact, in one place he explicitly affirms that the best model for understanding the church is the sacramental one (I, 224). The church as sacrament fits into an overall sacramental vision. God makes love visible in Jesus Christ who is the sacrament of this love and saving covenant. The church as a visible community of love and fellowship in the Holy Spirit is a sacrament endowed with sacraments to manifest God's gracious presence, love, and saving will (I, 348). This treatise on moral theology effectively uses the sacramental model to insist that the church itself live out the gospel message and thus be a sign to others and to the world. In his systematic discussion of creative freedom and fidelity our author concludes the chapter with a section on the church as the great sacrament of evangelical freedom (I, 158-161). (Note that the introduction to the chapter on page 105 refers to this section as VII, but in reality it is section VI. The chapter does not contain a section on education in and for freedom which the introduction to the chapter claims will be section VI.) It is interesting that this section speaks about the church as "embodiment of creative freedom and fidelity" and does not use the word sacrament. The church is called in God's freedom to be the sacrament of a free response to Christ the liberator. Precisely in this context the church must give more attention to its own prophetic ministry and to the role of prophets within the church. The church's own attitude toward freedom in its own life and structures is a sign of its own fidelity to Christ. The church should impose limits to creative liberty and fidelity only for the sake of freedom itself—to create favorable conditions for the growth of freedom everywhere and for all people. Words alone are not enough. The church in its life and practice must be a sign to the world of freedom. The church itself is called to be the great sacrament of conversion. The ecclesial community effectively calls others to conversion, reconciliation, and unity only to the extent that the church itself is a holy penitent (I, 426-429).

The unifying theme of the second volume is the truth that will make us free. It is not so much by abstract concepts but rather by images and symbols that the unconcealment of truth becomes liberating. Christ is the supreme and all-embracing symbol, the visible sign of the truth that saves. The church, and all Christians, must be a living sacrament of the truth that liberates (II, 5). The discussion of faith, hope, and love in the second volume insists on the understanding of the church as sacrament, although there is no explicit section on the sacramentality of the church in the discussion of love. All that the church is and has, all her dimensions and structures, should manifest to the world her faith in Christ and awaken and strengthen the faith of all (II, 223-224). Likewise, the sacramentality of the church requires her to be a sign in her total existence of the reality of hope (II, 406-407).

The church as sacrament also has an important role to play in what is often called social morality as distinguished from personal morality. The church herself in her own structures and positions must be a sign and a model to the world. The church's teaching in this area cannot be severed from convincing actions (III, 254-260). One of the great chal-

lenges facing our world today is peace. Here the church
is called to be an effective sacrament of peace and reconciliation for all human beings. If the church cannot live out
this reality of peace, the world will never be able to do so.
Throughout his work Häring makes a number of references
to the evil of sexism. Almost invariably in these considerations he emphasizes the need for the church to be a sacrament to the world (I, 139-140; II, 82, 89, 498-500, 511;
III, 138-139, 276, 309-310). The church must be critical of
the lack of women's participation in leadership roles in the
church, even prescinding from the question of ordination. It
is an urgent challenge to the church to give women a fully
proportionate share in decision-making processes in order to
make credible the call to society to overcome as quickly as
possible the discrimination against women.

Generally speaking, Häring effectively and coherently
employs what might be called a post-Vatican II ecclesiology
with emphasis on the sacramental model. One area in which
an older ecclesiology is somewhat more apparent is in the
discussion of love as ministry of salvation (II, 446-466).
Here too the book properly insists on the universal vocation
of all to the fullness of the discipleship of Christ and to share
in the redemptive task of the apostolate. The whole church
is apostolic. However, Häring finishes the section with a discussion of the official apostolate of the church which is based
on ordination. Lay people can participate in the official apostolate as collaborators in such functions as religious educators, organists, or even janitors, and thus in a certain sense
these people belong to the clergy. A special way of associat-
ing lay people with the official apostolate of the church is
Catholic Action with its organization created or officially approved by the hierarchy. For the laity there are two predominant ways of sharing in the apostolate and the ministry. The
first is the engagement of the individual by reason of one's
position, and the second is the organized action of the laity
under the direction of the hierarchy. In a different context,
Häring recognizes there are also numerous lay organizations
that carry out their ministerial, social, and charitable in-

itiatives on their own responsibility (III, 111-161). It seems that too much importance is given by Häring to the official apostolate or the hierarchical apostolate. Häring in this particular section of volume two should insist much more on the involvement of all in the apostolate and in the social mission of the church based on the baptismal commitment of all Christians.

This discussion has attempted to consider in greater depth some important aspects of Häring's moral theology: Christology, eschatology, optimism, and ecclesiology. By reason of the very breadth and depth of Häring's work this treatment remains very inadequate. All of the topics considered here could truly merit book-length studies in themselves. In addition, there are many other topics that have been mentioned throughout this review which truly deserve much deeper study; for example, Häring's approach to sin, conversion, the use of the Scriptures in moral theology, epistemology, and the role of the human sciences, especially anthropology. Aspiring doctoral students in moral theology can readily find many possible dissertation topics dealing with various aspects of Häring's moral theology.

IV. Content of Special Ethics

The final two volumes of *Free and Faithful in Christ* constitute what has traditionally been called special moral theology dealing with the specific areas of human existence as distinguished from the foundational and methodological concerns of the first volume. The most striking characteristic of these volumes is their breadth. There are very few people today who even venture to write a complete moral theology. One can readily understand why. The range of material to be covered is intimidating. In the process of writing these volumes Häring shows his wide-ranging interests and knowledge. His study includes the traditional material contained in the older manuals of moral theology but from an obviously contemporary and holistic viewpoint — faith, hope, charity, truth, secrecy, sexuality, medical ethics, and the material arranged in accord with the format followed in the Pastoral Constitution on the Church in the Modern World. In addition, there are many considerations which are included in the light of the signs of the times and because of the author's deep sensitivities — beauty, art, the mass media of communication, public opinion, a sense of humor, evangelization, ecumenism, atheism, and ecology. In the process Häring shows his familiarity with a wide range of sources not only in moral theology, systematic theology, and Scripture but also in psychology, sociology, philosophy, political science, and economics. His broad knowledge and interests are buttressed by his familiarity with the pertinent literature in all the major European languages. Häring's knowledge of the literature in so many different languages is unsurpassed by any contemporary. To write in a well-informed and sensitive way on such a broad range of topics and concerns is a monumental accomplishment. In general, Häring has done very well what few people would even dare to attempt.

The genre of the manual shares in the ambiguity of all human existence. The great benefit of the manual is a unified presentation of all the pertinent material in one set of volumes. Despite some of the weaknesses mentioned earlier, Häring presents a generally consistent, Christocentric approach which recognizes the importance of the scriptural message as well as the role of human understanding and the sciences. His treatment of the individual areas is knowledgable, sensitive, and creative. The final two volumes of *Free and Faithful in Christ* thus eminently fulfill the expectations of what one hopes to find in a manual of special moral theology.

There are also inherent drawbacks in the very genre of the manual. The attempt to put everything together means that the individual parts and aspects cannot be discussed in as exhaustive and thorough a manner as in a single monograph. For this reason it would be unfair to criticize any manual for not being the last word on a particular subject. The negative criticism would be even more unfair in the case of Bernard

Häring, who has already written so extensively on many of the topics considered here. This reader was constantly amazed at the breadth and depth of his considerations.

Take, for example, the area of medical ethics. Häring has previously written two books dealing with the topic,[10] but now the whole matter is found in 106 pages of the third volume (III, 3-109). Yet Häring covers the significant areas of interest remarkably well. He discusses the content questions of the meaning of human life, the beginning of human life, sterilization, artificial intervention in human reproduction, abortion, death, and dying. For anyone who is familiar with Häring's writings in these areas, his positions will not contain any surprises. In addition, as one would expect with Häring, the book gives a short Christian understanding of health and healing and describes the healing profession. Unlike many large tomes on the subject of medical ethics, *Free and Faithful in Christ* discusses the question of health delivery and health care policies. An important task of the church and of moral theology is to challenge the present system with its delivery of health care in large hospitals. There is need for more emphasis on a holistic approach and on preventive medicine. This section, as developed by Häring, is necessarily much more suggestive than programmatic. He raises the question if it would be well for the church to diminish the number of hospitals owned and staffed by her and to do more creative work in consciousness raising and in health education and maintenance (III, 53-56). There are many times when the professional moral theologian would like to push a particular point to greater depth, but the very nature of the work makes this impossible. Häring, for example, mentions that not every action which has the material aspect of suicide has the formal aspect of suicide. He uses the illustration of the person who sacrifices one's own life when faced with the situation of being brainwashed and forced to endanger the lives of many other people (III, 36). On the whole the discussion of medical ethics thus shows how amazingly well Häring can give a holistic and comprehensive exposition of the topic within the confines of space dictated by the manual itself.

Undoubtedly there are occasions in the book when the reader would wish for a more fully developed treatise. I reacted this way after reading his treatment of divorce and the pastoral care of divorced people, which comprises five pages (II, 538-543). Häring's theological, biblical, and pastoral concerns are evident in the short but very concise treatment which recognizes that marriage is indissoluble by grace. Indissolubility is a goal-commandment and a truly normative ideal for Christians, but it cannot be made into an absolute moral law. While recognizing the need for the church as a community to hold up this ideal, pastoral theology and practice must admit to the sacraments of penance and the eucharist those spouses involved in a second marriage who are sincerely longing for regular participation in the eucharistic life of the church, have sufficient reason to continue in their present union, are sorry for their past sins, and are striving to live in accord with the gospel. No one has written more sensitively than Häring on the issues of divorce and remarriage, and no one has been more "free and faithful" in charting new pastoral approaches within the church to the divorced and remarried. These approaches are marvelously condensed in these few pages, but one fears that the quick reader will never fully appreciate all that is being said. Despite the limitations of the manual format, Häring does remarkably well in dealing in a comprehensive way with a bewildering variety of issues.

It would be impossible to discuss at length all the various areas considered in these two volumes. Two areas, ecumenism and peace, will illustrate the approach and methods that Häring employs. An older moral theology obviously never discussed the reality of ecumenism in the moral life of Christians except perhaps under the rubric of condemned participation in sacred things or cooperation with heretics. The self-commitment of Christians to church unity should be a part of the fundamental option of all. The continual search for church unity is a true call for conversion which is both personal and structural. As individuals and as church we must recognize our sinfulness in the question of church unity. Conversion to Christ the prophet calls the church to move beyond frozen structures and doctrinal formulations which are not appropriate in the light of the contemporary signs of the times. A positive disposition toward pluralism is necessary in our search for truth. The claim for truth is absolute, but truth is always greater than our means of thought and expression. The universal church must appreciate and bring home the varied expressions, thought patterns, and coreflections which mark the different Christian experiences. Our author deals with the theoretical questions of belief and theology facing the ecumenical movement, and also discusses the rapprochement which is occurring in moral theology through the coming together of moral and dogmatic theology, of Eastern and Western traditions, of Protestant and Roman Catholic approaches.

On the practical level Häring proposes some interesting suggestions. In today's circumstances commitment to one's own tradition but also to the call for Christian unity might well be carried out through a "double membership" whereby the individual retains membership in one's own church but also belongs to an ecumenical community. *Free and Faithful* calls for a continuing ecumenical ministry to people in mixed marriages and advocates that spouses decide in common reflection and without anguish about the baptism and upbringing of children in one or the other church according to the greater chance to guarantee a true faith commitment. Throughout this discussion Häring insists on the need for creative and prophetic approaches and the willingness to make provisional or gradual solutions (II, 276-333). Perhaps here too Häring is overly optimistic and fails to appreciate all the obstacles in the way of church unity, especially of a structural nature, but his optimism is coupled with practical steps to advance truly the cause of church unity.

Häring's discussion of peace comes at the end of the third

volume and well illustrates the many aspects of Häring's moral theology (III, 391-426). The biblical and Christological aspects of peace are stressed. *Shalom* is a central concept in the Old Testament and in the life of the people of Israel. Luke presents Christ as the promised king of peace. *Shalom* is the greeting and gift which the risen Christ gives to his disciples. Renewed by the peace of Christ, all Christians are sent out as peacemakers. Yet the death of Jesus and many texts in the New Testament will not allow us to minimize the existence of conflict, but the resurrection of Jesus and the total biblical message of peace leave no doubt that the final word is not conflict but peace promised by God and Christ and proclaimed and fostered by peaceful disciples of Christ. According to biblical scholars the holy wars of extirpation waged in the name of God in the Book of Numbers and Judges probably never took place. These wars were the views of the Deuteronomists which were read back into an earlier historical time. Such views found in the Old Testament scriptures indicate the imperfect perception of even very religious people. The life of Israel in the Old Testament reveals the conflict between the mentality of the warrior tribes and peace prophecy, but in the Old Testament itself there is a growing awareness that the spirals of killing and war are a striking sign and consequence of sinfulness which God wants to stop. Jesus in the New Testament is totally opposed to nationalism, greed, and the lust for power. The contemporary signs of the times reinforce the biblical and Christological call to be peacemakers. People are becoming more conscious today of the unity of all human beings. The negative side of this reality is that the weapons in the arsenals of the world could today destroy the whole planet.

In his discussion of peace Häring quickly surveys the theory and practice existing in the history of the church. The just-war theory, which was first formulated for Christians by Augustine, obviously was influenced by the practice of the post-Constantinian church after the pacifism of the first three centuries. The primary intention of the great theologians in their just-war doctrine was to limit war. In the course of history, unfortunately, Christian thinkers have too often lacked the prophetic spirit crying out against war. There were all too many "king's priests" bereft of salvation knowledge. We must humbly recognize the evils involved in holy wars and crusades, in war against aborigines, and in the failure to condemn the massive bombing of civilian population centers in World War II.

Häring's emphasis is that the time has now come to liberate the world from the slavery of war and the curse of the arms race. He rejects the realism of Reinhold Niebuhr, who claimed that "immoral society" will never free itself from the curse of war. In view of the superabundant redemption in Christ peace is possible. To bring about this goal a number of means are discussed: conscientious objection and prophetic protest against war, nonviolence both as spirituality and as a tactic, and especially peace research and peace policy. The utopia of peace can be the sign of a new spirit and the result of the creative imagination that points in the right direction. This new spirit and attitude must also be embodied in structures. Models for a peaceful world order generally do not opt for a centralist world government but for functional peace agencies which can grow out of existing United Nations' structures. Peace education is most important. In typical Häring fashion the discussion ends with a section on the church as the sacrament of peace.

The emphasis throughout is on the goal of peace and the curse of war. Apparently Häring accepts the restricted formulation of the just-war theory as found in the Second Vatican Council, which maintains that with the present situation and structure of the world, government cannot be denied the right to legitimate defense once every means of peaceful settlement has been exhausted. This position is never really developed and defended by Häring. In an earlier section he briefly discussed violent revolutions and acknowledged their legitimacy as a last resort. However, the first question of conscience concerns the need to do everything in our power through nonviolence (III, 378-379). Our author is not a total pacifist but truly holds to the last resort aspect of violence, without ever really developing his position. Although his work makes an urgent call for radical disarmament, the author knows that this is unattainable at present, since the new spirit of peace has not yet taken root. He agrees with Thomas Merton that radical unilateral disarmament is naive at the present time, but unilateral initiatives in gradual steps are imperative.

The chapter on peace well illustrates Häring's approach in view of his holistic vision, Christological and eschatological dimensions, and prophetic, forward-moving thrust with more emphasis on the positive than on the negative. Perhaps the conditions for a just war at the present time should have been spelled out in greater detail with attention given to treating more specific problems such as the condemnation of the use of all nuclear weapons even if the arms themselves do not violate the just-war principles of discrimination. Also, in my judgment, Häring's prophetic emphasis might not take seriously enough the difficulty in changing the existing political structures. As is his wont, our author tries to emphasize the steps toward the utopia and the goal-commandment of peace. Chapter seven will indicate the similarities between Häring's approach to peace and the pastoral letter on peace issued by the American bishops.

Perhaps the major omission in Häring's special ethics is a discussion of liberation theology and some of the issues involved in this movement. There are comparatively few references to liberation theology throughout the book. Our author obviously agrees with the emphasis on the church's option for the poor. His insistence on the importance of nonviolent means might run counter to some but by no means to all proponents of liberation theology. In his discussion of faith Häring recognizes that we can rightly insist on the primacy of praxis, but it must be an intelligent practice that is related to the saving truth. Truly saving faith can never be merely an intellectual reality (II, 231). However, there is comparatively little emphasis on praxis throughout the book, no recognition of its importance in social ethics, and no in-depth theoretical understanding of praxis. The question of ideological suspicion does not come to the fore in Häring's approach even though he is aware of it. The book does recognize the importance of the cosmic, social, and structural dimensions, but in my judgment even more emphasis is needed. In the discussion of political and economic questions greater appreciation of the structural aspects and of sin could be brought together through a discussion of the sin in the world incarnated in unjust social and economic systems. My objection is not that Häring might disagree with liberation theology, but that he does not even dialogue with it.

In the light of the great number of areas and questions discussed in the last two volumes, many readers will undoubtedly disagree with Häring's discussion of particular topics. Personally I am amazed at the comparatively few differences I have with Häring's approach. Often my disagreements involve a different emphasis or nuance in approach. Häring's creativity in writing a section on art has already been pointed out, but his discussion fails to deal with the agony as well as the ecstasy of art. His understanding of beauty and art seems at times too optimistic and fails to recognize the struggles and sufferings of the artist (II, 116-130). In the treatment of lying I would opt for a greater acceptance of the distinction between lying and falsehood, based on the nature of lying understood in relational terms as a necessary way to protect secrets. Häring tries to avoid this distinction and heavily relies on the older mental reservation approach. His understanding of lying as related to Truth logically would make it more difficult for him to accept the more relational understanding of truth-telling in which the malice of lying consists in the violation of my neighbor's right to truth (II, 38-55). The discussion of sexuality seems to concentrate almost exclusively on genital sexuality, fecundity, and marriage. These aspects are most significant and important, but there are other aspects of sexuality. The book is also too negative in its approach to homosexuality, but perhaps an unfortunate use of English words contributes to the problem. We read, for example, "The church's faithfulness to her mission as sacrament of hope will constantly be tested by her attitude toward those who are, in one way or another, outlaws. I particularly mention homosexuals who need so much to be helped to discern between sin and suffering. Very often the afflicted person needs to be helped to accept the suffering implied in sex deviancy" (II, 414). Elsewhere Häring continues to use the word deviancy and associates homosexuality with other sexual deviations like sadism, masochism, fetishism, and beastiality (II, 564).

This section has tried through some specific illustrations to give an idea of Häring's approach to what used to be called special moral theology. His approach puts into practice all the many positive aspects of his more theoretical understanding of moral theology. The weaknesses mentioned in the second section of this critique are also present, but they are comparatively minor. There are some lacunae, and I personally have some comparatively few differences with the author.

V. Conclusion

Häring has chosen to write a complete treatise of moral theology for priests and laity. These aims also have some built-in limitations. A manual-type approach cannot claim to be exhaustive or definitive. *Free and Faithful in Christ* is primarily, and rightly, directed to "livers and doers" of the Christian life and not to thinkers. Despite these inherent limitations I believe there is a great need for such a work.

In the course of this lengthy, but ultimately very insufficient critical evaluation, some negative aspects have been pointed out. There are weaknesses in the way in which the author develops and integrates the subject matter as a whole and in some of its parts. In addition, I disagree somewhat with a few of Häring's underlying theological concepts and with his positions on a very small number of topics. But these negative criticisms are comparatively minor and insignificant in the light of the whole project. Moral theologians must take Häring's work seriously and enter into critical dialogue with him. In my judgment Häring has accomplished his task in a superlative way. There is no work existing today that can come close to Häring's as a holistic exposition of the Christian moral life for priests and laity.

NOTES

1. Bernard Häring, *Das Gesetz Christi: Moraltheologie dargestellt für Priester und Laien* (Freiburg i.Br.: Erich Wewel, 1954).

2. It has been translated into Chinese, English, French, Italian, Japanese, Croatian, Malayan, Dutch, Polish, Portugese, and Spanish.

3. H. Boelaars and R. Tremblay, eds., *In Libertatem Vocati Estis: Miscellanea Bernard Häring* (Rome: Academia Alfonsiana, 1977), pp. 13-30.

4. Bernard Häring, *Free and Faithful in Christ: Moral Theology for Clergy and Laity*, 3 vols. (New York: Seabury Press, 1978, 1979, 1981).

5. Bernard Häring, *Das Heilige und das Gute: Religion und Sittlichkeit in ihrem gegenseitigen Bezug* (Freiburg i.Br.: Erich Wewel, 1950).

6. Conversion is a central and well developed theme in *The Law of Christ*, I (Westminster, MD: Newman Press, 1961), pp. 387-481. For a later study of conversion see B. Häring, "La Conversion," in *Pastorale du péché*, ed. Ph. Delhaye (Tournai, Belgium: Desclée, 1961), pp. 65-145.

7. Josef Fuchs, *Human Values and Christian Morality* (Dublin: Gill and Macmillan, 1970), especially pp. 92-111.

8. Monika K. Hellwig, "Christology and Attitudes Toward Social Structures," in *Above Every Name: The Lordship of Christ and Social Systems*, ed. Thomas E. Clarke (New York: Paulist Press, 1980), pp. 13-34. This is an important article dealing with a most significant question.

9. Bernard Häring, *Embattled Witness: Memories of a Time of War* (New York: Seabury Press, 1976).

10. Bernard Häring, *Medical Ethics* (Notre Dame, Indiana: Fides Publishers, 1973); Häring, *Ethics of Manipulation: Issues in Medicine, Behavior Control, and Genetics* (New York: Seabury Press, 1975).

2: An Evaluation of Recent Works in Fundamental Moral Theology

This chapter will extend the scope of the first chapter and evaluate four other comparatively recent books dealing with fundamental moral theology. Anthologies or books treating specific topics in special moral theology will not be discussed.[1] The purpose is to consider various contemporary approaches to fundamental moral theology and to evaluate these works both in themselves and in their utility as textbooks. The authors to be considered are: Timothy O'Connell, Daniel Maguire, Enda McDonagh, and Franz Böckle.

As might be expected there are strengths and weaknesses in all these works. The primary interpretive key to be employed in this article is the *Sitz im Leben* of the book. The particular *Sitz im Leben* of each author helps to understand better what the book is trying to accomplish and at the same time serves to indicate some of the strengths and weaknessess of the particular volume.

Timothy O'Connell[2]

The *Sitz im Leben* of Timothy E. O'Connell's *Principles for a Catholic Morality* is the author's position as a professor of fundamental moral theology at St. Mary of the Lake Seminary of the Archdiocese of Chicago. O'Connell has attempted to write a modern manual of fundamental moral theology incorporating many of the contemporary developments in moral theology.

The first part of the book contains introductory essays on the meaning of moral theology, a history of moral theology, the themes of biblical morality, and Christ and moral theology. As a theologian, O'Connell is seeking not primarily truth but meaning. The ultimate test of theology is its meaningfulness or fidelity to Christian experience. The two major divisions of the work discuss the human moral person and the moral world in which the person lives and acts. Part two on the moral person considers the traditional topics of human action, the human person, sin and virtue, conscience, and adds short chapters on related dogmatic themes and the Christian vocation.

The section on the moral person relies heavily on the theory of the fundamental option. In following some contemporary transcendental Thomists (e.g., Fuchs), O'Connell distinguishes the human as agent, the level of categorical freedom, and the domain of objective knowledge from the human as person or subject, the level of core freedom, and the nonreflex knowledge of self as subject and not as object. The agent on the level of categorical freedom chooses certain objective or categorical actions such as to do this or that. However, in the core of the person the subject determines one's fundamental stance in a transcendental manner that literally transcends all categories. The fundamental option as such does not exist in and by itself. Many of our ordinary reactions remain only on the level of the categorical and involve the choosing and doing of a particular act, but other actions include a depth dimension involving the core freedom of the human person, choosing and determining oneself as subject in a fundamental stance. Mortal sin is a negative fundamental option which is a transcendental act on the level of core freedom and does not consist in the choice of a particular object or categorical action. Venial sin is a categorically wrong action which because of the impediments to a total human act does not involve the core freedom of the person in a fundamental option.

Principles for a Catholic Morality distinguishes three levels of conscience. Conscience/1 refers to a general sense of value and an awareness of personal responsibility. Conscience/2 is the judgment about a specific perception of value, and here people can disagree; for example, not all are agreed that gambling on horse racing is good or bad. Error can enter at this level. Conscience/3 is the consummately concrete judgment about the specific action which I ought to do here and now. This judgment of conscience/3 remains infallible. I have to do what I genuinely believe is right. Yes, conscience/3 may do what is objectively wrong because of its dependence on the fallible conscience/2, but we must always follow conscience, now properly understood as conscience/3. The role of authoritative church teaching comes into play on the level of conscience/2. As important as this role is, it is limited by the possibility of error, of incompleteness, and of inadequacy. Important as it is, this church teaching should never become a loyalty test for Catholics. The second part dealing with the human person closes with a short discussion of related dogmatic themes and the Christian vocation which insists on the temporal and growth aspects of the Christian life together with the unique calling of the individual given by God.

Part three concerns the moral world as distinguished from the moral person and deals with objective morality. The book here again fulfills its aim of trying to relate contemporary reflections to the tradition of Catholic moral theology. The author summarizes the scholastic tradition on natural law and then devotes the remaining chapters of the third part to a systematic understanding of natural law and its application to the objective morality of human acts. He traces the understanding of law, especially natural law, in the Scripture and in the historical tradition of the church. O'Connell indicates that at times in the considerations of the natural law the Greek concepts of givenness and facticity have prevailed over the Roman concept of reason. Thomas Aquinas appears to be somewhat ambivalent on this point.

Principles develops the theory of natural law which maintains that values are real, experiential, consequential, historical, and proportionate. One can see here the influence of the revisionist approach in contemporary Catholic moral theology. The right action is that action which contains the proportionately greatest maximization of good and minimization of evil. The values of the real world out there are concrete and "doing values" which are premoral values. Material norms govern these concrete premoral values and admit of exception. For example, do not kill is a material norm dealing with a premoral value which by its very nature must admit of some exceptions. Moral values are "being values" and refer to the qualities that should characterize the person—just, fair, honest, chaste. Formal norms govern the moral values, and they can be absolutely binding without any exceptions—be just, be fair, reasonable, etc.

This newer understanding of natural law and of the determination of the morality of acts results in a changed understanding of some of the traditional maxims of moral theology. There are no concrete and material acts (e.g., sexual relations) which can be said to be intrinsically evil and always wrong, never admitting any possible exceptions. Traditional theory explains that there are three sources of morality—object, end, and circumstances had to be good if the morality of the act was to be good. But in the revisionist perspective all these aspects are only premoral realities. The only source of objective morality is the deed and the relevant circumstances taken together. Also the newer position rejects the principle of double effect with its third condition that the good effect must not be produced by means of the evil effect. Positive and proportionate consequences can justify the means.

Yes, we can know the natural law. Our formulations are often inadequate, partial, and tentative, but this knowledge serves as the basis for our personal actions. A final chapter on human law discusses the binding force of human law and the virtue of epikeia, which appeals from the letter of the law to the spirit of the law. Part four consists of two concluding essays dealing with Christian morality and the present and the future of Catholic morality.

Principles takes the traditional concerns of the manuals of fundamental moral theology — the human act, conscience, natural law, sin, and virtue and explains them in the light of a moderately progressive, revisionist, contemporary Catholic morality with emphasis on the fundamental option, the rational aspect of natural law, and a proportionate-reason approach to moral norms. O'Connell has succeeded very well in what practically no one else has been willing or able to do. At the same time he has also tried to show exactly how this newer approach differs from the older approach, and he thus forms a bridge for his readers between the older and the newer concepts. In addition, O'Connell is a superb pedagogue. His thinking is clear and lucid; his style and writing are "textbookish" in the very best sense of that term.

However, there are also weaknesses and limitations, some of which come from the format and material content of the manual approach. *Principles*, for all its newness, retains the primary orientation of the manuals to train confessors for the sacrament of penance. This purpose is not quite so evident in O'Connell, but it remains predominant. The whole focus is primarily on the morality of acts and on the distinction between mortal and venial sin. The person is brought into the discussion especially in terms of the fundamental stance and fundamental option, but this consideration is developed to set up the distinction between mortal sin and venial sin. Continual conversion and growth are not developed. Virtue is mentioned, but little or nothing is said in a systematic way about the important relationships among the person, the virtues or character of the person, and one's acts. The implicit perspective of the work is that of the confessor judging the act of another and not the individual person responding to the call of God to become a disciple of the Lord and strive for holiness. A short last chapter admits that the science of the Christian life also involves spirituality which nourishes the interior life of the Christian and participation in a liturgical community. Moral theology only gives a partial view of the Christian life. I would rather emphasize that moral theology studies the whole Christian life, and spirituality and liturgy have to be incorporated into the whole picture to form a complete and total moral theology of the Christian life.

The narrow focus on the morality of acts and on the meaning and presence of sin means that practically no mention is made of the social, political, and cosmic aspects of the Christian life. The manual format clearly tends in this direction, and the author's emphasis on a transcendental philosophical approach also contributes to this lack. The transcendental approach has been criticized by political and liberation theologians for not giving enough importance to the social and political aspects of life and morality. The contemporary context has led to a great emphasis on the need to avoid the individualism of the older manuals of moral theology. The 1971 Synod of Bishops has maintained that actions on behalf of justice and participation in the transformation of the world form a constitutive dimension of the preaching of the gospel and of the mission of the church.[3] A contemporary book or course on Catholic moral theology must give significant emphasis to this dimension. Today the format and perspective of the older manuals are no longer totally apt or sufficient.

The manual or introductory book cannot be expected to probe deeply into all aspects of moral theology. O'Connell packs a great deal of information into his meaty and concise considerations, but at times the present volume shows the lack of a deeper approach or appears to propose solutions and approaches that are somewhat facile. It seems to me that his discussion of natural law or moral values as being proportional and consequentialist needs some further development and nuancing. At the very minimum O'Connell would help his own cause if he distinguished his position from that of utilitarianism. In his theory there is room for considerations other than consequences which would then readily differentiate his approach from that of utilitarianism. Also a more expanded version might have tried to respond at greater length to some of the arguments proposed against his proportionalism by thinkers such as Grisez.

His threefold division of conscience is a creative and contemporary development of a threefold distinction found in the manuals of moral theology. Conscience as the ultimate practical judgment about the morality of an act to be done by the agent is distinguished from synderesis, the innate habit of first principles, and from moral science which is an abstract judgment about the morality of an action. O'Connell uses this division very effectively. However, without adding too many extra paragraphs, he could have grounded his theory of conscience in the transcendental notion of the person which was developed earlier. The judgment of conscience is a virtually unconditioned judgment grounded in the thrust of the self-transcending subject toward the true and the good. Also, infallible is not the proper word to describe the judgment of conscience/3. The discussion of the teaching role of the church is integrated into the material on conscience, but there are many complex problems that even O'Connell cannot adequately cover in three and one half pages.

As a good pedagogue, O'Connell rightfully makes some very helpful distinctions, but at times there is the danger that such distinctions can too easily become dichotomies, or at least it is necessary to relate explicitly the aspects which are distinguished. I am thinking specifically of his distinctions between being and doing, subject and agent, formal and material.

A very important question concerns the meaning of the Christian aspect of moral theology and its relationship to philosophical ethics. In the main two sections of the book on the moral person and the moral world, the author generally does not invoke specifically Christian aspects except in his discussion in chapter twelve of the moral law in Scripture. The author himself willingly admits his approach here is philosophical. Four introductory essays, including two dealing with biblical morality and Christ and moral theology, prepare the way for the major sections of the book. The Chicago seminary professor maintains in these earlier essays that Christian ethics is humanistic ethics and for deeply theological reasons. He concludes, "Thus in a certain sense, moral theology is not theology at all. It is moral philosophy pursued by persons who are believers" (p. 41). He willingly admits that, as a result, in the major sections of the book he will be talking philosophy. In a concluding essay O'Connell explains the Christian influence in terms of vision, motivation, and formalities.

My own approach and perspective differ, but the following pages will show that the question remains very central and important in the discipline of moral theology. I maintain that the material content of moral theology or Christian ethics including concrete norms, attitudes, values, and dispositions cannot claim to be unique. Non-Christians can and do share the same understanding and actions. Christians in the past have too readily claimed attitudes such as self-sacrificing love as unique to Christians. History and experience remind us that many human beings have showed the same self-sacrificing love. Even though there is no unique content to Christian morality in the sense mentioned above, I still deny that Christian ethics is the same as philosophical ethics. Moral theology or Christian ethics is a thematic, reflexive, second-order discourse which studies the way in which the Christian life should be lived. The Christian existence as members of the Christian community marks our whole existence and everything we do including our approach to morality. Christian ethics or moral theology precisely because the discipline is "Christian" or "theological" must reflect on how this community understands the Christian moral life in the light of its own stories, Scriptures, symbols, traditions, and values. Even though the material content of Christian morality may not differ in principle from human morality, the way in which the Christian comes to these conclusions does depend on explicit Christian understandings. As will be pointed out later, some important secondary and complementary value is found in an approach which prescinds from the Christian aspect, but the primary methodology of moral theology must be explicitly theological and come from a faith perspective.

Daniel Maguire[4]

The *Sitz im Leben* of Daniel C. Maguire's *The Moral Choice* is the author's attempt as a college professor of Christian ethics to write an epistemology of ethics concentrating on the formal moral choice in the light of contemporary ethical debate and of today's moral issues. His scope is both narrower (an epistemology of ethics concentrating on the moral choice) and broader (the contemporary ethical debate and today's moral issues) than O'Connell's. Maguire does not attempt to update the older manual approach of moral theology, but rather in the context of a much broader dialogue he proposes his own methodology for moral choice which is explicitly based only on philosophical grounds but is open to use by all including religious ethicists and religious people. Maguire thus is attempting something limited but also quite new in terms of the historical development of moral theology.

The first two chapters reveal the author's wider context. The first chapter illustrates from sexuality, science, business, and politics the present muddle in the moralscape of contemporary, and especially, American life. *The Moral Choice* paints a negative picture of cultural and ethical disarray, including the cult of obscurity to which many intellectuals seem addicted and the very emasculation of ethics by those who claim to be ethicists.

There are two fundamental questions for ethical inquiry: What is morality? and What is the foundation of moral experience? Maguire begins his discussion by disagreeing with the relativists who reduce morality to custom, the survivalists who make survival the ultimate ethical category, the school of linguistic analysis which gives up philosophy and ethics for language, and the presumers who take the foundation of morality for granted. Maguire proposes a theory of ethical realism according to which morality is what befits or does not befit persons as persons. The foundation of morality is the experience of the value of persons and their environment, an experience which cannot be proved but only illustrated. This fundamental moral experience is an affective faith experience which must be understood in terms of process. The foundational moral experience calls for a proper love of self and a love of others which finds its first and minimal expression in terms of justice. The strategy of love is ethics which is understood as the art-science which seeks to bring sensitivity and method to the discernment of moral values.

The heart and center of Maguire's moral method is his "wheel model." The hub or center of the wheel contains the reality-revealing questions which supply the facts or data by uncovering the moral situation in all of its concrete, unique, empirical complexity. There are four reality-revealing questions: What, as the first question, fixes attention on the primary data (physical, psychological, systematic) by which we make our first cognitive contact? However, the what alone can never give us the final moral verdict. Without explicitly using the words, Maguire here differs from a physicalism which defines the human moral act in terms of the physical structure of the act. The second reality-revealing question asks: Why? How? Who? When? Where? The third question concerns foreseeable effects, while the fourth question deals with viable alternatives. The four reality-revealing questions are at the heart of the wheel and represent the expository aspect of the ethical enterprise. The nine spokes of the wheel model represent systematic concern for the second phase of the ethical enterprise — evaluation. Maguire, however, recognizes that in reality the expository or reality-revealing phase and the evaluational phase cannot be so neatly separated.

The nine spokes are ways of evaluation, but obviously all are not of equal value or importance. "Creative imagination is the supreme faculty of the moral person" (p. 189). Creative imagination is the power to perceive the possible within the actual. The conditions for creativity include excitement, quiet, work, malleability, and *kairos*. Principles as culturally based propositions or generalizations about what

befits or does not befit the behavior of human beings give
prima facie evidence but are always in some tension with the
unique circumstances of the case. Reason constitutes one of
the evaluative spokes, but there is a great gulf between
reasonable and rationalistic. Authority in all its different
forms constitutes another evaluative spoke, but emphasis on
authority has an underside as well as a good side. Affectivity
constitutes another evaluative mode. Systematic account
must also be taken of the value awareness that comes to us
from feeling or affectivity even though there is something
somewhat ineffable about affectivity. There is a feel of and
for moral truth. Two other evaluative spokes are individual
experience and group experience. Here again there are
dangers associated with both these aspects, and the Marquette University professor explicitly cautions against the
negative side of group influence with all its many limitations
and falsifications. Comedy and tragedy are two other modes
of evaluation. Humor performs many functions but especially acts as the bane of absolutism, whereas tragedy in
many ways can expand moral consciousness. However,
Maguire recognizes that comedy and tragedy as evaluative
spokes on the wheel do not function in the same way as the
others. The other seven spokes can serve as check points in
our evaluation of moral reality.

For Maguire conscience is the conscious self as attuned to
moral values and disvalues in the concrete. Conscience in
this sense is the moral person striving to make moral choices
and appropriating the moral message just described.
Maguire prefers to retire the word sin and speak of guilt
which can be understood in a taboo sense, an egoistic sense,
or a realistic sense.

There are many significant aspects in Maguire's work. He
gives great importance to the role of creative imagination,
and his own work itself is most creative. He is not following
the approach of the older manuals but has proposed an entirely new format. The author's creativity is seen not only in
his overall approach which proposes this new and different
format but also in his discussion of particular issues. Object,

end, and circumstances were the classical sources of morality, but Maguire now adds the notion of viable alternatives. One aspect of the wheel which is not all that new but which is often overlooked and forgotten in ethical methodologies is the insistence on affectivity and feeling. We have all had the experience described by Maguire of shrinking in horror before a certain idea or reality. Such a feeling can lead the agent to a more thorough investigation because of which one can then conceptualize what was already known through affectivity. Ethics cannot forget the important role of affectivity. Maguire also brings to the fore other aspects which are not often mentioned in the methodologies proposed for ethical decision-making such as the comic and the tragic.

Throughout the book one is impressed by the comprehensiveness of the approach and the insistence on complexity. The first four chapters give the reader a good overview of the contemporary muddle in the moralscape and of the different ethical approaches. The reader comes to dialogue with intuitionists, behaviorists, relativists, survivalists, and the followers of linguistic analysis. The author deftly situates his own moral realism in relation to these other approaches. One can only admire the way in which the book brings together so many diverse aspects in a clear and coherent way.

The emphasis on comprehensiveness and complexity is seen throughout the book. The great danger remains the exclusion of elements that should be considered. None of the evaluational spokes can be absolutized, but all must be considered. Affectivity is important, but there are dangers and pitfalls which are also present in affectivity. Maguire also reminds us that ethics must give due importance to both consistency and surprise. The discussion on authority is likewise comprehensive and balanced. Excessive reliance on authority can become a denial of our capacity to know moral truth, to reason, but at the same time authority properly understood is not an alien intrusion on the autonomy of the rational person but is part of a system of reliance and trust that should characterize human existence.

Another aspect of Maguire's comprehensiveness is seen in his emphasis on ethics as including not only the personal but also the social aspect. Too often books dealing with the moral choice tend to stress only the personal aspect. Maguire avoids this danger both by his many examples and also by maintaining that justice is the minimal manifestation of the foundational moral experience and the minimal manifestation of other love.

In his discussion of some important debates in contemporary ethics Maguire also opts for an approach based on comprehensiveness and complexity. Consequences are important in ethics, but an exclusive emphasis on consequences will be too narrow and too precarious. Consequentialism involves the glorification of ends at the expense of means and involves the danger of sacrificing the individual for the good of the whole. To ask if the end justifies the means is a bad question because ends and means must be judged in relational tension to one another and to all the pertinent circumstances. Teleology versus deontology is another misplaced debate. A realistic ethic must take account of both aspects. Granted these issues cannot be dealt with in great depth given the overall scope of the book, but the solutions proposed are appealing precisely because of their comprehensiveness.

The Marquette professor is obviously an excellent pedagogue, and the book can readily and easily be used by good college students. The wheel model has many pedagogical advantages as a way of describing ethical methodology which can easily be understood and appreciated by all. The book is obviously the product of the author's own classroom experience. Examples abound, perhaps too readily at times; but these cases and examples not only illustrate the method described but also engage the interest of the reader. Maguire's own writing style adds to the attractiveness of the book. His approach is engaging, enthusiastic, even exuberant, but at times the style borders on the breezy. This is no dry as dust textbook, for the author makes the quest of ethics and decision-making an exciting one.

Maguire, the university and college professor, unlike

O'Connell, the seminary professor, is not greatly interested in the older perspective of the manuals in their attempt to distinguish what is mortally sinful and what is not. Likewise, *The Moral Choice* does not expend a great effort relating its method to older approaches in the Catholic tradition. His scope is much broader — an ethic of moral choice which can be appropriated by all human beings.

The primary weaknesses I find in Maguire's approach stem above all from the rather narrow objective that he sets for himself. Anyone dealing with Christian ethics or moral theology must supplement what is found here. Throughout the book Maguire prescinds from the explicitly Christian aspect and presents a formal method for decision-making which is applicable to all. I agree that the same formal criteria apply to all human beings in their decision-making. Thus Maguire's approach is perfectly acceptable. However, as mentioned in the discussion of O'Connell, I believe that a Christian moral theology must include and work from an explicitly Christian faith perspective.

The narrow focus of *The Moral Choice* means that by definition it does not include topics other than a formal consideration of the moral choice. Above all a total moral theology must deal with anthropology, the person, and the moral growth of the person. Decision-making comes from the person and should be grounded in the person. Maguire does make some references to character, but they are not systematic and do not really contribute to an anthropology. The basic attitudes or virtues or character of the person, and in our case the Christian person, need to be expanded for a complete moral theology. The realities of faith, hope, and love should characterize the Christian person in addition to the realities of fidelity and integrity. In addition, the individual choice should be connected with the more basic orientation or choices of the person. Human acts themselves are ultimately related to the person as both subject and agent.

Another self-imposed limit on *The Moral Choice* is the formal character of the enterprise. The wheel itself has no material content but is to be used for all decision-making.

However, in each decision there are different values and meanings that are involved. Maguire thus brings in many practical illustrations to show how the wheel does work. On the whole his approach is satisfactory, but in each of these particular cases there is something more than the formal decision-making process at work. The material assessment of the values involved in the different cases and illustrations will obviously affect the outcome. People employing this same formal anthropology as described in the wheel model can and will come to different positions depending on their apprehension of the moral meaning and values involved. One would need a detailed analysis of each of these particular questions (such as Maguire does give in his other books on death, justice, and the Moral Majority)[5] to analyze how the material aspects of meaning and the perception of values enter into concrete decision-making.

Even within the legitimately narrow focus there are some questions that can be raised to Maguire. The author is very conscious that ethics is not an exact science. No methodology for decision-making can be an exact science. However, even with that said, there remain some questions especially about the relationship between and among the spokes of the wheel. Principles, for example, can be based on reason, analysis, group experience, or individual experience. Authority does not stand independently but is often intimately connected with one or the other spokes of the wheel. In addition to the question of overlapping between and among the spokes there is the more significant problem of conflicts and the resolution of those conflicts. How do you resolve possible conflicts among individual experience, group experience, reason, and authority? Such situations obviously are rather commonplace in human existence. Not all of the spokes are of equal value. How do they work together?

Questions can also be asked about the foundational moral experience to elicit a greater clarification. How does this differ from an intuitionist approach? How are norms or even the methodology proposed related to and grounded in this experience? There also appears to be some tension in the author's articulation of this experience. Usually Maguire speaks of the experience of the value of persons and their environment, but sometimes he speaks just of persons. What is the relationship between persons and environment? Sometimes he also speaks of the "inviolable sanctity of human life" (p. 81). Again, questions can be asked about the exact relationship between life and person, between the value and the sanctity of life and/or persons.

Yes, there are questions that can and should be raised to Maguire about his approach. However, it stands as a very creative attempt in the contemporary scene to deal with the moral choice. My major observation is the limited scope of the work in relationship to the total enterprise of moral theology.

Enda McDonagh

The *Sitz im Leben* of Enda McDonagh differs from that of the two previously considered authors. O'Connell and Maguire are primarily teachers writing for their respective students and academies. McDonagh is not writing primarily for his students in the classroom. The two books to be considered here, *Gift and Call* and *Doing the Truth*, are collections of essays and often very short essays.[6] What brings these volumes together is the attempt to develop a Christian theology of morality. By definition the works considered are not systematic but rather suggestive. Thus the books themselves could never really be used as a complete text for moral theology, nor can the approach in my judgment ever be a total approach. However, McDonagh's Christian theology of morality demands more attention than it has received from people in the discipline.

The Maynooth scholar recognizes that his approach is different from, but complementary to, what can properly be called moral theology. The usual approach, especially in the revised moral theology after the Second Vatican Council, begins with revelation and faith and draws out their meaning and significance for the moral life of the Christian. Moral existence is seen, lived, and studied in the light of the Christian faith. However, in the first four chapters of *Gift and Call* McDonagh develops a different approach beginning with moral experience common to all human beings rather than Christian revelation. Moral experience itself and not ethics is the starting point for McDonagh. After examining this moral experience common to all human beings and considered apart from faith, the theologian correlates or confronts this experience with faith in Jesus Christ.

According to McDonagh, reflection on moral experience reveals the existence of moral obligation in terms of a call which has an unconditional character about it. The final source of this obligation or call is another person or group of persons who call me or the group to recognize, respect, and respond. There is a reciprocity involved here, since the subject and the source of the call are both persons. We experience the coming of the other as gift but also at times as threat, so that this ambiguity is part of our moral experience. Our recognition, respect, and response differ insofar as we perceive the other as gift embodying call or as threat provoking fear. McDonagh sees the moral experience as involving self-transcendence. In transcending self to recognize, respect, and respond to the other there is involved a certain disintegration of the subject. "But this should then issue in a reintegration of subject and relationship at a deeper level of *communion* achieved through the reaching out in recognition, respect, and response, and at a deeper level of *differentiation*, achieved for the subject in a fuller self-identification, self-acceptance, and self-creation. In the ideal situation the interchange is mutual and the differentiation and communion are achieved by both" (p. 61).

When confronted or correlated with Christian faith, there is a coherence, illumination, and even an intrinsic connection between our moral experience and our Christian faith. The basic structure of Christian belief involves a gift-call structure. Salvation means that the loving divine initiative which comes to us is a call which we then recognize and respect and to which we respond. However, the checkered pattern of Judeo-Christian history also reminds us that the other can be perceived as threat-fear. The moments of recognition, respect, and response in the moral experience are parallel in the religious or faith experience of the Christian. Likewise the moral experience of personal integration following upon some disintegration corresponds to the Christian concept of conversion and sharing in the dying and rising of the Lord.

Not only is there convergence between the two experiences, but for the believer there is an intrinsic connection between the two. This intrinsic connection is above all seen in terms of Christian faith's ability to go beyond the question marks discovered at the limits of the analysis of moral experience. Christian faith understands the ultimate gift aspect of moral experience in terms of God's loving gift of self through Christ Jesus. Christian faith ultimately gives a satisfying explanation for the unconditionality of the moral call and the correlative inviolability of the person or human other. Christian faith also gives meaning to the problem of personal failure, the need for forgiveness, and the reality of death which now can be seen as a way to fulfillment rather than as an emptiness which throws doubt on the whole validity of the moral order.

Individual studies collected in *Gift and Call* and in the subsequent book of essays *Doing the Truth* apply this theory of a Christian theology of morality to some particular questions such as vocation. Of special interest are his essays on "Morality and Prayer" and "Morality and Spirituality" found in the later volume. In response to some inadequate understandings of these relationships proposed in the past (e.g., moral obligations to pray and the need to pray to obtain the light and strength for observing the moral law), the Irish theologian begins with his analysis of the moral experience apart from faith. One of the primary moral activities is thanksgiving for the presence of the other, a celebration of their presence as gift. The human response to the human other can and should by its own inherent dynamism expand into a response to the ultimate other; it can and should expand into prayer (*Doing the Truth*, pp. 40-57). The purpose of the essay on "Morality and Spirituality" is to root in ordinary experience some outstanding characteristics of Christian spirituality such as asceticism, humility, tolerance, celibacy, poverty, and obedience. Again the approach complements but does not supplement or replace the more conventional analysis which begins from Christian faith considerations (pp. 58-75).

McDonagh has come up with a novel and an intriguing approach which in my judgment merits more consideration than it has heretofore received. The Maynooth professor admits that this approach is complementary to the method that starts from faith perception in its dealing with morality. In my judgment his approach is quite legitimate and needed but also limited. What specifically can the theology of morality contribute? In my interpretation it serves in many ways the purpose of a foundational theology when applied to moral theology. In other words, it shows the basic congruence and coherence between Christian morality and the human experience of morality.

I also detect in McDonagh's whole approach a very apologetic purpose — a defense of Christian morality, primarily for those who in one way or another have become somewhat disillusioned with the Christian approach. There are indications in his writings that he is aware that many people have rejected Christian morality because of the poor and inadequate ways in which it has been presented (*Doing the Truth*, p. 43). The author in one place describes his own purpose as not a purely academic exercise but an attempt to deal on a pastoral level with the fact that many Christians find it difficult to connect immediately with and to accept a morality couched in strongly religious and Christian terms (pp. 60-61). It is precisely in this sense that I see his approach as apologetics. McDonagh, however, sees a somewhat less limited justification for his approach because he maintains that so many today, including Christians, actually experience the moral life in this way. His approach is, consequently, a fresh development of the traditional natural-law approach without the artificial limitations of that tradition which was based on a concept of pure nature abstracted from sin and grace.

However, I do not see such an approach as being the primary way in which the discipline of moral theology should go, but McDonagh's method can be complementary in a secondary way and for a number of different purposes. In fact, by his own admission his approach really constitutes a different type of discipline. In addition, it seems to me that the Christian in the existential order cannot help but have one's faith color and influence one's experience of morality. For the committed Christian or at least the persons striving to live a Christian life, moral experience cannot exist in a separate compartment apart from Christian faith. The existential reality is that the Christian person cannot experience morality without in some way seeing it influenced by the reality of faith. The moral experience which McDonagh talks about seems to be an abstraction which might be the experience of some even among disillusioned Christians. Existentially the Christian cannot separate faith from the moral experience in the same way that moral theology in the systematic realm cannot thematize the moral life apart from the realities of faith.

In addition I do not think that one can develop a systematic Christian theology of morality. The Irish theologian has given us only some fascinating illustrations, but I wonder if there is the ultimate difficulty and even impossibility of developing a systematic approach to both ethics and theology on the basis of his method. Notice that he usually speaks about a theology of morality and begins with moral experience, not a systematic ethics. Even granting McDonagh's starting point, a fundamental question can be raised. Is his understanding of moral experience accurate? Would all agree with him? I cannot help but think that his own Christian faith has influenced his understanding of the moral experience even though he claims this is an autonomous reality not connected with faith. This suspicion is fueled by the recognition that McDonagh earlier developed a moral theology based on an invitation-response model.[7]

McDonagh's approach is very sketchy and not systematically developed, but there are important emphases in his morality that are significant for contemporary moral theology and that need to be developed in any approach to the discipline. Father McDonagh insists that an analysis of moral life must involve more than acts and deal with the person and communities of persons. Spirituality, prayer, and liturgy are integral parts of Christian ethics. Both the personal and the social dimensions are stressed and equally attended to in his essays. The realities of limitation, sin, and death are also dealt with and not ignored.

In conclusion, McDonagh's approach is legitimate, intriguing, and complementary to other approaches. However, it is a limited approach and in my judgment can never be the primary methodological approach for moral theology as such.

Franz Böckle[8]

The *Sitz im Leben* of Franz Böckle's *Fundamental Moral Theology* is the Catholic theology faculty of a German university. Böckle must be seen in the context of the school of autonomous morality which began in Germany with the work of Alfons Auer, whose seminal article appeared in 1969, followed by a book in 1971.[9] There are some common thrusts to German autonomous morality. There is no unique content to Christian ethics, but moral norms and content are the same for all human beings. The morality of revelation is the true morality of reason. Morality is autonomous in the sense that the human person determines oneself as a rational being by one's own acts. This school in Germany, as is evident from Auer's first article, has also been reacting to the fact that often Catholic morality was presented as God's law given in revelation and coming extrinsically from outside the human person. This heteronomous understanding is rejected by the proponents of autonomous morality. Church authorities have to realize that their teachings on ethical norms must be reasonably convincing to all human beings. Autonomous morality claims to be in keeping with Aquinas and the best of the Catholic tradition which always grounded morality and ethics in the human. However, all must admit that at least the emphasis is different from that approach to moral theology proposed at the Second Vatican Council with its call for a theological anthropology in the context of a Christological and biblical approach.

As a university professor Böckle is interested in developing the scientific nature of moral theology. Our author rightly reacts to a restricted view of science that is limited to hypotheses which can be empirically tested. Such an understanding is much too limited and narrow. Since our contemporary world is conscious of the importance of questions of value and of meaning, science must also concern itself with nonhypothetical knowledge. At the same time problems also have arisen within the discipline of moral theology which has made certain moral judgments absolute. In this context Böckle wants to develop a fundamental moral theology.

The task of fundamental moral theology is to justify an ethical theory for the establishment of values and norms in the present social, intellectual, and cultural situation. This task suggests that a universally valid ethical theory based on reason should be elaborated into which the special insights arising from faith are to be incorporated as complementary and corrective elements. The Catholic tradition has recognized that the morality of revelation is the morality of reason. Böckle's primary goal is to make sure that the norms proposed are communicable to all human beings.

Fundamental Moral Theology must address two questions— why should we and what should we do? The why question is the ultimate basis of the moral claim which is the question about the basis and limits of human moral autonomy. The what question refers to the justification and claims to validity of moral statements. The what question has two parts—

the justification of morally relevant insights and the justification of concrete moral judgments. In keeping with the basic theory, the justification has to be done rationally. Part one of the book deals with the moral claim, while the second part deals with the justification of insights and norms.

Böckle develops what he calls a theonomous autonomy for the human moral subject. After discussing moral autonomy in the light of various philosophers, *Fundamental Moral Theology* gives a theological justification of moral autonomy which proves that faith in God and moral autonomy are not in conflict with each other. The Bonn University professor uses a transcendental understanding of the human person to ground his theonomous autonomy. The contradiction that a conditioned subject is unconditionally claimed by self or by other conditioned subjects ceases to exist when the moral claim is theonomously justified. (Note that the English translation on page 63 wrongly speaks here of an unconditioned subject.) The paradox of freedom remains. Freedom implies total dependence insofar as the human person receives as a gift the possibility of a free decision, but freedom also implies total independence insofar as the human person in one's choice confronts the only possibility of being free. In this theological vision the moral law is as a fact of reason nothing but the dependence of a personally free being, who is totally claimed in the freedom to have control over oneself. The paradox of finite liberty consists in the fact that the finite human person insofar as one is at the center of one's existence finds oneself in front of the Absolute Other. The human person truly becomes free and oneself only in relating to that Absolute Other. (Note again the inadequacies of the English translation which does not capitalize the terms and thus causes some ambiguity.)

This paradoxical situation is the source of the radical temptation and the basis of the possibility of alienation from oneself which is sin. Böckle develops both a phenomenological understanding of guilt and a theological approach to sin based on the theory of fundamental option. Despite the possibility and the reality of this contradiction in human existence (sin), the Christian is set free by Christ Jesus; but morality is theonomously autonomous.

Part two of *Fundamental Moral Theology* deals with the justification of norms. A first long section treats the Old Testament, the New Testament, the ethos of the early church, and natural moral law. The analysis of the biblical and ecclesial aspects comes to the conclusion that the concrete rules of biblical ethics were worked out by believers in the history of salvation in an attempt to make human society bearable and meaningful. Their material content is based on human reason and is neither mysterious nor exclusive. It must be and is possible to communicate to all people the consequences for human relationships that result from our faith in God and God's liberating law.

About thirty pages (pp. 199-233) are devoted to the question of the development and justification of morally relevant insights. Böckle recognizes that faith modifies our insight into goods and values, but we must always be able to communicate intelligibly our judgments about what is required of human action in this world to all other human beings. A short section of fifteen pages argues for a teleological basis for the justification of morally normative judgments, while an even shorter section on the church's contribution brings the book to a close.

The discussion of McDonagh's work sets the basis for my initial reaction to Böckle. The German professor offers a legitimate but in my judgment subordinate approach to moral theology. However, unlike McDonagh he does not refer to the validity of the other faith-based approach, nor does he explicitly refer to his own approach as complementary. Perhaps the method proposed by both McDonagh and Böckle can better be called a foundational moral theology which corresponds somewhat to the role foundational theology plays in the relationship to what is often, but unfortunately, called systematic theology. There is an important point in showing that Christian ethics is grounded in the understanding of the truly human. Especially in the university and scientific communities there is need to make and prove the basic assertion that Christian morality is truly human morality.

There are other advantages to the different approach proposed by Böckle and others. The Christian understanding of life in this world must in principle be able to be communicated to all other human beings if Christians are to have as significant an influence as possible on life in this world in the midst of a pluralistic society. Böckle is also correct in saying that too often in the past Christian morality has been expounded in an extrinsic way as if it were something imposed on human beings from outside and based on something in principle mysterious to all other human beings. Also at times some teachings of the hierarchical magisterium have been proposed with the same basic understanding. Such approaches will always be a temptation in the Christian community, but this temptation can be effectively met if there also exists the approach described by McDonagh and Böckle.

Although I agree that there is no unique material content in Christian ethics, I might justify my conclusion somewhat differently from Böckle. At least I am not entirely clear how he justifies his conclusion. In my judgment there is an important distinction between the older Catholic understanding of the natural and the contemporary understanding of the human. The older Catholic approach contrasted the natural with the supernatural as existing apart from grace and sin. Today the human refers to that which is historically and existentially present — human beings who are called by God to share in God's life and love, and the human world which is called to make ever more present the signs of the kingdom. As a concrete illustration of this theoretical understanding, human reason alone (i.e., apart from God's gracious self-gift) cannot fully understand and embrace the law of the cross, but all human beings in the present situation are able in principle to come to accept and to live out the reality of self-giving and suffering love. History also appears to support this contention.

In my judgment there is a complementary, but subordinate, place for the approach to moral theology found in

Franz Böckle's *Fundamental Moral Theology*. However, the term "autonomous morality," even with Böckle's modification of theonomous autonomy, seems ill chosen. Autonomy has connotations of individualism and fails to recognize the multiple relationships, responsibilities, and limitations which characterize human existence. I do not even believe that the contemporary world wants to see morality primarily in terms of autonomy. Think, for example, of the ecological aspects of human existence. Many problems have been caused in the past precisely because of human autonomy forgetting the limitations of existing in and with ecosystems. I prefer other terms such as the fully human or the truly human, both of which are found in the Pastoral Constitution on the Church in the Modern World of the Second Vatican Council. The fully or the truly human insists on the intrinsic character of Christian morality and its humanness but avoids some of the poor connotations of the word autonomy. At the same time, the fully or the truly human indicates the difference with the natural which in an earlier time was distinguished and separated from the supernatural.

Another limited aspect of *Fundamental Moral Theology* is the matter treated. Again, one cannot criticize an author for the limits placed on a book, but at least these limits mean that the book cannot be used as the only textbook in a course on moral theology. The questions of moral obligation and the justification of moral insights and judgments are the only issues discussed. Nothing is said, for example, about the person with the vision, character, and virtues which influence human actions as well as the growth and development of the person. Nor is anything said about the community which shapes the person by its story and traditions. Such considerations belong to all ethics and must bring in the explicitly Christian aspect in moral theology. There is also a limited aspect to the way in which the three main questions are explicitly treated in this book. The short section on the justification of norms is inadequate in the light of the contemporary debate. Much more can and should be said about this issue. Böckle, in a manner similar to O'Connell, makes a significant distinction between goods and values which could help advance the continuing discussion. Goods are realities which have an existence independently of personal thinking and willing—such as life, physical bodily integrity—and institutional goods—such as marriage, family, and the state. Values refer to the somewhat formal virtues which really exist only as qualities of the will such as justice, faith, fidelity, and solidarity. Böckle uses this distinction to explain his differences with Germain Grisez.

There is a further difficulty with the style of the book. As mentioned, greater emphasis could have been given to the justification of norms. The overall development itself could be streamlined somewhat and made clearer. Above all, the translation hinders a ready grasp of what the author is saying and at times is even erroneous.

In conclusion, these two chapters have evaluated and critiqued five significant contemporary authors in moral theology. The hermeneutic tool describing the *Sitz im Leben* of each book has been used to interpret and critique the authors considered. The relative strengths and weaknesses have been pointed out, but each author has important things to say to the ongoing discussion in contemporary moral theology.

If I had to choose one book as a basic text in Catholic fundamental moral theology for an upper-level college, or graduate, or seminary course, I would choose the first volume of Häring. There are problems and weaknesses with Häring's work as have already been mentioned. The reason for such a decision stems from the completeness of Häring's approach which involves all the aspects that should be included in moral theology, his holistic vision, and his explicitly Christian approach. However, Häring also needs to be supplemented by what other authors such as Maguire and O'Connell propose. McDonagh and Böckle develop a very significant but subordinate approach to moral theology which must be mentioned in all courses and which could rightly be used as a basis for special courses in a graduate setting. The

contributions of all these authors augur well for the continued growth of the discipline of moral theology.

NOTES

1. Much discussion in American moral theology in the last few
years has centered on the question of norms. Many articles have
been written on this subject. The books dealing with this issue have
tended to be collections of essays. For the recent history of the discussion giving all sides in the debate see Charles E. Curran and Richard
A. McCormick, eds., *Readings in Moral Theology No. 1: Moral Norms
and Catholic Tradition* (New York: Paulist Press, 1979). For the
thought of Richard McCormick and comments on it see Richard
A. McCormick and Paul Ramsey, eds., *Doing Evil to Achieve Good:
Moral Choice in Conflict Situations* (Chicago: Loyola University Press,
1978). For opponents of a revisionist position, see William E. May,
ed., *Principles of Catholic Moral Life* (Chicago: Franciscan Herald
Press, 1980).

2. Timothy E. O'Connell, *Principles for a Catholic Morality* (New
York: Seabury Press, 1978).

3. "Justice in the World," n. 6, found in *The Gospel of Peace and
Justice: Catholic Social Teaching Since Pope John,* ed. Joseph Gremil-
lion (Maryknoll, New York: Orbis Books, 1976), p. 514.

4. Daniel C. Maguire, *The Moral Choice* (Garden City, New
York: Doubleday, 1978; paperback ed., Minneapolis: Winston
Press, 1979).

5. Daniel C. Maguire, *Death by Choice* (Garden City, New York:
Doubleday and Co., 1974; paperback ed., New York: Schocken
Books, 1975); Maguire, *A New American Justice: Ending the White Male
Monopolies* (Garden City, New York: Doubleday, 1980; paperback
ed., Minneapolis: Winston Press, 1982); Maguire, *The New Subver-
sives: Anti-Americanism of the New Right* (New York: Crossroad
Publishing Co., 1982).

6. Enda McDonagh, *Gift and Call: Towards a Christian Theology
of Morality* (St. Meinrad, IN: Abbey Press, 1975); McDonagh, *Doing the Truth: The Quest for Moral Theology* (Notre Dame, IN: University of Notre Dame Press, 1979).

7. Enda McDonagh, *Invitation and Response: A Collection of Essays in Moral Theology* (New York: Sheed and Ward, 1972).

8. Franz Böckle, *Fundamental Moral Theology* (New York: Pueblo, 1980).

9. Alfons Auer, "Nach dem Erscheinen der Enzyklika 'Humanae Vitae', Zehn Thesen Über die Findung sittlicher Weisungen," *Theologisches Quartalschrift* 149 (1969): 75-85; Auer, *Autonome Moral und Christilicher Glaube* (Dusseldorf: Patmos, 1971).

PART TWO

Sexual and Biomedical Ethics

3: Moral Theology and Homosexuality

This chapter will consider the question of homosexuality from the perspective of moral theology in three different sections. The first part will discuss some aspects of moral theology with particular attention given to the relationship between moral theology and the Christian life. The second section will examine four different contemporary approaches in moral theology to the question of homosexuality. The final part will develop my own approach of moral theology to homosexuality.

I

Moral theology as a discipline has been in the process of change and development in the last fifteen years. Many of these changes occurring in moral theology in terms of its general methodology are very pertinent to the evaluation of the particular question of the morality of homosexuality and of homosexual acts. Catholic moral theology has traditionally employed the natural-law approach, but within the discipline itself there has recently been much discussion about the precise meaning and adequacy of the natural-law methodology. Natural law is a complex reality that involves at least two distinct questions from the perspective of moral methodology. The theological aspect of natural law concerns the sources in which Christian ethics finds ethical wisdom and knowledge. Natural-law theory maintains that the sources of moral theology are not only faith, revelation, and Jesus Christ but also and even primarily human reason and human nature. A very significant question then involves the exact

73

relationship between faith and revelation, on the one hand, and reason and human nature, on the other hand. The philosophical aspect of the question of natural law refers to the precise meaning of human nature and human reason.[1]

A concomitant question in contemporary moral theology concerns the place of moral norms in the Christian life and the way in which norms are ultimately established. Some maintain that the existing norms (e.g., adultery is always wrong; remarriage after divorce is always wrong; torture is always wrong) have been arrived at in a deontological manner. The Christian conscience declares such actions are wrong and incompatible with Christian existence no matter what the consequences because the actions directly violate the order willed by God or go against fundamental goods and values in the Christian life. Others maintain that the existing norms have been established and should be justified (or questioned) on teleological grounds. The Christian community comes to the conclusion that certain actions are wrong because generally speaking no proportionate reason exists which would justify doing what is prohibited in these cases.[2] These methodological questions now being discussed in moral theology greatly influence the approach one takes to the question of homosexuality.

There are other significant methodological questions in moral theology that also have an important bearing on the approach to homosexuality. The proper way for the discipline to use the Sacred Scripture has received much attention in recent literature. All must recognize both the importance and the limitations of the scriptural witness for moral theology.[3] One very striking illustration of this problem is found in the different liberation theologies. Latin American liberation theology makes strong appeal to the Scripture and finds there firm support for its position in the Exodus story, in the emphasis on the struggle against oppression and injustice, and in the privileged position of the poor.[4] Feminist liberation theology is confronted with a different reality. Here many parts of Scripture seem to support a basic inequality of the sexes. These differences point out the need for biblical theology and moral theology to employ a proper hermeneutic in understanding the data of the Scriptures and their relationship to contemporary reality.[5] Another significant problem concerns the use of the empirical sciences in moral theology. This question often comes to the fore in areas touching on economics, political science, sociology, and psychology. These two methodological questions assume significant importance in any ethical evaluation of homosexuality and of homosexual acts.[6]

Another very significant theoretical and practical question, especially in terms of life in the Christian community, concerns the relationship between church authority, moral theology, and the life of the individual believer. All Christian churches claim an authority to preach the Word and describe the Christian way of life. Roman Catholic ecclesiology recognizes a special hierarchical teaching office in the church. Only in the last fifteen years have Catholic theologians and Catholic practice explicitly faced up to a discussion of the possibility of dissent from authoritative, authentic, noninfallible hierarchical teaching.[7] Chapter nine will discuss this very important question in greater detail.

These questions have been briefly mentioned at the beginning to indicate that a study of homosexuality must of its very nature also involve a discussion about the methodology to be employed in moral theology. The second part of this study will examine four different positions on homosexuality as well as the different methodologies employed in these positions. However, it will be impossible to examine at length all the methodological presuppositions of the four questions. Of necessity only the more salient and specific aspects of the methodologies will be discussed.

This first part will now explore in greater depth the relationship between moral theology and the living of the Christian life. Such a consideration should help to clarify what is the role and function of moral theology. The particular relationship under consideration is a variation of the broader question of the relationship between theory and practice.

In general, moral theology studies the Christian life and

the way in which the Christian should live and act. In the first two chapters I have insisted that moral theology must deal with more than just the moral evaluation of particular acts. Moral theology and Christian living involve much more than just actions. This discipline must also consider the attitudes, dispositions, and character of the Christian person. Also, goals, ideals, values, institutions, and structures form a very important part of moral theology. An older moral theology too often limited itself to a consideration of the morality of actions and usually to the minimal aspect of what constituted right and wrong.

Moral theology studies the Christian moral life, but every Christian is called upon to live the Christian life. Is every Christian a moral theologian? What relationship is there between studying the Christian life and living the Christian life?

Every single Christian is called upon to respond to the good news of God's love made present in Jesus Christ through the power of the Spirit. This response is often referred to in the Christian tradition in terms of the twofold commandment of love — love of God and love of neighbor. All Christians are called through the gift of the Spirit to respond freely in conscience to this call. By our decisions and actions we make ourselves who we are. We shape our character. In addition, by our actions we try to bring about a greater peace and justice in the world in which we live. The Constitution on the Church of the Second Vatican Council maintains that all Christians are called to perfection and holiness.[8]

Perhaps the question can best be phrased in this manner: Is the moral theologian a better living Christian than those who have never studied moral theology? A theologian must point out that such a question is somewhat crass and has Pelagian overtones, but the query focuses very well the issue to be discussed. The same question can be raised about any professional ethicist, i.e., one who studies ethics. Are ethicists better living people or better decision-makers than those who have never systematically studied ethics?

From personal experience I can answer the question! Moral theologians are not necessarily the best living Christians. Ethicists are not necessarily the best living human beings and the best decision-makers. An old spiritual axiom rightly maintains that it is much more important and significant to practice compassion than to be able to define compassion. There might be a tinge of anti-intellectualism in the axiom, but the basic reality is true. There are many very good living Christian people who have never studied moral theology. Many of us who have professionally studied moral theology would readily admit our failure to respond as we should to the gracious call of God in Jesus Christ.

What then is the relationship between moral theology and the living of the Christian life? Moral theology studies the Christian life in a systematic, thematic, and reflective way. Moral theology involves second-order discourse and seeks to understand the Christian moral life in a systematic way. But every Christian is called to live the fullness of the Christian life. Every Christian has the gift of the Spirit and is called to bring forth the fruits of the Spirit. The Christian lives on the level of first-order discourse and ordinarily does not stand back to reflect in a systematic, thematic, and reflective way on the Christian life. This does not mean that the Christian person should not be reflective about one's own life, but this reflection is not of a scientific nature involving the demands of consistency and coherency on the level of theory.

Perhaps an analogy will help to understand better the relationship between moral theology and the living of the Christian life. How do you respond to the following question? Are psychiatrists the most mature, emotionally well-balanced and developed people you know? Without denigrating a particular profession, most people would respond negatively to that question. Yet most people recognize that psychiatrists have a significant role to play at times in mental and emotional well-being. The psychiatrist studies systematically, thematically, and reflectively the meaning of mental and emotional health and development. However, there are many people who have never read Freud or Jung or any theories of psychology and psychiatry who are emotionally mature and well-balanced human beings. What then is the role of psychiatry? Psychiatry studies on the level of second-order discourse human emotional development and maturity. Especially when problems arise in one's psychic world, then the psychiatrist can try to help the individual to locate the problem and correct it. Psychiatry can contribute to a better understanding and better living of human life, but every single human being possesses the basic human instinct to live an emotionally mature and well-balanced existence.

Moral theology has somewhat the same relationship to Christian moral life as psychiatry has to human emotional and psychic health. Moral theology operates on the level of theory trying to explain systematically and in a consistent and coherent way all the aspects of the moral life. People can lead good Christian lives without moral theology, but this discipline involves a critical approach of a scientific nature which helps in evaluating how Christians should live and act.

In keeping with the understanding of moral theology proposed here, the role of moral theology in the church will be less than the role often given to moral theology in the past. In the past the impression was often given that Christian practice was based on and followed from the theory developed in moral theology. The Catholic natural-law theory was the basis on which it was decided that a particular practice or action was in conformity or not with the Christian understanding of human existence. There is some truth in this understanding. However, history would seem to indicate this was not always true. Many accepted practices in the church came about first, and only later was the natural-law theory developed to explain the already-existing moral practices. The Christian community itself in the light of all the help it has been given through the gift of the Spirit, including a hierarchical teaching function, came to the recognition that some actions were right and that other actions were wrong. The second-order discourse of theory and systematization came later to explain in a systematic way why this particular action was right or wrong and how it fit in with an overall Christian understanding.

There is an analogy between the relationship of the individual Christian to moral theology and the relationship of the church as a whole to moral theology. The individual Christian by no means has to be a moral theologian, but moral theology offers help especially in time of crises and difficulties. The church itself has very often arrived at its own particular moral positions and teachings and then only later fully explained them and understood them in the light of a coherent and systematic theory. Moral theology is significant and important for critically understanding the Christian moral life. But this second-order discourse with its insistence on a rigorous scientific development is not the only way in which the church comes to accept a particular practice or reject a particular practice or action.

The relationship between theory and practice in moral matters in the church today is reciprocal. Sometimes a new practice will develop and ultimately be accepted in the church community, thereby calling for a change in the theory. The development which took place in the church's attitude to religious liberty well illustrates this reality. The lived experience and reality of religious liberty in the context of modern democratic societies came before the development of a theory to explain consistently and coherently this reality. The lived experience came first and only later was a theory developed to explain why the practice of religious liberty was consonant with Catholic self-understanding.[9]

However, not every new practice that comes along is necessarily good. Moral theology on the level of second-order discourse, together with all the other moral insights available to the Christian community, can and should serve as a basis for rejecting some new possible developments and practices. The just-war theory, for example, evolved in the Catholic tradition as a way of dealing with the morality of arms and warfare. The principle of discrimination in the just-war theory forbids the direct killing of noncombatants. In the light of this theory the Second Vatican Council declared "any act of war aimed indiscriminately at the destruction of entire cities or extensive areas along with their populations is a crime against God and man himself. It merits unequivocal and unhesitating condemnation."[10] This theory rightly and strongly condemns using nuclear weapons against cities. Chapters five and six, will show how the teaching of the American bishops and the moral theology presupposed in such teaching criticize American nuclear policies.

This reciprocal relationship between theory and practice is obviously operating in the contemporary discussions about sexuality in the life of the Roman Catholic Church and in moral theology. A glance at the literature of the past few years indicates how extensive the discussion has been. It is obvious that practice is changing within the Catholic Church on a number of questions dealing with human sexuality. The most obvious example is contraception. At the Synod of Bishops in Rome in 1980, Archbishop Quinn, the then president of the National Conference of Catholic Bishops, reported the figures from a study which concluded that 76.5 percent of married American Catholic women were using some form of birth regulation and that 94 percent of these women were using methods condemned by the church.[11] This changing practice has met with different theoretical reactions. Some have proposed a theory which accepts and justifies the practice, while other theologians condemn such practices on the basis of their theoretical understanding of moral theology and of human sexuality.[12] There can be no doubt that some of the recent developments and changes in the methodologies proposed in moral theology stem from a dissatisfaction with the past approach to questions of sexuality.

My understanding of moral theology recognizes that there is this reciprocal relationship between theory and practice, so not only does theory have some influence on practice but practice also has some influence on theory. The contemporary discussion on homosexuality takes place within this context. There is disagreement both about the morality of homosexuality and of homosexual acts and about the moral theory involved. A mutual relationship exists between one's approach to the theory of moral theology and to the practical appreciation and understanding of homosexuality. The point is that one cannot discuss the question of homosexuality without also discussing the question of moral theology and its methodology. In the light of this understanding of moral theology and its relationship to life and practice, the second section of this study will examine different approaches to the meaning and morality of homosexuality and homosexual acts. One point needs to be repeated. This discussion is prescinding from the very significant question of the role of official hierarchical church teaching in relationship to both the moral life of the Christian and moral theology.

II

This section will now consider and analyze four different approaches to the morality of homosexuality, paying attention both to the methodological approach taken by the various authors and to their substantive conclusions about homosexuality and homosexual acts. The four authors to be considered are John Harvey; John McNeill; the authors of *Human Sexuality*, the report of the Committee on the Study of Human Sexuality of the Catholic Theological Society of America; and Edward Malloy. The order of consideration is based on the chronological order of their writings.

John Harvey has been publishing in the area of homosexuality for over twenty-five years. No Catholic moral theologian has devoted more time or effort to this study. Perhaps the most synthetic discussion is his article in the *New Catholic Encyclopedia*.[13]

Harvey's methodological approach to the morality of homosexual acts is the natural-law approach found in the manuals of traditional moral theology. Homosexual acts are wrong because "such an act cannot fulfill the procreative purpose of the sexual faculty and is therefore an inordinate use of that faculty." This methodological approach begins with the recognition that every human person has a human nature, and one must live in accord with human nature. In human nature there are a number of built-in inclinations and faculties, including the faculty of human sexuality. Human reason sees in the faculty the God-given purpose and finality of procreation. Every sexual act must be open to the possibility of procreation. Human beings cannot directly go against the procreative purpose of human sexuality. Once procreation can completely be separated from the sexual act, then any kind of sexual act can be justified. The heavy emphasis is on the procreational aspect, and there is only a brief reference to going against the natural attraction of man for woman, which leads to the foundation of the basic stable unit of society, the family. The condemnation of homosexual acts in Scripture and in the traditional teaching of the church is in keeping with the reasons proposed.[14]

In addition to the question of the objective morality of homosexual acts, Harvey also considers the homosexual orientation itself and the subjective responsibility for homosexual actions. The homosexual orientation is not bad or evil, and the individual is not usually responsible for it. Homosexual acts are always objectively wrong, but responsibility for these might be lessened because of circumstances that take away one's freedom. The pastoral solution is to develop self-control through asceticism and live a celibate existence.[15]

The critique of Harvey's theory will begin with consistency. In general his theory is consistent, coherent, and logically based on the nature and function of the sexual faculty. However, there is one point which might be raised against the consistency of the theory. Harvey admits that the homosexual condition itself is not wrong or evil. One could argue that the homosexual is truly acting in accord with one's nature and therefore is doing no wrong. Harvey would probably respond that human nature is not only the existing reality but also the plan of right reason willed by God and found in the essential teleology of the sexual faculty itself. By benignly recognizing that the homosexual orientation is not evil in itself, Harvey might be giving some backing to the arguments of his opponents. In general, however, his theory is quite consistent.

My problem with his theory can be stated rather succinctly. The sexual faculty and acts should never be seen apart from the person and the person's relationship to other persons. I would argue that for the good of the person or for the good of the marital relationship one can interfere with the procreative aspect of the sexual act through the use of contraception. To see the meaning of human sexuality primarily in the nature and finality of the sexual faculty does not seem to give enough importance to the contributions of history and culture to the meaning of human sexuality. The theory tends to be ahistorical. I have often described this type of theory as being guilty of physicalism. The physical structure of the act becomes normative, and no one can ever interfere with the physical act. This problem comes to the fore especially in the theory's condemnation of artificial contraception. Harvey's theory serves to ground norms that are always obliging because they are based on the essential natural order willed by God. There is no room for possible exceptions or for the recognition that secondary precepts of the natural law oblige only as generally happens (*ut in pluribus*) and admit of exceptions in unique circumstances. Think of the famous case often mentioned in the literature of Christian ethics about Mrs. Bergmeier. In the story as first narrated by Joseph Fletcher, Mrs. Bergmeier seduced a prison guard and became pregnant so that as a result of her pregnant status she would be released from the horrors of the prison camp and sent home.[16]

A very important consideration concerns the relationship between sexuality and procreation. No one can deny (except for the cases of artificial insemination and *in vitro* fertilization) that procreation takes place through sexual relations. Traditional Roman Catholic moral theology has stressed procreation as an end or good of sexuality and has condemned artificial contraception as an unwarranted interference in the procreative nature of the sexual act. On the other hand, the Catholic Church has allowed sterile people to marry. In addition, there has been much development in terms of the understanding of the role of procreative intent in marriage and sexuality. At one time it was thought that only a procreative intent saved the sexual act in marriage from being wrong. Now it is accepted in Catholic teaching that husband and wife can intend that their sexual relations not be procreative, and they can even purposely choose the time when the wife is not fertile. There is some relationship between sexuality and procreation, but that relationship is very difficult to define and very difficult to use as a criterion for absolute moral condemnations.

John J. McNeill, a Jesuit priest, philosopher, and theologian, wrote some articles on homosexuality in *The Homiletic and Pastoral Review* in 1970 and published *The Church and the Homosexual* in 1976. The book was finally published with ecclesiastical permission from his Jesuit superiors after a delay of two years. However, that permission itself was later rescinded.[17]

McNeill reacts to the overemphasis on nature, reason, and law in the traditional approach to sexuality in moral theology. The human person is understood primarily in terms of radical freedom. The older approach has stressed the natural and biological rather than the personal, which is truly what is unique about the human. Human sexuality participates in radical human freedom. Whatever participates in human freedom cannot receive its total explanation in terms of causal determinism. We are born male or female biologically speaking, but we become men or women through a free human process of education. What it means to be a man or woman in a given society or culture is a free, human cultural creation. In the light of this emphasis on the person and on the freedom of the person, the basic moral norm for sexuality is love. A general consideration of the scriptural data leads to the same conclusion that sexual relations can be justified morally if they are a true expression of human love. Intrapersonal love is the ideal human context for sexual expression. The practical norms governing human sexual expression are derived from the concept of the human person as an end in himself or herself and from the necessary conditions of possibility for genuine intrapersonal love relationship. Among these conditions are such norms as mutuality, fidelity, and unselfishness.[18]

McNeill logically must and does deal with two factors that have often been proposed as bases for the traditional position condemning homosexual acts — the procreative aspect of human sexuality and the male-female complementarity. The nature of the love relationship, not the procreative aspect, is the norm for sexual expression. His argument here is rather curious. The Catholic Church continues to condemn any voluntary separation of the coequal purposes of sexual behavior, procreation and mutual love. The genuine homosexual does not fall under this condemnation since the procreative aspect is not eliminated by a free voluntary choice of the individual. The homosexual couple should be compared with the sterile heterosexual couple who are not able to procreate.[19] I think a better case could be made primarily through disagreeing with the teaching that artificial contraception is always wrong. McNeill's own methodology logically must condemn artificial contraception. One can appreciate that he is trying to find arguments for a position within traditionally accepted Catholic teaching, but McNeill seems to be stretching too much and conceding too much with this particular argument.

Male-female complementarity cannot be proposed as the norm, nor as the God-given reality, nor as the divine image in human existence. What makes one male or female is not biology but a free, human cultural creation. In the course of history look at all the problems of the domination of the female by the male that have resulted from the apparently God-given complementarity between male and female. The critical theologian should try to liberate humanity from these poor sexual stereotypes. The primary God-given ideal goal of human sexual development is that people should fashion cultural identities that make it possible for human beings to achieve the fullness of a true personal relationship of sexual love. Since it seems to be God's plan that 10 percent of human beings do not conform to the accepted heterosexual pattern, these homosexual people should not be cut off from the goal of human sexual development in terms of a personal relationship of sexual love. To make the biological male-female complementarity the basis of the moral norm for sexuality would deny human freedom its important role.[20] In the light of this theory McNeill maintains that for the genuine homosexual, or the invert, which is the word he frequently uses, a sexual relationship characterized by mutuality, unselfishness, and fidelity is a good.

The Scriptures and tradition need to be properly interpreted in the light of historical, cultural, and psychological realities of their own times. The Scriptures condemn perverse homosexual activity engaged in by otherwise truly heterosexual individuals as an expression of contempt or self-centered lust and usually associated with some form of idol worship. Both the Scriptures and the historical tradition did not know the phenomenon of inversion, and therefore they cannot be judged as condemning the homosexual acts of genuine homosexual inverts in the context of a loving relationship.[21] *The Church and the Homosexual* also cites data from the human sciences to indicate that many homosexuals have avoided the traps of promiscuity and depersonalized sex by entering into mature homosexual relationships with one partner and with the intention of fidelity and mutual support.[22]

In terms of critique there is an overall consistency to McNeill's approach with its emphasis on freedom and love and the denial of the procreative aspect and the male-female complementarity. However, I have some disagreements with McNeill's concept of the person as radical freedom and think there is some problem of consistency in his own approach. McNeill insists on understanding the person in terms of radical freedom. On the other hand he is inclined to agree with the position that the homosexual condition "is the result of an unconscious psychological process which lies radically outside the conscious, and therefore, free self-determination of the individual."[23] If there are certain aspects of our

makeup and sexuality that we cannot change, then our freedom is not as radical as this author claims. In addition, the
Jesuit theologian justifies homosexual acts only for the genuine homosexual or invert. However, if the human person
is to be defined in terms of radical freedom alone, it would
seem that one must consistently also accept the fact that such
actions could also be justified for the person who is not a
genuine homosexual. It seems that the sexual orientation of
the person as well as freedom enters into McNeill's own position. I agree that there are many things about ourselves that
we cannot change, but as a result one has to conclude that
our freedom is more limited and situated.

My basic philosophical disagreement with McNeill centers on this question of anthropology. In my judgment human freedom is more situated and limited. Consider human
experience. Human beings are quite limited by our heredity
and our environment. All people experience tiredness and
fatigue. We cannot for a long time avoid the basic human
need for rest and recreation. We are limited by our bodies
to being in only one place at one time. Some existential
thinkers see every human choice as a sacrifice. When we
choose to do one thing, we recognize our limitations and in-
abilities to do many other possible choices at the same time.
Yes, we have freedom in the sense of determining our own
fate through our actions, but we are also limited by our
multiple relationships with others, the world, and even with
ourselves. In terms of our relationship with the world, the
whole ecological debate has made us aware that our freedom
is very limited. Too often in the past, in the name of freedom
and self-determination, human beings have abused the finite
resources of our planet earth and the complex ecosystems
that are present and necessary for our world.

Contemporary theology has also been discussing the
understanding of the human person. Johannes Metz
disagrees with the transcendental Thomism of his mentor
Karl Rahner with its primary emphasis on the freedom of
the self-transcending subject. Such a position according to
Metz fails to give enough importance to the political and

social aspects of reality.[24] I too agree that human anthropology cannot be reduced to radical freedom because human freedom is more situated and limited, and more importance must be given to the social, political, and cosmic dimensions of human existence.

McNeill's anthropology logically sees sexuality in terms of radical human freedom. My anthropology gives more importance to the structures of human sexuality. Human sexuality is an embodied sexuality, and embodiment remains an important part of human sexuality as such. Too often radical freedom can imply a dualism between spirit and body in the human being. Body is an important aspect of all human anthropology. The embodiment of human sexuality in terms of male-female differences and complementarity is an important aspect of the meaning of human sexuality. Unfortunately, this complementarity too often in the past has been used by males to dominate females. But complementarity of itself does not necessarily involve the use of stereotypical sex roles which have been so prejudicial to women. Male-female complementarity is a part of human sexuality, for our sexuality is an embodied sexuality and our anthropology is an embodied anthropology. As a consequence, I do not accept McNeill's contention that male-female complementarity does not enter into the meaning of human sexuality and the norms governing human sexuality.

A third approach to homosexuality is that published by the Committee on the Study of Human Sexuality of the Catholic Theological Society of America, published under the title *Human Sexuality: New Directions in American Catholic Thought*.[25] The authors—Anthony Kosnik, William Carroll, Agnes Cunningham, Ronald Modras, and James Schulte— refer to homosexuality in the context of their broader discussion. Their approach logically begins with a definition of human sexuality and its meaning. These authors insist on an embodied view of human existence. Subjectivity is embodied in either a male or female body. Kosnik et al. are of the opinion that the two sexes experience themselves in subtly different ways by reason of their differences in bodily struc-

ture. The genital impulse is predisposed in favor of heterosexual union. It is in the genital union that the intertwining
of subjectivities of human existence has the potential for
fullest realization.[26]

The next step involves the approach to be taken in determining moral norms governing sexuality. There are three
different levels of moral evaluation. The first level is that of
the universal principle which governs all human sexuality
and is described as the need for sexuality to serve creative
growth toward integration. The second level of moral evaluation describes the particular moral values associated with
sexuality — self-liberation, other-enrichment, honesty, fidelity, service to life, social responsibility, and joy. The third
level of moral evaluation concerns the concrete norms, rules,
precepts, or guidelines which govern human sexuality in light
of protecting the values of human sexuality mentioned above.
These norms indicate what Christian experience has proven
to occur generally (*ut in pluribus*). To the extent these norms
refer to concrete physical actions (e.g., masturbation) without specifying particular circumstances or intentions, they
cannot be regarded as universal or absolute moral norms.[27]
In reviewing the literature on homosexuality the book summarizes four different approaches to the question: (1)
Homosexual acts are intrinsically evil. (2) Homosexual acts
are essentially imperfect. (3) Homosexual acts are to be evaluated in terms of their relational significance. (4) Homosexual acts are essentially good and natural. The authors
exclude both the first and the fourth solutions. They express some problems with both the second and the third approaches, but these approaches are more compatible with
the understanding of sexuality developed in their report.[28]

My primary negative criticism of this approach is the lack
of consistency. In developing the meaning of human sexuality the report emphasizes the male and female aspects of
human sexuality and the complementariness involved. However, the seven values of human sexuality, which constitute
the second level of the moral evaluation, do not incorporate
the male and female aspect of sexuality. If maleness and

femaleness are so significant for the meaning of human sexuality, this should appear in the values that are to be found
and protected in sexuality. The book opts for either the second or third of the four positions found in the contemporary
literature. The second position makes heterosexual relationships the ideal, but the third position bases everything on the
quality of the relationship. This third position logically follows on the basis of the seven values of human sexuality
posed in the moral evaluation. But on the basis of the insistence on the male-female complementarity in the definition
of human sexuality, the authors would logically have to reject the third position.

The crux of the inconsistency is that the meaning of sexuality accepts a male-female complementarity, but the values
of sexuality do not seem to incorporate this reality. For this
reason one can rightly criticize the values proposed for being
overly general and not specifically referring to human sexuality as such in all its specifics. One could argue that very
many different human realities should embody these same
seven basic values.

Edward A. Malloy has developed a fourth approach to
homosexuality in his recent book *Homosexuality and the Christian Way of Life*.[29] In his own words Malloy characterizes his
approach as a response to the revisionists. The revisionists
are those who have proposed that homosexual acts in the
context of a faithful, stable, mutual relationship can be morally justified and acceptable. Malloy believes that the revisionists have not made their case and sets out to prove that
claim in his book.[30]

Malloy compares the homosexual way of life with the
Christian way of life. He concludes the section of the book
on the homosexual way of life in this way:

> The central claim of this section of the book can be phrased in
> the following manner. The homosexual way of life is a pattern
> of social organization that takes certain characteristic forms
> which find a common focus in the ultimate commitment to
> unrestricted personal sexual freedom. Whatever other values
> individual homosexuals may hold and pursue, this liberation
> conviction is at the heart of their common identity with other

homosexuals. To accept homosexuality as a way of life is to call into question any attempt to enforce sexual standards of a more restrictive sort, whether based on political, social or religious grounds.[31]

The Christian way of life inculcates three virtues in the realm of sexuality. Chastity is the disciplined determination of appropriate sexual behavior according to the degree of the relationship of the partners. Love is the ultimate sharing of mutual concern according to the natural stages of attraction, passion, friendship, and sacrificial service. Faithfulness to promise involves the patient endurance and the voluntary exchange of the reciprocal commitment according to the community-based meaning of exclusivity and permanence. In the light of these values the church has seen monogamous marriage as the context that best promotes full realization of sexual expression. The homosexual way of life as described earlier is irreconcilable with the Christian way of life, for it is opposed to the three basic values of chastity, love, and faithfulness. Some individual homosexuals may achieve these virtues, but it is in spite of the homosexual way of life. The homosexual way of life is centered on the pursuit of unrestricted sexual pleasure.[32]

Malloy devotes a chapter to explaining and refuting the position of the ethical revisionists whom he divides into the moderate revisionists — who accept homosexual acts within a stable, exclusive, relationship — and radical revisionists. He maintains that the revisionists have not won the day, and their arguments are not convincing.[33] In the closing section on pastoral responses to the homosexual, Malloy admits that homosexual couples consciously committed to a permanent and exclusive relationship offer the best hope for the preservation of Christian values by active homosexuals. For those incapable of a celibate existence such a private arrangement is preferable to the other alternatives. However, the celibate option for Christian homosexuals should continue to be presented as the most consistent response to the Christian ethical view.[34]

My primary negative criticism of Malloy is his failure really to join the issue. No Catholic moral theologian defends the homosexual way of life as he has described it and defined it. In condemning the homosexual way of life he is really condemning a straw person and not entering into true dialogue with other theologians on this issue. There is also a problem with the way in which he has divided revisionists into moderate and radical revisionists. According to him moderate revisionists are those who maintain the need for a stable and faithful relationship. However, he never properly distinguishes the radical revisionists from the moderate revisionists. Malloy puts both McNeill and Kosnik et al. under the category of radical revisionists, but both of them also insist very much on the importance of a mutual, faithful relationship. Also, this reader was somewhat surprised to find in the final pastoral section at the end of the book some limited acceptance of homosexual couples committed to a permanent and exclusive relationship. Nothing in the book really prepares the reader for this. Such a position is crying out for further elucidation, especially in the light of everything else that Malloy has said. How does this position differ from the moderate revisionist position? What is the basis for such a pastoral practice? What exactly does he mean by the possibility of limited acceptance of such a relationship?

In my judgment a very significant difference between Malloy and the revisionists is the assumption about the possibility of a homosexual couple living in a faithful and exclusive relationship. Malloy implies this is possible only for a very few. The revisionists maintain there is a greater possibility for such relationships especially if they can openly be accepted and supported both in society and in the church.

III

Since I have developed my own approach to homosexuality in previous publications, there is no need to repeat what has been said before.[35] This section will briefly set forth my own position and then try to respond to some of the objections that have been or can be brought against it.

My position affirms that for an irreversible, constitutional, or genuine homosexual, homosexual acts in the context of a loving relationship striving for permanency are objectively morally good. On the other hand, the ideal meaning of human sexual relationships is in terms of male and female. My assumption is that the genuine homosexual orientation is irreversible. Those who can must strive for heterosexual orientation, but this is not possible for the genuine or irreversible homosexual.

This position on homosexuality fits into a broader theory — a theory or theology of compromise. According to this theory, because of the presence of the sin of the world, Christians are justified in doing certain acts which would not be justified without the presence of such sin of the world. In the past many Catholic theologians justified private property on the basis of the presence of sin in the world and maintained that if there were no such sin, there would be no private property. Note well that the sin of the world does not refer to personal guilt, fault, or sin. The objective condition is existing independently of one's own responsibility or guilt. But this objective situation is not a good. It is an evil, but not a moral evil. Christians are called, in general, to struggle against such evil, but it is not always possible to overcome it. Consider again the justification and acceptance of private property. Such is the case of the genuine and irreversible homosexual.

Perhaps this position can be clarified in the process of responding to objections. As a mediating position, this approach can be questioned both by those who hold to the traditionally accepted approach and by those who hold for a more radical position.

How can one abandon the traditional approach which has been existing in the church for so long? Our knowledge of psychology has only developed in comparatively recent times. We know much more today than we ever did before about the human psyche and the human person. The genuine or constitutional homosexual is a reality that was explicitly unknown in the past. Within the Catholic theological tradition John Harvey made a great innovation by emphasizing the distinction between the homosexual orientation and the homosexual act. The literature of moral theology was not even explicitly aware of this distinction until very recently. Obviously my own approach would go further than that of Harvey, but it is based ultimately on an understanding coming to us from the human sciences which was unavailable to those who lived earlier. Also the official church teaching has changed significantly in the importance it now gives to the relationality aspect of sexuality, as illustrated by the greater importance given to the union of love as an end of marriage.

If a permanent homosexual orientation can justify homosexual acts of the person, what about other orientations? Does the permanent attraction or orientation to animals justify beastiality? What about child molesting? Recall that not all the acts of the constitutional homosexual are justified. These acts must be seen within the context of a loving, faithful relationship striving for permanency. It is precisely this relationship which is missing in the other cases.

But does God not give people the strength and the grace to keep his law? If the homosexual orientation is somehow connected with the sin of the world, should not the Christian be able to overcome it with God's help? Perhaps an analogy will help. The possibility of the moral justification of going to war, which has long been held in the Catholic theological tradition, obviously is related to the sin of the world. All are called to work for peace, but resort to arms as a last resort has been an acceptable option for Christians in this world. The fullness of the kingdom is not yet here. Those who think the moderate revisionist position goes too far must maintain that all constitutional homosexuals are called by God to celibacy. I believe that celibacy is a charism in the church given to certain individuals, but it is not automatically given to all people with a permanent homosexual orientation.

The more radical position also raises objections. Why are heterosexuality and heterosexual acts the ideal? Why is it necessary even to postulate an ideal? I interpret the Scriptures and the tradition as pointing to the ideal meaning of human sexuality as involving the complementarity of male and female. My understanding of human sexuality as embodied also comes to the conclusion that male-female complementarity is the ideal meaning of human sexuality. Also there are social and pastoral reasons supporting heterosexuality as the ideal. In the process of psychosexual development many people go through different phases, including at times a homosexual phase. Heterosexuality as the ideal gives a direction and guide in this process of development.

Does this position still treat homosexuals as second-class people? All persons are to be respected as persons. Homosexuality should not be identified with personality. Homosexuality is not the ideal, but this does not mean that the person is of less dignity. One might make a comparison with the ideal of human physical existence as meaning a human being with all one's limbs and faculties. To be blind or deaf or missing an arm is not the ideal. It is a real lack, but this in no way affects the equal dignity of the person. So too in the case of homosexuality, the person as such is still deserving of just as much respect as any other person.

Why employ the term and the understanding of sin of the world? There is no doubt that reference to the sin of the world can cause some problems. But the sin of the world refers to the sinful structures and realities present in our world and in no way to personal guilt, blame, or responsibility. The phrase "sin of the world" is used to emphasize that heterosexuality is the ideal. I want to distinguish carefully between finitude and sin, a distinction some moral theologians today are not that insistent on making clear.[36] In my judgment there are both important theoretical and practical reasons for making a distinction between finitude and sin. The Roman Catholic theological tradition has recognized that there is a form of human limitation which comes from finitude, but there is another form of limitation which comes from sin. The distinction also has practical ramifications. Finitude is part of our makeup and will always characterize human existence in this world. The reality of finitude is not something less than the ideal. The sin of the world bespeaks a true lack — something which falls short of the human ideal. My use of the phrase sin of the world is connected with the understanding of heterosexuality as the ideal. However, for the constitutional homosexual, homosexual acts in the context of a loving relationship striving for permanency are objectively morally good.

This chapter has attempted to discuss homosexuality from the perspective of moral theology. The first section considered some aspects of moral theology itself, especially the relationship between theory and moral life. The second part examined and critiqued four different approaches to the question, while the final section has proposed and explained my own mediating position.

NOTES

1. For my position see Charles E. Curran, *Themes in Fundamental Moral Theology* (Notre Dame, IN: University of Notre Dame Press, 1977), pp. 27-80. For a different approach see William E. May, "Natural Law and Objective Morality: A Thomistic Perspective," in *Principles of Catholic Moral Life*, ed. William E. May (Chicago: Franciscan Herald Press, 1980), pp. 151-190. The best source for a review and critique of developments in moral theology in the last fifteen years is Richard A. McCormick, *Notes on Moral Theology 1965 through 1980* (Washington, D.C.: University Press of America, 1981).

2. For different approaches to this question, see Charles E. Curran and Richard A. McCormick, eds., *Readings in Moral Theology No. 1: Moral Norms and Catholic Tradition* (New York: Paulist Press, 1979).

3. See Bruce C. Birch and Larry L. Rasmussen, *Bible and Ethics in the Christian Life* (Minneapolis: Augsburg Publishing House, 1976).

4. Anthony J. Tambasco, *Juan Luis Segundo and First-World Ethics: The Bible for Ethics* (Washington, D.C.: University Press of America, 1981).

5. Elizabeth Schüssler-Fiorenza, "Discipleship and Patriarchy: Early Christian Ethos and Christian Ethics in a Feminist Theological Perspective," *The Annual of the Society of Christian Ethics* (1982), pp. 131-172.

6. I have discussed both of these methodological questions in the context of the question of homosexuality in *Catholic Moral*

Theology in Dialogue, paperback ed. (Notre Dame, IN: University of Notre Dame Press, 1976), pp. 186-197.

7. Charles E. Curran and Richard A. McCormick, eds., *Readings in Moral Theology No. 3: The Magisterium and Morality* (New York: Paulist Press, 1982).

8. Constitution on the Church, chapter 5, par. 39-42.

9. Richard J. Regan, *Conflict and Consensus: Religious Freedom and the Second Vatican Council* (New York: Macmillan Co., 1967). The Declaration on Religious Freedom itself begins with the recognition of the demand and the desire of contemporary people for religious liberty, and it declares these desires to be greatly in accord with truth and justice.

10. Pastoral Constitution on the Church in the Modern World, par. 80.

11. Archbishop John R. Quinn, "New Context for Contraception Teaching," *Origins: N.C. Documentary Service* 10 (October 9, 1980): 263-267.

12. Joseph A. Selling, "The Reaction to *Humanae Vitae*: A Study in Special and Fundamental Theology" (S.T.D. diss., Catholic University of Louvain, 1977).

13. John F. Harvey, "Homosexuality," *New Catholic Encyclopedia* (New York: McGraw-Hill, 1967), vol. 7, pp. 116-119. For Harvey's criticism of some contemporary approaches, see John F. Harvey, "Contemporary Theological Views," in John R. Cavanagh, *Counseling the Homosexual* (Huntington, IN: Our Sunday Visitor Press, 1977), pp. 222-238. Cavanagh's own position will be discussed in chapter eight.

14. Harvey, *New Catholic Encyclopedia*, vol. 7, pp. 117-118.

15. Ibid.

16. Joseph Fletcher, *Situation Ethics: The New Morality* (Philadelphia: Westminster Press, 1966), pp. 164-165.

17. John J. McNeill, "The Christian Male Homosexual," *The Homiletic and Pastoral Review* 70 (1970): 667-677, 747-758, 828-836; *The Church and the Homosexual* (New York: Pocket Books, 1978).

18. McNeill, *The Church and the Homosexual*, pp. 111-117, 207-208.

19. Ibid., pp. 110-111.

20. Ibid., pp. 114-116.

21. Ibid., pp. 76-77.

22. Ibid., pp. 77, 118-135. It should be pointed out in passing that McNeill develops his approach in dialogue with and in

distinction from my own theory (ibid., pp. 41-47). However, McNeill has misinterpreted my position. For confirmation of this see Lisa Sowle Cahill, "Homosexuality," in *Homosexuality and Ethics*, ed. Edward Batchelor, Jr. (New York: Pilgrim Press, 1980), pp. 225-227.

23. Ibid., p. 190.

24. Johannes B. Metz, *Theology of the World* (New York: Herder and Herder, 1969), pp. 107-125; Metz, "Foreword," in Karl Rahner, *Spirit in the World* (New York: Herder and Herder, 1968), pp. xiii-xix.

25. Anthony Kosnik, William Carroll, Agnes Cunningham, Ronald Modras, and James Schulte, *Human Sexuality: New Directions in American Catholic Thought* (New York: Paulist Press, 1977).

26. Ibid., pp. 82-85.

27. Ibid., pp. 96-97.

28. Ibid., pp. 200-209.

29. Edward A. Malloy, *Homosexuality and the Christian Way of Life* (Washington, D.C.: University Press of America, 1981).

30. Ibid., pp. viii-ix.

31. Ibid., p. 181.

32. Ibid., pp. 322-328.

33. Ibid., pp. 243-286.

34. Ibid., pp. 359-360.

35. Curran, *Catholic Moral Theology in Dialogue*, pp. 184-219; Curran, *Transition and Tradition in Moral Theology* (Notre Dame, IN: University of Notre Dame Press, 1979), pp. 59-80.

36. Joseph Fuchs, "The Sin of the World and Normative Morality," *Gregorianum* 61 (1980): 60.

4: Biomedical Science, Morality, and the Human Future

This chapter approaches the question of biomedical science, morality, and the human future from the perspective of Christian theological ethics in the Roman Catholic tradition. Part one describes some of the critical concerns that are being discussed in contemporary bioethics, but the primary purpose of the first part is to explain why these problems have come to the attention of our society. Part two, from the perspective of Christian ethics, proposes a general approach for understanding and evaluating biomedical science and technology in relation to our human existence. Part three considers some important concepts in Christian ethics and how they shape an approach to the question of biomedical science, morality, and the human future. These concepts are not static but are very much influenced by experience and ongoing dialogue.[1]

I

Part one surveys some of the problems and questions that are being discussed in contemporary bioethics. Above all this section tries to explain why these problems have arisen and become so acute today. The major contention maintains that these questions have arisen because of the tremendous advances that have occurred in biomedical science and technology. Science is understood in the broader sense of the empirical knowledge of the human; technology is defined as applied science by which human beings are able to control and influence human existence. Human beings have a greater power than ever before to control and influence our human existence because of the advances in science and technology.

Great progress has been made in medical and genetic knowledge and technologies in our own lifetimes. Consider the phenomenal progress in the one area of drug therapy. The antibiotics, the antihistamines, and the psychoactive drugs, three of what are now the eight major classes of prescribed therapeutic drugs, were unknown forty years ago. The sulfas and the vitamins, two other major classes of drugs, were introduced between the two world wars. Barbiturates and hormones were discovered somewhat earlier in the century. Before this century only narcotic drugs were known, but today's representatives of this class, with the exceptions of morphine and codeine, are recently developed drugs.[2] A momentary reflection calls to mind the startling advances in all aspects of medicine in our day — the control of fertility, complicated heart transplants and operations, a greatly increased life expectancy. However, these biomedical developments have also brought with them new and perplexing ethical dilemmas.

Since 1960 there has been an ever-growing interest in biomedical ethics. Before 1960 there was little or no attention paid to medical ethics by most people and disciplines. There were few ethical problems because the criterion of good medicine and the criterion of good ethics were one and the same. The whole purpose of medicine was to care for and cure the individual patient. Whatever the doctor did was directed to the goal of helping the individual patient. Ethics proposed exactly the same criterion — any medical procedure, therapy, or treatment is good if it is to the benefit of the individual patient. Since both medicine and ethics recognized the same basic criterion, there were few if any areas of conflict.

The very fact that contemporary developments in medicine and genetics give us greater knowledge and power constitutes a general reason for more awareness of ethical problems about our use of this power. However, these newer developments in many areas raise an entirely new set of ethical questions precisely because the purpose and goal of biomedical knowledge, power, and technology are no longer restricted to the cure and care of the individual patient. The following questions illustrate the basic contention that ethical problems have arisen because of the greater knowledge and power that human beings possess and because through this power biomedical interventions no longer are always destined to help the individual, who is somehow exposed to danger or even harmed in the process itself. The purpose of this section is not to solve all these problems but rather to give intelligibility and understanding to the more basic question of why these problems constitute ethical questions and dilemmas.[3]

First, consider transplants between living human beings. One of the great medical advances in the decade of the 1950s was the successful transplant of a kidney from one living person to another living person who had no kidney function and needed a kidney in order to live. The donor had two kidneys, so that the loss of one, while exposing the individual to some possible future danger, did not constitute any immediate, grave danger for the donor. Because of the problem of rejection in transplants, the donations usually came from a twin or a sibling of the person who needed the kidney. Through such a donation the kidney recipient was able to live. Kidney transplants marked a tremendous achievement of medical science and technology. However, kidney transplants between living persons also raised an entirely new ethical dilemma. Perhaps for the first time in medical history some harm was being done to a person by medical technology not in order to help that particular person but in order to help another. Harm was done to X in order to help Y. No longer was the unique purpose of medical technology the good of the individual patient. The new ethical problem created by this advance was not insoluble, but it indicated the types of problems that would be increasingly faced in the future.[4]

Experimentation is a second illustration of the basic contention that biomedical progress has brought with it new ethical dilemmas. The phenomenal progress of contemporary medical science and technology would have been impossible without experimentation. It is very important to recognize the distinction between therapy and experimentation. Therapy is done for the good of the individual patient. Experimentation is not done for the good of the individual subject but for the good of medical knowledge or of some future patients. Sometimes a doctor may suggest to the patient the use of an experimental drug, but this is not experimentation in the strict sense of the term. In this case the whole purpose of taking the drug is to cure or help the individual patient. The ethical problem in experimentation comes from the fact that the individual subject of the experimentation is exposed to some harm not for the individual's good but for the good of science or of some future patients. Without experimentation progress in medical technology and drugs would be practically impossible, but abuses connected with experimentation have often been documented.[5] Recall the experimentation with people suffering from syphilis in Tuskegee, Alabama, in the late 1930s and 1940s. Even after penicillin was recognized as the ordinary treatment for syphilis it was not given to the people involved in this experiment.[6]

The fundamental ethical concern in experimentation is to protect the freedom, dignity, and autonomy of the subject of experimentation. As a free agent the subject must cooperate with the researcher in the quest of new knowledge. The subject is a free and autonomous person and not just an object. To protect the person and dignity of the subject, ethicists and lawyers, as a basic minimum, call for the need for informed consent. However, in practice there are many obstacles to ensuring informed consent. Statistics reveal that the vast majority of experiments occur in the charity wards of hospitals and not in the private rooms. A person in the hospital, and especially a poor person, is very vulnerable. Many would find it impossible to say no to what "the doctor" wants. To safeguard the rights of the individual person, it is very important to distinguish in theory and in practice between therapy and experimentation, between the doctor and the researcher. Not everyone wearing a white coat in a hospital is a doctor whose primary concern is the good of the individual patient. Experimentation can be morally acceptable under the proper conditions, but the rights of the subject can readily be infringed upon.

Death and dying constitute a third area of moral dilemmas today, and, again, medical progress has made the problem more acute.[7] Medical technology today can prolong life for even an indefinite period. In a previous generation there were no respirators, to say nothing of the whole phalanx of technologies that are used in the modern hospital. Is there a moral obligation to do everything possible to keep human life in existence? In our society all of us in one way or another, either with regard to ourselves personally or with regard to a loved one, will probably face the decision of whether or not to pull the plug. From my ethical perspective there is no moral obligation to do everything possible to prolong human existence.

Doctors, lawyers, and ethicists today are raising the question about the definition of death or the criterion for determining if death has occurred. Until recently all accepted the common criterion of the lack of breathing as a sign of death. However, that criterion is not always helpful today precisely because modern medical technology can keep breathing going indefintely. A new criterion is necessary, and most of these new approaches center on brain death.

A fifth problem area brought about by medical progress concerns behavior control.[8] Through drugs and electrical impulses deviant human behavior can be somewhat controlled. Human beings today possess this awesome power. Some have suggested behavior-control techniques as a substitute not only for mental hospitals but also for prisons. Obviously the attempts to control and regulate the behavior of others raise a host of ethical problems.

A sixth problem area concerns genetic engineering and human reproduction. The so-called test-tube baby is now a reality. Conception can occur outside the womb in a Petri dish (not a test tube), and the conceptus can then be implanted in the womb of a woman and brought to birth. In the future even more startling ways of reproducing may become actualities. These actual and possible procedures raise significant ethical questions about the nature of human parenthood, the beginning of human life, the problem of mistakes and mishaps, and the power of human beings to control their destiny.

A seventh and final consideration concerns priorities in medicine. The priorities question owes much of its acuteness to developing technologies and takes many different forms. One aspect of the priorities question concerns who will receive lifesaving treatment when such technologies are available to only a limited number. Some people claim that we should not play God and make such life-and-death decisions. However, we have no choice; one way or another these decisions will be made. My primary ethical concern is to safeguard the basic equality of all human beings in making these decisions. After medical considerations are taken into account, the basic equality of all human lives can ordinarily best be safeguarded by a lottery or "a first come, first served" method of selection. Otherwise we become involved in the unacceptable role of deciding that some human lives are more valuable than others.

Another important aspect of the priorities question concerns the investment of our funds and our talents. Should we spend huge amounts on exotic lifesaving technologies for a few or invest in more mundane realities such as maternal health care and infant mortality problems? Should more concern and funding be directed to preventive health care rather than to forms of cure? As a society do we not have an obligation to make sure that all our people have access to basic medical care? These are some of the important priority questions which we as a nation must face.

This first part has tried to give an overall view of some of the more important ethical questions raised by the technological progress which has occurred in modern medicine and genetics. In addition to raising the problems, the purpose was to give some understanding about why and how these problems have arisen, but no attempt has been made to solve or discuss these problems in any detail.

II

Part two of this study proposes a general framework for understanding and evaluating science and technology, especially biomedical science and technology, from the perspective of theological ethics in the Catholic tradition. Three theses will be developed: (1) Theological ethics must be open to the data of science and the possibilities provided by technology. (2) Too often in the past practical suspicion characterized the reaction of the Catholic tradition to science. (3) Although important, the scientific and the technological are limited and not totally identified with the human. These three theses attempt to establish an approach to understanding the importance and the limitations of science and technology. There is much debate in the world today about whether science and technology are good or bad.[9] My own approach tries to avoid simplistic extremes. These three theses point to the fact that science and technology constitute human goods but limited goods.

The first thesis maintains that theological ethics must be open to the data of science and to the possibilities of technology. My understanding of Christian ethics (obviously Christian ethicists, as practitioners of any discipline, do not always agree among themselves) posits a basic openness to human reason, human science, and the possibilities for human betterment afforded by technology.

The first reason for a basic openness to science and technology stems from an acceptance of the goodness of human reason and the recognition that faith and reason can never contradict one another. Some religious and theological traditions are quite wary of human reason, but the Roman Catholic tradition has at least in theory insisted on the goodness of human reason and its ability to arrive at true wisdom and knowledge. The medieval theologians strongly insisted that faith and reason can never contradict one another. Faith is God's gift to us, but so is human reason.[10] Some of the first scientists were themselves theologians — Albert the Great, Roger Bacon. The best of the Catholic tradition has always been willing to sponsor universities and the search for the truth through human reason. Thomas Aquinas, the most significant figure in the Catholic theological tradition, well illustrates the harmony which the tradition asserts as existing between faith and reason. The genius of Aquinas was to take the thought of a pagan philosopher who never knew Jesus and to use this philosophy to explain and understand better the mysteries of the Christian faith. Reason and science are not opposed to our Christian understanding, but rather they can enhance and contribute greatly to our understanding of the human.

A second reason for a theoretical openness to what science can discover and to what technology can do comes from a theological recognition of the goodness of the natural and of the human. Christian theology has constantly struggled with the problem of the relationship between the divine and the human, between grace and nature. The Catholic tradition has insisted that there is no incompatibility between grace and nature. Grace does not destroy nature, but rather builds on nature. The older Catholic understanding of the relationship between grace and nature must be criticized for a number of reasons, but its basic acceptance of the goodness of the natural and of the human remains true.

There are theologies which, for various reasons, do not accept the basic goodness of the natural and of the human. Some theologians maintain that sin has utterly marred and destroyed the goodness of the human. In my judgment, as will be explained later, some theological traditions, including the Roman Catholic, have not given enough importance to the reality of sin, but sin can never totally negate the goodness of the human, which is God's creation. Sin infects and affects but does not destroy the goodness of the human. Other theologians downplay the human and human capacities because they want to stress more the power, the glory, and the majesty of God. It is a false dilemma to think that in order to emphasize the glory and the power of the divine, one has to minimize the glory and the power of the human. Precisely through the gift of creation human beings share in the power, the goodness, and the glory of God. Participation and mediation aptly describe the relationship between the divine and the human. Thomas Aquinas based his whole ethic on the human being who is an image of God precisely on the basis of intellect, free will, and the power of self-determination.[11] My theological perspective affirms the goodness of the human and the goodness of reason with a consequent openness to the discoveries of science and to the possibilities provided by technology.

The second thesis is basically historical and recognizes that the Catholic theological tradition has not always lived up to its theoretical affirmation that there can be no contradiction between faith and reason. Too often in the midst of tensions this tradition lost the courage of its basic assertion that faith and reason cannot contradict one another. At times there grew up suspicion or even hostility between Catholic faith or theology and science. History provides many examples of this suspicion and hostility toward science. Think, for example, of the Galileo case. In the nineteenth century, theology, and especially Catholic theology, felt threatened by the teaching of biology on evolution. Later there seemed to be a great opposition between theology and psychiatry and psychotherapy. Theologians in the twentieth century were often suspicious of the application of the tools of historical criticism to the Scriptures. There is no need to delay any longer over the thesis that historically there has often been suspicion, and at times even hostility, between theology and human sciences. However, this attitude was in basic contradiction to the assertion that faith and reason cannot contradict one another.

The third thesis recognizes the limitations of science and technology, which must always be in the service of the truly human. There is not a perfect identity between the human and the scientific or technological. A first limitation comes from the fact that the human embraces much more than the scientific and the technological. The human realities of freedom, wonder, awe, and suffering all transcend the empirical and the technological. Empirical science and technology can never solve the deeper human problems of meaning, of relationships, and of life and death itself. Empirical science and technology can contribute much to the meaning and enhancing of the human, but there are important aspects of the human that transcend the empirical and the technological.

Since the human is not totally identical with the scientific, there are times when the human must say no to the scientific and to the technological. A good practical illustration of saying no to the technological in the name of the human is shutting off the respirator and allowing the person to die in peace. Actually the problem of whether human beings must do everything possible to keep human life in existence goes back a long time. In the sixteenth century the question was raised about the obligation to undergo surgery to save one's life if the operation involved excruciating pain. Remember that anesthesia was first successfully used only in the middle of the nineteenth century. The Catholic theological tradition accepted the conclusion that excruciating pain generally excuses one from the obligation of undergoing surgery even if surgery is the only way to save one's life.[12]

A second source of limitation comes from the limitation of any one particular science or technology. There are many different sciences which contribute to our understanding of the human. The human moral judgment must take into consideration all these different aspects of the human—the psychological, the sociological, the hygenic, the eugenic, the medical, etc. In our complex human reality nothing is perfect from every one of these perspectives. The human judgment in a sense is the ultimate judgment which relativizes all the other particular judgments of the individual empirical sciences. The perspective of any one empirical science can never be equated with the total human perspective.

Two illustrations show the limitations of any one science in relation to the other scientific perspectives and to the truly human perspective. The first example concerns the science of sociology, which is interested in assembling data about how systems and people act and respond. However, sometimes in order to find out this data it might be necessary to invade the privacy of individuals or to deceive them. At times society should say no to possible sociological investigations precisely because they violate important human rights. In the name of the truly human the sociological perspective must be controlled and at times even limited. There is some knowledge we do not have the moral right to acquire because of the bad means that must be used in the acquisition of such knowledge.

A second illustration comes from genetic engineering and reproductive technologies. Scientists today talk about the future possibility of cloning human beings. Cloning is most easily understood as the xeroxing of human beings. One can produce genetic twins of the original by transplanting the nucleus of the cell. It might be biologically and genetically possible in the future to reproduce one thousand Einsteins or multiple "copies" of other famous and succesful people. Think of the tremendous advantages available to the human race. But, on second thought, such a development might cause many problems. Consider, for example, the psychological problems which might ensue. Even now we know the problems that exist for children of famous parents. There are also problems for twins achieving their identity vis-à-vis one another. How are a thousand Einsteins ever going to achieve their own individuality as human persons. The biological and the genetic are not the only perspectives that must be considered in the whole question of cloning. These illustrations point up the limitations of any one empirical science which must always be related to all the other scientific perspectives and to the fully human perspective.

A third source of limitation comes from the different opinions within any one particular empirical science or technology. This problem is acute for all lay people who lack scientific expertise in a particular area or field. In psychology should I follow Skinner or Erickson? In economics is Friedman or Galbraith correct? One of the great ethical dilemmas facing society today is the use of nuclear power. Are nuclear reactors safe? The expert opinion seems to be quite divided. Within most disciplines (including Christian ethics) there exists a great diversity of opinions. The differences within one science add to the complexity of many of the problems which face the modern world. However, from our perspective these differences of opinion show the limitations existing within any one science in terms of its relationship to the fully human.

This part of the study has proposed a framework for understanding and evaluating the scientific and the technological. In brief, empirical science and technology might be described as limited goods. They are goods which can contribute to our understanding and developing of the human, but they are also limited and must constantly be under the control and direction of the human.

III

Part three of this study examines four important concepts in theological ethics which provide a framework for the approach to be taken to the questions involving biomedical science, morality, and the human future. Theological ethics is not unaffected by human experience, for the discipline is not an a priori construct. Interdisciplinary dialogue about science and technology affords theological ethics an opportunity to examine critically some of its own concepts. We are constantly trying to understand better our basic religious and theological concepts in the light of our experience. On the other hand, there always exists the danger that human experience might distort some of these basic religious and theological ideas and principles. This section discusses four important concepts in theological ethics — the understanding of God, anthropology, human progress, and the proper

ethical model. These important concepts have a great influence on how one approaches the question of science,
morality, and the human future.

Our understandings of God and of how God works in the
world are very much influenced by human experience. Ask
yourself this question: Do you think of God as a Chinese
woman? However, God can just as easily be visualized as a
Chinese woman as a white, European or American male.
The Scriptures remind us that no one has ever seen God.
Our understanding of God will always be colored by our
own experience. But at the same time we must always be
careful not to distort the concept of God because of our own
limited experience. God may surprise us all when she finally
reveals herself! There is always the danger of committing the
great idolatry—making God into our own image and like-
ness. Christian America has too often identified God with its
own national goals, aims, and adventures.

In terms of theological ethics an older concept tended to
see God and God's role in the world in a static way. In both
the Catholic natural-law approach and in the Lutheran theory God was seen primarily in terms of ordering our world.
From this it was easy for theological ethics to talk about the
eternal and immutable plan of God for our world. One of
the dangers with such an approach is that what is a historically conditioned reality too easily becomes identified with
the immutable plan of God. An older Catholic understanding called for the union of church and state as the ideal form
of relationship. In reality this abstract ideal was greatly influenced by the historical reality introduced by Constantine.

Contemporary theological ethics generally proposes a
more active understanding of God's working in the world.
Liberation theology, which was developed in a Catholic context in South America but has also evolved in feminist and
black perspectives, tends to see God acting in the world and
in history to bring about the liberation and freedom of
human beings.[13] The good news of the gospel is the story of
liberation from sin, but freedom from sin includes freedom
from all the oppressive social, political, and economic circumstances which too often oppress people today.

I am in basic agreement with the thrust of the image and role of God proposed in liberation theology, but I want to add some amendments or modifications. Liberation involves a long, hard struggle, and it will never be fully accomplished in this world. The conclusion from this modification is not that Christians should accept the status quo, but that Christians must recognize that the struggle for liberation will never be totally successful in this imperfect world in which we live. Freedom is a multifaceted reality and embraces many different aspects. At times it is easy to forget certain aspects of unfreedom, especially in our own lives. In our own society the teen-agers are usually held up as the most free and liberated people in society. If this is true, why do they have a dress code which is more strict than that of any private boarding school of the past generation? Why do all teen-agers think they have to wear jeans? Latin American liberation theologians see oppression primarily in economic realities; feminist theologians often see oppression primarily in sexist oppression. There is a danger of limiting oppression to just one area and forgetting the other important areas of oppression.

In general, a contemporary concept of God's role in the world stresses the humanizing and freeing activity of God to bring about peace and justice. In general such an approach is acceptable, but one must always be alert to the danger of too easily identifying God's own work with our own narrow perspectives or particular causes. In addition, the recognition of a dynamic presence of God in history cannot deny the important continuities that are a part of human existence. The danger of forgetting that the fullness of God's work and kingdom will only come at the end of time has already been pointed out. Later considerations will call attention to the continuing presence of sin in our world.

Anthropology is another very significant and fundamental concept in Christian ethics. One important aspect of this question involves an optimistic or pessimistic view of the human. The diversity in theological ethics includes both extremes. Harvey Cox, in the 1960s, proposed a very optimistic anthropology. Cox does not forget the reality of sin, but for him the primary human sin is *acedia*, or sloth — the failure to take responsibility for the world in which we live. The great temptation of human beings is "to leave it to the snake" and not take initiative and responsibility for the world. Sloth underestimates human abilities and powers.[14] On the other hand, Paul Ramsey, a Methodist theologian from Princeton, maintains that the great sin of human beings is pride. Human beings tend to claim too much for themselves and forget about their inherent limitations and sinfulness. Pride, or claiming too much power, is the root of all the evils in the world. The great human temptation is to play God.[15]

My approach to anthropology is based on the stance that I propose for Christian ethics. The Christian looks at the world and at all reality in the light of the fivefold Christian mysteries of creation, sin, incarnation, redemption, and resurrection destiny. Such a stance recognizes a basic goodness about human beings grounded in the mysteries of creation, incarnation, and redemption. At the same time, the presence of sin infects and affects all of human reality, and the future of resurrection destiny reminds human beings of our incompleteness and limitations in this world. Such a stance or perspective avoids the extremes of optimism and pessimism and grounds what might be called a critically open perspective. Power and technology can be used for good, but the dangers of misuse are always present. Such a realistic stance reminds contemporary human beings that genetic planners are no more immune from the finitude and sinfulness of human life than public-policy and foreign-policy planners.

From a more philosophical perspective of anthropology some contemporaries see the human person as a self-creator.[16] Such a concept recognizes that through science and technology human beings have acquired great power over human existence. No one can deny that human beings have greater power than ever before precisely because of many technological advances, but the image of the human person as a self-creator goes too far. The creator is the one who makes something out of nothing. Unfortunately, but in my judgment it is more accurate to say fortunately, human beings start with something and not with nothing. We start with the realities of our embodied selves and the world in which we live. Human beings exist among many limitations. We live in only one space in the universe and in one comparatively short period of time. We tire and become fatigued. There are many things we cannot do because of our limitations. Yes, human beings are creative, but they are also limited. Consider for a moment our ability to speak and communicate. This ability to speak signals the transcendence and the creativity of human beings, but still our ability to communicate through speech is quite limited. Human beings must use many words, and all of us have experienced the frustration of not being able to communicate how we really feel or believe. Human beings are both creative and limited.

An anthropology which understands the human person in the image of a self-creator tends to see human activity only in terms of freedom and to reduce all ethical issues to freedom. Freedom remains a very important ethical consideration, but it is not the only ethical consideration. The fact that the person involved or all persons concerned agree to something does not make it right. There are other ethical realities in addition to our freedom. The stress on freedom alone also fails to recognize the many limitations which characterize human existence. The ecological crisis and the population problem remind human beings of limitations. Human beings are not free to intervene any way they want in the environment. There exist complex ecological systems which must be respected. There are limits to what we can and should do. A contemporary emphasis on small is beautiful has arisen as a reaction to the failure to recognize the limits to creativity and freedom.

A third important concept in Christian ethics is the understanding of human progress. No one can deny the tremendous technological progress which has occurred. The progress in biomedical science and technology was mentioned at the beginning of this study. Consider the fabulous technological progress in transportation. In one generation human beings went from the horse drawn carriage to space flight. At first glance technological progress seems to be always progressive. The newer development builds upon and improves on the older. Such progress appears to be constantly going forward with each new discovery becoming another step on the way to utopia.

At the very minimum technological progress is not the same as truly human progress. Human progress does not occur in such a constantly developing, ever-improving direction. Why is it that we still read Shakespeare, listen to Beethoven, and admire the paintings of Giotto or van Gogh? Too often the allure of technological progress deceives human beings into thinking that truly human progress involves a constant improvement, with the newer always better than the old.

A deeper reflection recognizes that technological progress itself is ambivalent and does not necessarily involve progressive growth. In the enchantment with technological progress many human beings forget about the negative effects of that progress. The pollution of our air, the impurity of our waters, the screeching sounds of cars and airplanes in our ears, and the devastation of our ecological resources all remind us of the ambivalence of technological progress.

There is even a more fundamental question to raise about human progress: Is there such a thing as truly human progress in our world? A glance back over the history of human existence seems to give contradictory evidence. In more primitive times human beings threw stones at one another; in the modern world human beings are prepared to hurl deadly nuclear weapons at fellow dwellers on planet earth with the possible consequence of even extinguishing human life in apocalyptic destruction. On the other hand, there seems to have been some progress in our recognition of the freedom and dignity of human beings with a basic set of inalienable rights. In general both from historical observations and from my theological stance with its fivefold Christian mysteries, I think there has been some truly human progress in this world. But this progress is slow, limited, difficult, and often marred with regressions along the way. The Christian gospel calls human beings to strive for true progress and a greater presence of the kingdom in this world, but the fullness of the kingdom will only come at the end of time.

A fourth important concept in Christian ethics concerns the model employed for understanding the Christian life. In the space allotted it is impossible to develop this question at great depth. The only purpose of this consideration is to show that a technological model is inadequate for understanding Christian and human ethical life. The technological model of human existence sees the person primarily as a maker or a doer. The technological model emphasizes the control and power of the human being who is a maker. According to this model the human being has the ability to shape and direct all that comes into one's hands. Take the simple example of the carpenter shaping wood into a table. However, both theology and human experience remind us that we do not have such control over our human lives and existence. There are many things which happen to us in our life which we do not want. Human existence would probably be quite dull if we had full power and control over our lives. There is a great difference between a technological model of human existence and a proper theological, ethical understanding.

The technological model cannot come to grips with the reality of human suffering. Again, human experience and theology both recognize the problem of suffering. The book of Genesis was originally written not to explain the reality of creation but to come to grips with the problem of how evil and suffering can exist in the world in the light of a belief in a good and gracious God who made all things. Evil and suffering raise a continual problem for believers—for Job, for Jesus, for the survivors and witnesses of Auschwitz. The technological model of human existence with its emphasis on human power and control cannot deal with the reality of suffering. The Christian perspective sees suffering in the light of the paschal mystery of Jesus. Jesus gave a redemptive quality to suffering. Through the suffering of the cross Jesus overcame the power of evil and sin.

The Christian tradition recognizes the reality of suffering, sees suffering in the light of the Cross and resurrection of Jesus, but ultimately must admit the mystery of suffering. Likewise, the Christian tradition must honestly admit that its own approach to suffering in the past has at times been deficient. The Marxist critique of religion and of Christianity contains some truth. All too often Christians were given the advice to put up with their suffering and to endure the present vale of tears because their reward would be great in heaven. Faced with the reality of evil, Christians are called upon to struggle to overcome it; but in this world, evil and suffering will always continue to exist. A technological model has no place for the reality of suffering. A Christian vision tries to deal with this reality but in the past has occasionally proposed distorted and one-sided approaches.

The technological model of human existence is interested in results, effects, and success. When applied to human existence, such a model sees human value in terms of what one does, makes, or accomplishes. The whole of the Judeo-Christian tradition cries out against such an understanding of human value and dignity. Who are the privileged people in the kingdom of God? Are they the rich, the powerful, the doers? No, the privileged people in the kingdom of God are the poor, the lowly, the outcast, and the children. Human values and dignity do not ultimately depend on what one does, makes, or accomplishes.

A technological model applied to human existence tends to result in a total ethical consequentialism. The best illustration of such a strict consequentialism is utilitarianism with its criterion of the greatest good of the greatest number. But too often the greatest good of the greatest number leaves out the weak, the handicapped, the poor, the oppressed. In my judgment a Christian approach to human existence and ethics cannot accept such a utilitarian approach.

This entire consideration of the differences between a technological model applied to human existence and a Christian approach well exemplifies what was said earlier about the technological. Science and technology constitute limited goods, but the human and the Christian involve more than just the scientific and the technological.

This chapter has tried to give an overview and a perspective on the questions of biomedical science, morality, and the human future. Part one surveyed many of the existing questions but especially tried to explain why these problems have arisen today. Part two offered a perspective which views the scientific and the technological as limited human goods. Part three provided some general theological perspectives for approaching particular problems.

NOTES

1. Many aspects touched upon in this paper are developed in Charles E. Curran, *Issues in Sexual and Medical Ethics* (Notre Dame, IN: University of Notre Dame Press, 1978).

2. Bernard Barber et al., *Research on Human Subjects* (New York: Russell Sage Foundation, 1973), p. 1.

3. Two important reference tools in the area of bioethics should be mentioned: Warren T. Reich, ed., *Encyclopedia of Bioethics*, 4 vols. (New York: The Free Press, 1978); LeRoy Walters, ed., *Bibliography of Bioethics*, (Detroit: Gale Research Co., 1975-). A new volume of this bibliography is published every year.

4. James B. Nelson, *Human Medicine: Ethical Perspectives on Medical Issues* (Minneapolis: Augsburg Publishing House, 1973), pp. 149-170.

5. For an exhaustive study of human experimentation see Jay Katz, *Experimentation with Human Beings* (New York: Russell Sage Foundation, 1972).

6. R. H. Kampmeier, "Final Report on the 'Tuskegee Syphilis Study'," *Southern Medical Journal* 67 (November 1974):1349-1353.

7. See President's Comission for the Study of Ethical Problems in Medicine and Biomedical and Behavioral Research, *Deciding to Forego Life-Sustaining Treatment* (Washington, D.C.: U.S. Government Printing Office, 1983).

8. For a discussion of behavior control from various perspectives see Willard Gaylin, Joel Meister, and Robert Neville, eds., *Operating on the Mind* (New York: Basic Books, 1975).

9. In July 1979 the World Council of Churches sponsored a Conference on Faith, Science and the Future which was held at the Massachusetts Institute of Technology, July 12-24. This conference and the publications connected with it discussed in great detail and from many different perspectives the understanding of science and technology in the light of Christian faith. For the results of the conference see *Faith and Science in an Unjust World*, vol. 1: *Plenary Presentations*, ed. Roger L. Shinn (Philadelphia: Fortress Press, 1980); *Faith and Science in an Unjust World*, vol. 2: *Reports and Recommendations*, ed. Paul Abrecht (Philadelphia: Fortress Press, 1980). A preparatory volume was published before the conference: Paul Abrecht, ed., *Faith, Science and the Future* (Philadelphia: Fortress Press, 1979).

10. Vatican Council I, 3rd session, Dogmatic Constitution *Dei Filius*, Cap. 4, *De fide at ratione*, in *Enchiridion symbolorum definitionum et declarationum de rebus fidei at morum*, ed. H. Denzinger, A. Schönmetzer, 32nd. ed. (Barcelona: Herder, 1963), n. 3017. See also Fifth Lateran Council, Denzinger, n. 1441.

11. Thomas Aquinas, *Summa Theologiae, I^a II^{ae},* prologue.

12. Daniel A. Cronin, *The Moral Law in Regard to the Ordinary and Extraordinary Means of Conserving Life* (Rome: Pontifical Gregorian University, 1958).

13. The best-known examples of liberation theology in the South American context are Gustavo Gutierrez, *A Theology of Liberation* (Maryknoll, NY: Orbis Books, 1973), and Juan Luis Segundo, *The Liberation of Theology* (Maryknoll, NY: Orbis Books, 1976).

14. Harvey G. Cox, *On Not Leaving It to the Snake* (New York: Macmillian, 1967), especially pp. ix-xix.

15. Paul Ramsey, *Fabricated Man: The Ethics of Genetic Control* (New Haven, CT: Yale University Press, 1970), pp. 90, 151-159.

16. For a discussion of the creativity and freedom of human beings in the light of modern genetics see John J. McNeill, "Freedom and the Future," *Theological Studies* 33 (1972): 503-530.

PART THREE

Social Ethics

5: An Analysis of the American Bishops' Pastoral Letter on Peace and War

On May 3, 1983, the American Catholic bishops, by a vote of 238 in favor to 9 opposed issued a pastoral letter on peace and war entitled "The Challenge of Peace: God's Promise and Our Response."[1] A committee of bishops chaired by Archbishop (now Cardinal) Bernardin of Chicago began working on the document in spring of 1981. The committee had many meetings, heard testimony from over thirty-five expert witnesses, and issued a first draft in June 1982. A second draft was sent to the bishops in October 1982 and discussed at the annual bishops' meeting in Washington in November. The third draft was issued in early spring of 1983 and served as the basis for the final document approved at the May meeting of the bishops.[2]

Synopsis of the Pastoral Letter

In my judgment there are three realities that set the perspective and background for the teaching found in the letter. The letter begins with a recognition of what might be called the most significant of the signs of the times — we live in a moment of supreme crisis because of the possibility of the destruction of our world through the use of nuclear weapons. This present-day reality is balanced off by the call for peace as both a gospel imperative and a moral challenge arising from the interdependent world in which we live. In the present situation nations still retain as a last resort the right to self-defense within moral limits, but all of us are called to work for peace. The building of peace is the way to prevent war.

The pastoral letter is divided into four parts. In proposing ways of building peace "Part III: The Promotion of Peace: Proposals and Policies" appeals to the need for structural change, while "Part IV: The Pastoral Challenge and Response" calls for a change of heart and education. Catholic teaching consistently recognizes the international common good and calls for structures commensurate to that good. We can begin by strengthening existing structures such as the United Nations. The absence of adequate structures at the present time places an even greater responsibility on the part of the individual states who are called to interpret their own national interest in the light of the larger global interest. One must realistically assess the contemporary world situation dominated by the superpowers in a divided world. The bishops recognize the fact of a Soviet threat and a Soviet imperial drive for hegemony in some regions of major strategic interest. We as a nation have failed at times to live up to our own ideals, but at least we do enjoy political freedom. Although there are major differences between American and Soviet philosophies and political systems, the undeniable truth is that objective mutual interests do exist between the superpowers. These mutual interests furnish the starting point for structural change, beginning with negotiations between the superpowers, which can and must occur in order to insure peace. Nonviolent means of conflict resolution must also be developed. Part four insists on the importance of change of heart and education, and concludes by addressing the many different individuals involved in the work for peace — pastoral ministers; educators; parents; the young; men and women in the military, in defense industries, in science, and in the media; public officials; and Catholics as citizens.

The challenge to work for peace exists side by side with the justification for governments to go to war in self-defense as a last resort and in a limited manner. We Christians must recognize the reality of the paradox we face in our world as it exists. We must continue to recognize our belief that peace is possible and necessary and yet acknowledge that limited force in self-defense might be justified. The first two parts of the letter consider the Christian approaches to the use of force and to nuclear deterrence.

"Part I: Peace in the Modern World: Religious Perspectives and Principles" begins by justifying the need for such a document, by differentiating the different levels of teaching authority in the letter, and by briefly describing the methodology to be used and the audiences to be addressed. A scriptural section is followed by a description of our eschatological situation in the "already but not yet of Christian existence." The moral choice for the kingdom involves a commitment to work for peace, but the preservation of peace and the protection of human rights are to be accomplished in a world marked by sin. There is always a strong presumption in favor of peace, but limited self-defense cannot be denied to nations in our world. While governments must defend their people against unjust aggression, individuals may either be pacifists or support a legitimate use of limited force in self-defense. The document then spells out the just-war criteria under the traditional headings of *jus ad bellum* (just cause, competent authority, comparative justice, right understanding, last resort, probability of success, and proportionality) and of *jus in bello* (principles of discrimination and proportionality). A final section justifies nonviolence as a choice for some individuals. Pacifism and just war are distinct but interdependent methods of evaluating warfare, with each contributing to the full moral vision we need in pursuit of human peace.

"Part II: War and Peace in the Modern World: Problems and Principles" applies these principles of a just war to the contemporary scene. Since this section will be analyzed later in greater detail, a brief description will suffice. In the light of the distinctive capability of nuclear weapons we are faced with the necessary and urgent task of saying no to the use of nuclear weapons. The pastoral letter takes three positions on the use of nuclear weapons: no use of nuclear weapons against civilian population targets; no first use of nuclear weapons; while highly skeptical of the possibility of limiting any nuclear war, the bishops do not absolutely reject the use of counterforce nuclear weapons (as distinguished from counterpopulation or countervalue) in response to a nuclear attack. The letter gives a strictly conditioned moral acceptance of a limited nuclear deterrence which can never be the basis for a true peace. More specifically the bishops accept a limited counterforce deterrent which is not destabilizing, does not possess hard-target kill capability, and is limited to preventing nuclear war and not to fighting a limited nuclear war. Sufficiency to deter a nuclear war and not superiority in the arms race is another limiting criterion of moral deterrence.

The primary purpose of this study is to give an analysis of the pastoral letter. The first section will discuss the various tensions that arose in writing the drafts of the letter. The second and longest section will analyze the ethical teaching on just war and its application to nuclear use and deterrence. The third section will briefly consider the ecclesiological aspects of the document.

Tensions Experienced in the Drafting

Throughout the drafting process the bishops were in dialogue with and even opposed by a number of different groups within the church and without. Within the church the relationship with Rome and with other national hierarchies was a predominant consideration. The Vatican Council and the popes have spoken on these issues. Obviously the American bishops were not going to be in opposition with the official teaching of the universal church. However, the early drafts clearly indicated that the pastoral letter intended to be more specific and concrete than the earlier documents of the universal church. At the same time there was a possible tension with other national hierarchies, especially those within

Europe. It was well known that some French and German bishops were opposed to the condemnation of the first use of nuclear weapons since both the NATO and the French defense systems rely on the threat of limited nuclear weapons to deter attack even by conventional forces of the enemy. The universal church obviously is concerned that different national hierarchies might come to different moral conclusions on these issues.

These possible tensions with Rome and with other European hierarchies occasioned a special consultation in Rome among representatives of the American bishops' conference, European bishops' conferences, and officials of the Vatican. A synopsis of the meeting written by the Reverend Jan Schotte of the Pontifical Commission on Justice and Peace was sent to all American bishops in March 1983 and subsequently has been published.[3] Cardinal Ratzinger, the prefect of the Congregation for the Doctrine of the Faith, chaired this meeting and proposed five points for discussion: bishops' conferences as such do not have a *mandatum docendi*; the need to be clear when the bishops are speaking as bishops and invoking their teaching authority; the use of scripture in the American document; the presumption of a dualism involving both a just-war tradition and a nonviolent tradition in the church; and the application of fundamental moral principles to the nuclear-arms issue, especially taking into account the geopolitical context.

Within the church itself in the United States, as might be expected, there were disagreements with the proposed draft from both the "left" and the "right." Both positions were somewhat vocal during the drafting process. The "left" wanted a more prophetic statement based on gospel values which would not compromise and would forthrightly condemn all use of nuclear arms and call for unilateral nuclear disarmament.[4] In the end many advocates of this position were somewhat satisfied with the bishops' pastoral because they understood the document as moving somewhat in this direction and as taking a negative stand against the existing deterrent policy of this country. Numerically speaking the "right" was stronger than the "left." On a somewhat general level they questioned the competency of the bishops to become involved in such complex political issues. More specifically there was a feeling that the draft was too idealistic and did not recognize the complexities and realities in the existing world situation with the resulting need at times to use and to threaten to use nuclear weapons. The most significant statement of this position was a draft pastoral letter written by the lay theologian and philosopher Michael Novak, which was signed by a number of Catholics and published in its entirety in both the *National Review* and *Catholicism in Crisis*.[5]

Another source of tension involved the relationship between the American bishops and the American government. Stories appeared in the press that the American government was tring to go to Rome to force the American bishops to soften some of the earlier drafts. The press tended to see the changes made in subsequent drafts primarily in terms of the relationship between the bishops and the administration. Although the bishops do not call for a unilateral disarmament, they certainly are critical of many aspects of American policies. Reagan administration spokespersons tended to criticize very strongly the second draft of the letter but then were much less negative about the third draft. In my judgment this change on their part was more of a tactical maneuver. There can be no doubt that by their opposition to the second draft they gave more importance and significance to the bishops' document. The reaction by the administration and the press to the third draft was such that Archbishop Roach, the president of the American Bishops' Conference, and Archbishop Bernardin issued a news release pointing out the many areas in which the third draft disagreed with American policy.[6] The third draft did back down somewhat by substituting "curb" for "halt" with reference to bilateral agreements on the arms race, but the substance of the third draft was basically the same as the second. Despite the addition of some more "realistic" wording, and a few corresponding changes, the third draft went beyond the second draft and condemned counterpopulation deterrence. The final document clearly shows that the American bishops no longer feel the need to prove their loyalty and patriotism by an uncritical acceptance of American policy. Within the last few years this critical attitude of the American bishops toward the American government has been growing, but the pastoral letter marks a very significant development in this movement.[7] A further tension involved ethical theory and will be discussed in detail in the following section.

Ethical Analysis of the Teaching on Nuclear Use and Deterrence

The pastoral letter recognizes that individuals within the church can follow either a pacifist approach or the just-war theory. Despite some questioning in the Roman meeting that nonviolence has not been a second tradition within the church alongside the just-war theory, the final document is very strong in its suppport of nonviolence.[8] The bishops affirm that the theme of Christian nonviolence and pacifism has echoed and reechoed, sometimes more strongly and sometimes more faintly, from the beginning of the Christian tradition down to our own day. The specific section in the pastoral on the value of nonviolence twice quotes the Pastoral Constitution on the Church in the Modern World. The text refers to the praise that the Council Fathers gave "to those who renounce the use of violence in the vindication of their rights." However, the pastoral letter in this its major discussion of nonviolence does not add the condition found in the very same sentence of the Constitution on the Church in the Modern World (n. 78), namely, "provided this can be done without injury to the rights and duties of others or of the community itself." There can be no doubt that the bishops are quite absolute in their acceptance of pacifism as one option for the individual Catholic conscience and insist that such an option has been a tradition in the church. However, the pastoral letter recognizes that governments have an obligation to defend their people against unjust aggression and cannot adopt a totally pacifist perspective.

The letter addresses the question about the use of nuclear weapons in the light of the just-war theory. The third draft made one curious addition to the criteria related to the *jus ad bellum* which was not found in the second draft and is usually not found in the tradition—comparative justice. Under this criterion the draft recognizes defects in the American system but insisits there is a greater justice in our society in which basic human rights are at least recognized as compared to tyrannical and totalitarian regimes.[9] The final document retains this curious criterion but eliminates the assessment that our political system is comparatively more just and uses the category to emphasize the presumption against war.[10] Thus the bishops finally retain this criterion but use it differently from the purpose it seems to have had in the third draft.

The most significant question in ethical theory concerns the relationship between nuclear use and deterrence. This chapter will briefly explain, analyze, and criticize the different drafts of the letter on this important point. On the question of the use of nuclear weapons the drafts show relatively little change.[11] Step one consistently condemns the use of nuclear weapons or any weapons used against population centers or civilian targets. Step two condemns the first use of nuclear weapons. The third draft abhors the concept of initiating nuclear war on however restricted a scale. Such a war is an unjustifiable moral risk because of the danger of escalation. However, obviously in response to the concerns of some European bishops, the draft goes on to say, "Therefore, a serious moral obligation exists to develop defensive strategies as rapidly as possible to preclude any justification for using nuclear weapons in response to non-nuclear attacks." One could conclude that until such defense strategies are developed the first use of nuclear weapons might not be completely ruled out. Cardinal Ratzinger has interpreted the document in this way.[12] The final version is somewhat changed. The first sentence, as a result of an amendment made by Archbishop Quinn in Chicago, reverts to the language of the second draft and reads: "We do not perceive any situation in which the deliberate initiation of nuclear warfare on however restricted a scale can be morally justified." However, the same paragraph still contains the first part of the statement as found in the third draft maintaining that a serious moral obligation exists to develop nonnuclear strategies as rapidly as possible. There could very well be a contradiction between these two sentences in the same short paragraph. The new opening sentence seems to say that no situation can justify first use, but the final sentence could be interpreted to leave open the possibility of such use until one has fulfilled the moral obligation of developing nonnuclear defensive strategies. Perhaps this possible contradiction indicates one of the problems in trying to amend a document in a meeting of three hundred people.

The third step in the use of nuclear weapons deals with what is technically called retaliatory (as distinguished from first use) counterforce (as distinguished from countercity, counterpopulation, or countervalue) use. The first draft recognizes that Christians and others of good will may differ as to whether nuclear weapons of this type may ever be used. I describe the position taken here in the first draft as a reluctant noncondemnation of such use, with the major problems being the difficulty of keeping such use limited and the danger of accident or misjudgment. The subsequent drafts are in basic continuity with the first but somewhat more skeptical about even the possibility of keeping a nuclear war limited. In the final version there is no absolute moral condemnation of retaliatory counterforce use of nuclear weapons, but like the third draft, the final document remains highly skeptical about keeping such use of nuclear weapons limited.

What about the consistency of the bishops' position on the use of nuclear weapons? An argument can certainly be made for consistency. In the case of a defensive retaliatory use of

counterforce nuclear weapons there might be a proportionate reason justifying the risk that nuclear war will become
unlimited, while there is no proportionate reason that could
justify the first use of such weapons. However, the whole
thrust of the letter insists on the impossibility of keeping nuclear war limited. Also in the case of retaliation why are
counterforce nuclear weapons necessary if conventional weapons could often accomplish the necessary purpose? Can the
bishops perceive any situation in which the retaliatory use of
counterforce nuclear weapons on however restricted a scale
could be morally justified? I think the whole thrust of the
bishops' argument goes against any use of counterforce nuclear weapons as first use or in retaliation. However, in
fairness, the pastoral letter does not advocate such retaliatory counterforce use but rather does not absolutely rule out
such use.

There is another very important reason why the pastoral
letter does not absolutely rule out all counterforce nuclear
weapons. The position on deterrence is intimately connected
with the position on use. The bishops do not want to demand unilateral disarmament because it would be destabilizing. They are willing to accept some nuclear deterrence in
a conditioned way. In many ways it is this position on deterrence which logically has a great effect on their not categorically condemning all counterforce use of nuclear weapons.
Here we enter the very difficult ethical problem of the relationship between use and deterrence. There has been much
development within the drafts of the pastoral letter on the
kind of deterrence acceptable, the relationship between
use and deterrence, and the moral theory governing these
considerations.

The first draft proposes a unique two-tiered approach to
deterrence.[13] The first tier is a marginally or barely justifiable deterrent policy. The draft explicitly recognizes that it
has left the door open and has not absolutely condemned
counterforce use in order to justify some deterrence. The
draft maintains that it is wrong to threaten to do what you
cannot morally do. Here the draft quotes the 1976 pastoral
letter issued by the American bishops "To Live in Christ

Jesus." Consequently it is wrong to threaten to attack civilian population centers or to threaten to initiate nuclear war. Since some retaliatory counterforce use might be justifiable, one can legitimately threaten and deter with such counterforce nuclear weapons.

The second tier of deterrence in the first draft is the toleration of countercity or counterpopulation deterrence. The draft, quoting from official government documents, assumes that American policy involves a counterpopulation deterrence which cannot be approved outright. The draft then justifies the toleration of such an evil on the basis of the lesser of two evils in order to avoid the greater evil of destabilizing the international ordering by requiring the unilateral disarmament of our counterpopulation deterrence. In arriving at this judgment the draft quotes extensively from the testimony of Cardinal Krol before the Senate Foreign Relations Committee in 1979 on the SALT II treaty. The draft does not approve such deterrence but merely tolerates it as long as there is hope that negotiations will lead to meaningful and continuing reduction of nuclear stockpiles.

The second draft drops the two-tiered approach to deterrence.[14] The discussion of deterrence on the basis of the *US Military Posture Statement for FY 1983* understands American deterrent policy as involving the willingness to threaten and strike targets of value in the Soviet Union. Such targets of value either explicitly include the civilian population or include individual targets which essentially would involve killing a large number of civilians.

The document recognizes the moral and political paradox of deterrence which by threatening the use of such nuclear weapons has apparently prevented their use. The Pastoral Constitution on the Church in the Modern World is then cited in this regard. The draft quotes the pertinent parts of the 1976 bishops' pastoral letter "To Live in Christ Jesus"—not only is it wrong to attack civilian populations but it is also wrong to threaten to attack them as part of a strategy of deterrence. Then the Krol document is cited with its toleration, but not approval, of countervalue or countercity deterrence provided through negotiations there is meaningful progress toward reducing and phasing out altogether nuclear deterrence and the threat of mutual assured destruction.

The second draft goes on to quote something new, the June 1982 address of Pope John Paul II to the United Nations. (The address was actually given by Cardinal Casaroli, who read the Pope's document.) The Pope said: "In current conditions deterrence based on balance, certainly not as an end in itself, but as a step on the way toward a progressive disarmament may still be judged morally acceptable." The draft in the light of this gives a strictly conditional moral acceptance to deterrence and later develops the limits of deterrence. There are negative elements connected with deterrence including "the intention to use strategic nuclear weapons which would violate the principles of discrimination and proportionality." This fact and other negative dimensions make the arms race with deterrence as its key element a sinful situation which must be changed. However, such a situation can still be morally acceptable provided it is a step toward progressive disarmament. Note the reasoning is basically the reasoning of the 1979 Krol testimony, but the conclusion is taken from the Pope.

However, there is a serious ethical problem in the Krol testimony. The 1976 pastoral letter "To Live in Christ Jesus" deals with all aspects of the moral life and devotes only a few paragraphs to the nuclear question.[15] However, this document contains a sentence that has not been in previous statements of the universal hierarchical magisterium or of the American bishops — not only is it wrong to attack civilian populations but it is also wrong to threaten to attack them as part of a strategy of deterrence. This sentence caused no great excitement at the time, but it was to have a great influence later. This statement basically maintains that it is morally wrong to threaten to do what you cannot morally do, apparently because the threat involves the immoral intention to do the moral evil. One could thus logically conclude that counterpopulation deterrence is morally wrong and must be condemned.

The Krol testimony in 1979 tries to answer the dilemma.[16] Deterrence aims to prevent the use of nuclear weapons, but it does so by an expressed threat to attack the civilian populations of the adversaries. This wrong declared intention explains the Catholic dissatisfaction with deterrence. As the second draft says explicitly, for this reason such deterrence cannot be accepted but only tolerated.

However, the Krol testimony involves a novel use of toleration. Yes, the Catholic tradition has traditionally recognized especially in social and political ethics that one can tolerate an evil in order to avoid a greater evil or to bring about a greater good. The classic example is the toleration of laws allowing public prostitution. However, in the Krol testimony one is tolerating one's own immoral intention to do moral evil. To intend to do moral evil in the Catholic theological tradition is morally wrong. It cannot be approved or tolerated; it must be condemned.

Moral theologians identified with a more conservative approach to moral theology accused such an approach of consequentialism.[17] The moral evil of an immoral intention is justified by the good effects that come from such deterrence — namely, the prevention of the use of nuclear weapons. Such an ethical theory, it was pointed out, would put the bishops in support of revisionist Catholic moral theology which accepts the morality of contraception and sterilization, and questions the absolute condemnation of direct abortion. The revisionist position says that these evils which are called premoral or nonmoral evils can be justified by a proportionate reason. Obviously the framers of the bishops' letter did not want to be accused of proposing a moral theory that would logically lead them to justify positions contrary to hierarchical magisterial teaching in the area of sexual morality.

However, revisionists do not necessarily accept the reasoning of the Krol testimony and of the second draft. The novel use of tolerating one's own moral evil was pointed out by revisionists. Most revisionists would agree that one cannot intend to do moral evil. The theory of proportionalism maintains that one can do premoral evil if there is a proportionate reason but not moral evil. To do moral evil or to intend to do moral evil is always wrong.[18] Thus revisionists too pointed out problems in the reasoning of the Krol testimony and of the second draft. It is wrong to identify such reasoning with the revisionist theory of proportionalism.

Such intramural Catholic debate pointed out the ethical problem in the theory proposed in the Krol testimony which was accepted somewhat in the first draft (the second tier of tolerated deterrence) and wholeheartedly accepted in the second draft. Archbishop Bernardin alluded to these problems on a number of occasions. At the discussion of the second draft at the November 1982 meeting of the American bishops and at the January 1983 meeting in Rome, Bernardin indicated that the committee was not yet totally satisfied with the theoretical argument in the second draft on the morality of deterrence.[19]

One other important change occurred during the time of preparation of the third draft. The tension between the early drafts and American policy has already been pointed out. It was well known that the Reagan administration was somewhat upset with the drafts. The administration and the bishops' committee were in dialogue. There was a very significant letter of William Clark, the national security advisor, to Cardinal Bernardin on January 15, 1983. The letter stated very clearly, "For moral, political, and military reasons the United States does not target the Soviet civilian population as such." We target only the war-making capability of the Soviet Union — its armed forces and the industrial capacity to sustain war.[20] This letter is very important. In the Krol testimony and in the first and second drafts the bishops assume and cite official documents to show that the United States deterrent policy involves countervalue and not just counterforce deterrence. Now they have a document asserting that the United States nuclear deterrence is counterforce and not counterpopulation.

All the above considerations set the stage for the third draft. In the third draft the section on deterrence in principle and practice begins with an explanation of the concept and development of deterrent policy.[21] Particularly significant is the relationship between "declaratory policy" (the public explanations of our strategies, intentions, and capabilities) and "action policy" (the actual planning and targeting policies to be followed in a nuclear attack). Without going into detail the letter recognizes that there has been substantial continuity in American action policy despite real changes in declaratory policy. (However, as will be highlighted below, the bishops themselves thought there was a different targeting policy in their earlier drafts.)

The section on the moral assessment of deterrence begins by citing the Second Vatican Council and discussing various aspects of the question. The 1976 pastoral letter and the Krol testimony are both mentioned and summarized together in one short papagraph with no mention of the teaching on the specifics of deterrence and the moral theory behind it. Pope John Paul II's address to the United Nations in June 1983 is quoted at length as are other statements by the Pope. The draft concludes that in light of the need to prevent nuclear war from ever occurring and to protect and preserve justice, freedom, and independence, deterrence not as an end in itself but as a step on the way to progressive disarmament may be judged as morally acceptable. However, there are moral limits to deterrence just as there are to use. Specifically, it is not morally acceptable to intend to kill the innocent as part of a strategy of deterring nuclear war. The draft appreciates the clarifications given in the letter from William Clark and in the annual report of Secretary Weinberger to Congress maintaining that it is not American policy to target enemy populations. Although such a policy does not go against the principle of discrimination, there still remains the question of proportionality, namely, that attacks on military targets would involve massive and disproportionate civilian casualties.

The third draft like its predecessors then spells out the implications of its strictly conditioned moral acceptance of deterrence. Proposals for fighting a limited nuclear war are not acceptable, for the whole purpose of deterrence is to prevent the use of nuclear weapons. Sufficiency to deter and not superiority must be the moral criterion. Any theoretical or practical changes must be assessed on whether they aid or impair steps toward progressive disarmament. The document then goes on to spell out some specifics in the light of this understanding. Basically the draft calls for a conditioned acceptance of limited counterforce deterrence, with no appearance of first-strike capability, not possessing hard-target kill capability, which is aimed at preventing nuclear war and not at fighting a limited nuclear war.

The final version of the letter approved by the bishops is in basic and almost verbal agreement with the moral theory and general judgments about deterrence found in the third draft.[22] There are only comparatively minor changes from what has been outlined above. The final letter does include a citation from the Krol testimony, but the quote does not deal with toleration or the moral theory behind toleration. The final version relegates the Clark letter and the Weinberger report to the footnotes but explains their content in the text as no targeting of civilian populations.

One can understand better the position of the pastoral letter on deterrence by comparing it with the conciliar and papal statements so often cited in the document itself. It is true that the bishops do not go against the papal and conciliar teaching, but they do take significant steps beyond such teaching. The pope and the council never directly opposed countercity or counterpopulation deterrence. The bishops now, at least on the level of targeting policies, oppose counterpopulation deterrence. The pope has never accepted the principle that countercity deterrence involves the immoral intention to do what is morally wrong. The bishops accept the principle and therefore cannot accept counterpopulation deterrence. The pope consequently has not ruled out the moral acceptance of a bluff strategy, but the bishops do not accept any bluff strategy in terms of targeting policies of deterrence. These are three significant differences between the papal position and that of the American bishops.

The bishops in the course of their drafting process changed their ethical theory and their position on counterpopulation nuclear deterrence. The unanswered question is, Why? Our analysis has shown that the two most important factors were the recognition of the problem connected with the theory of toleration of such deterrence and the changed factual recognition that American deterrence was not targeted on population centers as such.

The theory of toleration proposed in the Krol testimony

and in the first draft does have some problems in terms of the Catholic theological tradition. However, the bishops could have rejected this theory and still accepted a counter-city deterrence. Logically they would then have to reject the 1976 statement that one cannot threaten to use what one cannot morally use. Pope John Paul II has not condemned countercity deterrence. They could have used the general arguments proposed by the pope without getting into the particulars which caused the problem in the Krol testimony and in the first two drafts. Did they change because of their changed understanding of the factual situation? Once they realized that American policy does not involve the targeting of population centers, then they would not run into much American opposition in condemning countercity deterrence. However, the bishops were certainly willing in many other instances to oppose American and NATO policy.

Perhaps they changed because they came to realize that a limited counterforce deterrence is sufficient to achieve the purpose of deterrence — to prevent the use of nuclear weapons. Perhaps they are merely following through on the logic of their argument to limit deterrence as much as possible. What they did not think was sufficient in the first draft they decided to be sufficient deterrence by the time of writing the third draft.

Another question can be raised. The final document ties use and deterrence very closely together by maintaining that one cannot threaten to do what one cannot morally do. Another ethical option is to claim that there is a great separation between the order of deterrence and the order of use. So great is this distinction that to threaten to deter does not necessarily involve a moral intention to use. Such a position is maintained by those who accept, in one way or another, a theory of bluff. Such a theory could maintain an absolute prohibition against all use of nuclears (a position perhaps logically contained in the bishops' own argument on use) but still accept some deterrence. I personally lean toward this position, even though it is not without its own problems.

The very fact that the bishops have related use and deterrence so very closely raises other problems for the bishops. Is it the need to hold to some deterrence that prevents their total condemnation of the use of nuclear weapons? If this is so, perhaps they should give this as one of their reasons. A second question concerns the exact relationship between use and deterrence. The pastoral letter wants to put the two together, but the final document seems to allow room for much greater deterrence (granted it is still quite limited) than it does for use.

This analysis has shown that the greatest changes in the course of drafting the document involve the theory about deterrence and the substantive question of countercity deterrence. The thorny question of deterrence and the ethical theory supporting it will continue to be the most important subject for further ethical investigation.

Ecclesiological Aspects

A somewhat brief and final consideration must be directed to the ecclesiological implications of this letter. In this light two aspects — the process itself and the recognition of the possibility of dissent from specific teaching — deserve attention. The process itself was quite different from that followed in most previous documents put out by the American bishops, although there has been a refreshing attempt to have broad-based consultation in some catechetical documents. In this case there were meetings of the committee with people involved on all sides of the issue. The people consulted represented all shades of opinion, and no position was a priori excluded. The first draft was sent to all the bishops and marked confidential. However, within a few days the content of the pastoral letter was published in the media. The second and third drafts were publicly released to the press and the general public after they were sent to the bishops. Likewise the final meeting in Chicago, at which amendments were proposed, voted on, and the final document approved, was open to the press. Many bishops in their individual dioceses encouraged study and discussion of the various drafts as they were proposed. Often in the past, episcopal statements — especially those dealing with questions of social ethics — were prepared with no participation from outside and very little involvement by the individual bishops. As a result, even the bishops themselves did not really "own" these documents. Many Roman Catholics today are very surprised to learn about the existence of the body of teachings which the American bishops have issued on social questions in the last fifteen years.[23]

The process itself greatly helped and abetted the purpose of making Catholics and the general public much more aware of the moral issues involved in this question. The best teaching device is no longer merely a letter coming from on high which will probably be read and studied by very few. The public and participatory process thus enhanced the teaching aspect and the influence of the letter, to say nothing about the internal strength of the document itself.

Perhaps even more importantly the process has set a precedent for the future. The consultative process indicates that the whole church was involved in preparing the document. If further documents on other subjects are to be credible, they must be willing to follow the same process. Unfortunately, in other areas of morality there has not been as great a willingness to bring about a dialogue involving the whole church.

A second ecclesiological implication concerns the possibility of dissent and the existence of pluralism within the church on specific ethical issues. At the Rome meeting in January 1983 great emphasis was attached to the need to distinguish the different levels of authoritative teaching involved in the document. The third draft and the pastoral letter itself distinguish universally binding moral principles, statements of recent popes and of Vatican II, and the application of moral principles to particular judgments. In the application of principles the letter realizes that prudential judgments are involved based on circumstances which can be changed or be interpreted differently by people of good will. Such moral judgments made in specific cases do not bind in conscience but are to be given serious attention and consideration by Catholics in making their moral choices.[24]

Such an ecclesiology recognizes a "big church" in that there will always be room for disagreement, pluralism, and dissent on specific complex questions, although the letter carefully avoids using the term "dissent." The bishops rightly insist that the unity of the church is not to be found on such specific questions. The basic principle behind such a statement is that in these areas one cannot attain a certitude that excludes the possibility of error. In my judgment such an approach logically must recognize the possibility of dissent in other areas of church teaching where one cannot claim to preclude the possibility of error. The following chapter will develop these ecclesiological aspects in greater detail.

This study has attempted to analyze the American bishops' pastoral letter on peace and war. The content of the teaching was briefly explained and some of the tensions in the drafting process were mentioned. The major section involved an ethical analysis of the document concentrating on the theory and the teaching on nuclear use and deterrence. A final short section considered the ecclesiological implications of the document. In conclusion, I do not think that it is an exaggeration to say that this letter is perhaps the most important and significant document ever issued by the American bishops.

NOTES

1. "The Pastoral Letter on War and Peace: The Challenge of Peace: God's Promise and Our Response," *Origins* 13 (1983): 1-32.

2. "First Draft: Pastoral Letter on War and Peace," *National Catholic Reporter* 18 (July 2, 1982: 11f; "Second Draft: Pastoral Letter on War and Peace," *Origins* 12 (1982): 305-328; "Third Draft: Pastoral Letter on War and Peace," *Origins* 12 (1983): 697-728. For the sake of clarity I have used the similar generic title for the different drafts.

3. "Rome Consultation on Peace and Disarmament: A Vatican Synthesis," *Origins* 12 (1983): 691-695.

4. Arthur Jones, "What Is Evil Is Evil: An Alternative Pastoral Letter," *National Catholic Reporter* 19 (April 15, 1983): 14.

5. Michael Novak, "Moral Clarity in the Nuclear Age: A Letter from Catholic Clergy and Laity," *Catholicism in Crisis* 1 (March 1983): 3-23.

6. National Catholic Office for Information, "News Release," April 8, 1983.

7. J. Brian Benestad and Francis J. Butler, eds., *Quest for Justice: A Compendium of Statements of the United States Catholic Bishops on the Political and Social Order 1966-1980* (Washington, D.C.: United States Catholic Conference, 1981).

8. *Origins* 13 (1983): 12, 13.

9. *Origins* 12 (1982): 707.

10. *Origins* 13 (1983): 10.

11. *National Catholic Reporter* 18 (July 2, 1982): p.11; *Origins* 12 (1982): 314, 315; *Origins* 12 (1983): 711, 712; *Origins* 13 (1983): 14-16.

12. *N.C. News Service*, Thursday, May 19, 1983, p. 1.

13. *National Catholic Reporter* 18 (July 2, 1982): 11, 12.

14. *Origins* 12 (1982): 315-318.

15. Benestad and Butler, *Quest for Justice*, pp. 43-45.

16. Cardinal John Krol, "SALT II: A Statement of Support," *Origins* 9 (1979): 195-199.

17. Germain Grisez, "The Moral Implications of a Nuclear Deterrent," *Center Journal* 2 (Winter 1982): 9-24.

18. Richard A. McCormick, "Ambiguity in Moral Choice" and "A Commentary on the Commentaries," in *Doing Evil to Achieve Good: Moral Choice in Conflict Situations*, ed. Richard A. McCormick and Paul Ramsey (Chicago: Loyola University Press, 1978), pp. 7–53 and 193-267.

19. Archbishop Joseph Bernardin, "Address to the November 1982 Bishops' Meeting," *Origins* 12 (1982): 397; *Origins* 12 (1983): 692.

20. *Origins* 12 (1983): 714.

21. Ibid., pp. 713-716.

22. *Origins* 13 (1983): 16-19.

23. Benestad and Butler, *Quest for Justice*.

24. *Origins* 12 (1982): 700; *Origins* 13 (1983): 2, 3.

6: Roman Catholic Teaching on Peace and War in a Broader Theological Context

This chapter will continue to examine the positions on peace, war, deterrence, and disarmament proposed in the Roman Catholic Church. The previous chapter proposed an ethical analysis of the teaching of the American bishops' pastoral letter on nuclear weapons. This chapter will proceed in a different manner. The first part will briefly summarize the present teaching of the Roman Catholic Church as this is found in the documents of the universal hierarchical teaching authority and in the statements representing the American bishops as a whole. Then the main body of the chapter will analyze the official Roman Catholic teaching on peace, war, and disarmament in the light of the broader perspective of moral theology by giving special attention to three important areas — ethical theory, eschatology, and ecclesiology.

I. Official Roman Catholic Teaching

The most authoritative recent statement of the teaching of the Roman Catholic Church on peace and war is found in the Pastoral Constitution on the Church in the Modern World of the Second Vatican Council. There have been and continue to be discussions about the exact teaching of Vatican II, but the main outlines of these teachings are, in my judgment, clear. The document calls on Christians to cooperate with all people in securing a peace based on justice and love. The constitution, known by its Latin name *Gaudium et Spes*, stresses the need for peace rooted in the hearts of all but also recognizes the need to set up structures and institutions to bring about that peace. Since human beings are sinful, "the threat of war hangs over them and will hang over them until the return of Christ."[1] However, it is our duty to work for the time that war will be completely outlawed by international consent. This goal requires the establishment of some effective universal public authority to safeguard peace.[2]

The council further recognizes that the savagery and horror of war are magnified by the new weapons of massive destruction and devastation. "All these considerations compel us to undertake an evaluation of war with an entirely new attitude."[3] The exact meaning of this sentence is not clear. The footnote is to the statement of Pope John XXIII in the Encyclical *Pacem in Terris* which maintains war is no longer an apt means of vindicating violated rights. There has been some doubt about the interpretation of this particular passage from *Pacem in Terris*, but it seems that the pope was not taking away the right to war as a means of self-defense but only as a means of vindicating rights which had already been violated.[4] In the text itself of *Gaudium et Spes*, after the statement about the need for an entirely new attitude, the pastoral constitution applies without explicitly saying so the just-war principle of discrimination to the use of nuclear weapons.

There are some significant new developments in the teaching of the Catholic Church as found in this document. For the first time pacifism and nonviolence are recognized as acceptable approaches within the Roman Catholic Church. *Gaudium et Spes* also calls for the state to make humane provisions for those who because of conscience refuse to bear arms provided they accept some other form of service to the human community. No distinction is made between conscientious objection and selective conscientious objection.[5]

However, the document does not abandon the just-war tradition and obviously employs that tradition in its approach. Since war has not been rooted out of human affairs and since there is no effective international institution, governments cannot be denied the right to legitimate defense once every means of peaceful settlement has been exhausted. Even in self-defense there are limits on the ways in which war and violence are employed.[6] The strongest condemnation of the whole council is an explicit application of the just-war principle of discrimination. "Any act of war aimed indiscriminately at the destruction of entire cities or of extensive areas along with their population is a crime against God and humanity. It merits unequivocal and unhesitating condemnation."[7] Note that the condemnation does not include all nuclear weapons but only indiscriminate weapons.

The arms race is condemned as an utterly treacherous trap and one which affects the poor to an intolerable degree. It is not a safe way to preserve a true peace. The peace of a sort resulting from the present balance is not authentic and true peace.[8] In light of the present world realities all must work to end the arms race and "to make a true beginning of disarmament, not indeed a unilateral disarmament, but one proceding at an equal pace according to agreement, and backed up by authentic and workable safeguards."[9] Subsequent papal teaching has been in continuity with the proposals of the Second Vatican Council.[10]

In the light of the teaching of the Vatican Council and of other subsequent papal utterances, the American bishops have made corporate statements about the issues. The most significant statements according to Archbishop Bernardin, the chair of the committee which drafted the pastoral letter, are the pastoral letter "Human Life in Our Day" (1968), the pastoral reflection "To Live in Christ Jesus" (1976), Cardinal Krol's congressional testimony representing the official policy of the United States Catholic Conference on the SALT II treaty (1979), and the Administrative Board's statement on registration and the draft (1980).[11]

"Human Life in Our Day" and subsequent statements acknowledge the continuing legitimacy of service in the military as a service to society. However, in accord with the Vatican Council document, the bishops also accept the legitimacy of Christian pacifism and call for the recognition of both conscientious objection and selective conscientious objection by our legal system.[12]

While half the pastoral letter "Human Life in Our Day" is addressed to the family of nations and the issues of peace and war, the pastoral reflection "To Live in Christ Jesus" discusses all aspects of the Christian life and devotes about two pages to peace issues.[13] This document succinctly summarizes the material found in the universal and American documents already considered. Chapter five has discussed the one new aspect found in this document — the claim that it is not only wrong to attack civilian populations but it is also wrong to threaten to attack them as part of a strategy of deterrence. The document does not explicitly raise the questions of how deterrence can continue to exist in the light of this or how deterrence can be effective without someone's having the intention to use the weapons.

Cardinal Krol's congressional testimony in 1979 on the ratification of the SALT II treaty discusses the nuclear question at greater length.[14] The cardinal is very precise and exact in introducing his testimony. On such specific issues as the SALT treaty there is a divergence of views within the Roman Catholic Church. The position he adopts is not the unanimous position of all the bishops or of all Catholics, but it is the official policy of the United States Catholic Conference. The testimony maintains that the first and primary moral imperative is to prevent the use of any nuclear weapons. The previous chapter has discussed Krol's approach to deterrence. Likewise there is no need to repeat here the summary of the American bishops' pastoral letter on peace and war.

The main thrust of this chapter is to analyze this teaching in the light of the broader perspective of Catholic moral theology. Three areas of moral theology will be considered —

ethical theory, eschatology, and ecclesiology. Is this approach to peace and war intimately related to and even grounded in broader theological understandings in the Roman Catholic theological tradition?

II. General Ethical Theory

In my judgment the most distinctive aspect of Roman Catholic ethics is the insistence on mediation. Mediation is characteristic of Roman Catholic theology in general. Karl Barth maintained that his biggest problem with Roman Catholicism was its *and.*[15] This comment points to the Catholic insistence on *and*—Scripture and tradition, faith and reason, God and human beings, faith and works, Jesus and the church. The Catholic tradition has opposed the axiom "the Scripture alone," because the Scripture must always be made concrete and contemporary through the continuing work of the Spirit in the church in the light of the historical, cultural, and social circumstances of the times. Catholic theology has rejected the axiom "to God alone belongs the glory," because the human being is a sharer and participator in the glory of God. Catholic ecclesiology insists on the church as a visible society mediating the word and work of the risen Lord. The believer is a part of this community of the church and through the church community is related to the risen Lord.

Major problems have occurred in the Catholic tradition when the true concept of mediation was forgotten. At times the second element in the couplet was given independent value and seemed to exist on its own apart from the first. Think of the older Catholic approach to Scripture and tradition as two different sources of revelation. An older apologetic thought that reason could conclusively prove the existence of God. A previous morality so emphasized work that the charge of Pelagianism was rightly raised because of the failure to see faith being active in works. An older ecclesiology absolutized the institution of the church and in its triumphalism failed to see that the whole reality and meaning of the church are in terms of mediation. However, all these abuses were abuses precisely because they forgot the reality of mediation or participation.

As applied to moral theology, mediation can be seen in a number of different ways. The traditional natural-law theory, especially from the perspective of theology, well illustrates the reality of mediation. To know what human beings are to do, this approach does not appeal immediately and directly to God or God's plan or will. Yes, the plan of God is the ultimate norm of human morality, but the natural law is precisely the participation of the eternal plan in the rational creature. Human reason reflecting on human nature can arrive at the plan of God. In a similar manner, as chapter four has pointed out, the faith vision of the Christian is mediated in and through human reason and human sciences. In the best of the Catholic tradition there can never be a dichotomy or opposition between faith and reason. If anything, the older manuals erred by absolutizing human reason in itself and failing to understand reason as mediating faith. In this light, approaches to the realities of peace and war often prescinded from faith and scriptural perspectives. However, these faith perspectives cannot exist alone but must be mediated through human reason. One cannot jump immediately from scriptural citations to complex specific moral issues without the mediating use of reason.

This emphasis on mediation in Catholic social ethics is illustrated in the tradition by the tendency for moral theology to give a very specific and minute analysis of moral questions. Compare, for example, *A Living Wage* published by John A. Ryan in 1906 with *Christianity and the Social Crisis* written by Walter Rauschenbusch in 1907.[16] These two men were the leading figures in the Roman Catholic and Protestant social ethics of their day. Rauschenbusch's book deals in a very broad way, as the title indicates, with Christianity and the social crisis. Ryan deals with one comparatively small concern — a living wage. The Catholic author discusses various theories of wage justice and argues for a living wage by insisting on the fact that God created the world for the sustenance of all and that access to the bounty of the earth becomes available to most people only through the expenditure of useful labor. In addition to a thorough and detailed form of reasoning, Ryan also employs economic theory and statistics in his book. A living family wage for an average size family of four or five children is at least six hundred dollars a year in American cities, and more is needed in the larger cities. Ryan makes out a family budget to prove his contention. Ryan's work well illustrates the fact that Catholic moral theology has used reason and the sciences as mediating realities in coming to its specific ethical conclusions. Obviously there are other factors such as confessional practice which also strongly influence the Catholic tendency to be quite specific in its ethical analysis and conclusions.

The recognition of mediation means that morality becomes very concrete but also that moral appeals must employ and appropriate the data of all the human sciences. Too often there has been a tendency to claim that many issues involve only economic or political decisions and not moral decisions. However, there is a moral aspect to these decisions, and most truly human decisions are moral decisions even though they involve much data from the human sciences. John Ryan can again illustrate the Catholic tradition in this regard. The very first sentence in Ryan's unpublished licentiate dissertation makes the point: "Every free economic action has ethical relations, and is subject to ethical laws."[17] Thus in the contemporary discussions of peace and war, the issues of deterrence and disarmament are not merely political problems but are truly moral and ethical issues.

A mediated ethic which recognizes the need to become concrete and specific through the use of the data of the sciences must logically acknowledge that solutions employing such data cannot claim too great a degree of certitude. The human sciences are not able to provide certitude without the fear of error. Church teachings in moral theology must recognize the inability to achieve absolute certitude on complex specific issues. This realization lies behind the caution given by Cardinal Krol when he testified for the United States Catholic Conference on the SALT II treaty. The testimony supported the treaty but also recognized many shortcomings in it. The cardinal distinguished between the principles of Catholic morality and the positions taken on a particular issue such as the SALT II treaty. Krol carefully recognized that his testimony did not represent the unanimous position of all Catholics or of all the Catholic bishops or even of the Administrative Board of the Catholic bishops. It was nonetheless the official policy of the United States Catholic Conference.

The outstanding characteristic of all the drafts of the pastoral letter of the American bishops, especially in comparison with the documents of the universal church, is the emphasis on specifics. In this sense the pastoral letter goes beyond but not necessarily against the papal and conciliar statements. The pastoral letter explicitly calls attention to the specific character of many of its proposals and distinguishes these proposals from the broader level of moral principles. Such specific proposals are prudential judgments which cannot and do not claim to have the same moral and doctrinal authority as the more general moral principles. Catholics can legitimately disagree with these judgments. The principle of mediation thus recognizes that on a specific complex issue or judgment one cannot claim a certitude that excludes the possibility of error.

The traditional Catholic emphasis on mediation in moral theology, together with other influences, recognizes that social reform and social justice require not only a change of heart but also a change of institutions and structures. This emphasis has always been present in Roman Catholicism with its integral vision of the world and is illustrated in the social teaching of the popes beginning with the encyclical *Rerum Novarum* of 1891. Change of heart alone is not enough, but a change of institutions and structures is also necessary. In fact, the official Catholic social teaching in the last century could rightly be criticized for not giving enough importance to interior dispositions, or the change of heart.

Documents such as *Rerum Novarum* concentrate on structural change and only at the very end briefly mention the need for interior personal change. This recognition of the need for both a change of heart and a change of structures is also present in the official Catholic teachings on peace, war, and deterrence. *Gaudium et Spes* sees peace as resulting from justice and love and as being deeply rooted in the hearts of individuals. However, to bring about peace in our world certain political structures are required. The goal of completely eliminating war requires the establishment of some universal, public authority acknowledged as such by all and endowed with effective power. In the meantime, everything must be done to strengthen trust in existing institutions and structures. The rejection of a call for unilateral disarmament echoes the need for systems and institutions which can assure the peace. The structural aspect of securing peace is most important. Part three of the pastoral letter entitled "The Promotion of Peace: Proposals and Policies" stresses the structural changes necessary, whereas the fourth part, "The Pastoral Challenge and Response," emphasizes the need for conversion and education.

The discussion of Catholic ethical theory has thus far concentrated on the characteristic aspect of mediation and its consequences for ethics in general and specifically for official Catholic teaching on peace, war, and disarmament. There is one other aspect of Catholic ethical thinking which should be mentioned — the contemporary debate about the existence and grounding of norms. Within the discussion about peace and war in the Catholic tradition there can be no doubt that a very strong pacifist tendency has emerged during the last few years.[18] This pacifism takes many different forms and has many different groundings and formulations. One form of pacifism is the pacifism of the Catholic Worker movement associated with Dorothy Day and such "traditional" Catholic pacifists as Gordon Zahn.[19] In my judgment their approach can best be described as Christian witness pacifism. The gospel calls the Christian to bear witness to Jesus who did not take up arms or engage in violence. The primary emphasis is on bearing witness.

The Christian is not primarily concerned with efficacy, for in the end results are in the hands of God. The Catholic action communities of the 1960's, often called in the media the Catholic left, also held pacifist positions but in a different way.[20] They were totally committed to nonviolence but saw nonviolence not primarily as a witness but as an effective and efficacious means of social change. A third group might be called nuclear pacifist, but the term pacifists is here used in a very equivocal manner because many of these people are not absolute pacifists. The growth and influence of the pacifist movement in Roman Catholicism are readily evident. The conditioned acceptance of pacifism by Vatican II as a legitimate Catholic option both has been brought about by this contemporary movement and has also contributed to the growth of the pacifist movement.

While pacifism has been growing within Roman Catholic circles, another development has occurred in Catholic ethical theory which in general tends to argue against an absolute pacifism. Since the middle 1960s a growing number of Catholic moral theologians have questioned the existence and grounding of absolute moral norms.[21] The revisionists maintain that the older approach has often identified the human moral act with the physical stucture of the act. The physical structure, in such instances as contraception and the concept of directly doing evil, constitutes a premoral evil which can be justified for a proportionate reason. Sometimes the terms deontological and teleological are used to describe the two approaches. The older, or deontological, approach maintains that certain actions are always wrong no matter what the consequences. The teleological approach maintains that premoral evil can be done if there is a proportionate reason. I prefer to describe the revisionist approach as emphasizing a more relational understanding which refuses to absolutize any one value.

The revisionist approach to the moral theory about the existence and grounding of norms tends to be in opposition to the growing emphasis on pacifism in the literature dealing only with peace and war issues. Peace and no killing are absolutized; violence is never permitted. The revisionist approach would see violence or killing as a premoral evil which could be justified by a proportionate reason. Peace exists in relationship to other values or virtues; sometimes in the name of justice, for example, violence might become morally acceptable. These two different developments — one in the specific question of peace and war and the other in the area of moral theory — have been growing in the last few years without any interaction. Those writing on pacifism tend to be interested only in the pacifism issue and have not entered into the current methodological discussion in Catholic moral theology. As a proponent of a revisionist approach in moral theory I see such an approach as another reason why I personally or the church as a whole cannot accept an absolute pacifist position.

The revisionist approach to the grounding and existence of norms, however, must come to grips with the just-war principle which traditionally has forbidden the direct killing of noncombatants. Can such killing be only a premoral evil which is justified for a proportionate reason? Many of the revisionists have explicitly considered this question and concluded that there is a moral norm in this case because there is no proportionate reason that could ever justify such killing in warfare.[22] More dialogue and discussion would be helpful in this area.

In general there appears to be a consistency between the Roman Catholic teaching on peace, war, and disarmament and the understanding of Roman Catholic ethics as accepting the reality of mediation with all of its ramifications. In addition recent revisionist developments in ethical theory also argue against an absolute pacifism and seem to be opposed to the line of reasoning proposed by the growing number of recent Catholic advocates of pacifism.

III. Eschatology

Eschatology has been a subject of increasing interest in the last few decades in Christian theology especially in terms of such discussions as secularization, the meaning of history, and the social mission of the church. My own approach to eschatology is in terms of the fivefold stance I propose for moral theology.[23] The Christian looks at the world and reality in terms of the fivefold mysteries of creation, sin, incarnation, redemption, and resurrection destiny. Creation reminds us of the goodness and finitude of all that was made by God. Sin affects everything human but cannot totally destroy the goodness of creation. The incarnation recalls that God has destined all of created reality to be joined in the work of Jesus. Redemption means that the saving love of God is already present in our midst, but the fullness of the eschaton always remains future and will never occur in this world. In general terms this eschatological vision corresponds to the type proposed by H. Richard Niebuhr of Christ transforming culture.[24]

What has been explained above in terms of eschatology can also be expressed in other theological terms and under other aspects of theology. The doctrine of God corresponding to this eschatological approach understands God's action in terms of creating, preserving, and redeeming. The corresponding theological anthropology sees the Christian person in the light of all these different mysteries.

In the discussion on peace and war, especially in *Gaudium et Spes*, the Catholic teaching seems to adopt such an eschatology. Some of the other parts of *Gaudium et Spes* (especially chapters 1, 2, and 3 of part I), with their intention of emphasizing the christological aspect of reality, so overstress the resurrection and redemption that they fail to recognize that the fullness of the eschaton will always lie outside history. The discussion of the nature of peace seems to present a more adequate eschatology in keeping with the stance mentioned above.[25] Peace results from the harmony built into human society by its divine founder and actuated by human beings as they thirst after greater justice, but because of the presence of sin this is not enough. Peace is likewise the fruit of love which goes beyond what justice can provide. This earthly peace results from the peace of Christ, who through the cross reconciled all to God. Because of our sinfulness the threat of war will hang over us until the return of Christ. There are some indications that perhaps the fullness of the eschaton as future is somewhat slighted in these formulations, but on the whole the eschatological vision of this paragraph of *Gaudium et Spes* coheres with the stance mentioned above.

A significant change between the first and the second drafts of the pastoral letter of the American bishops underscores the need for such an eschatological perspective. The first draft begins with an introduction based on the Scriptures giving a picture of the kingdom as embracing peace and the living out of the Sermon on the Mount. The next section treats of peace in the modern world and the different stands that Christians take toward peace and violence in this world.[26] The second draft, after the biblical section entitled "Peace and the Kingdom," adds an important section on "Kingdom and History" which recognizes the imperfect and sinful realities of the present in relation to the eschatological fullness.[27] Only in the light of this eschatological perspective does the draft then develop the different approaches which Christians take with regard to peace and force in our world. The second and subsequent drafts also have, near the very beginning, a short section describing the Catholic social tradition. Here the letter refers to the biblical vision of the world created and sustained by God, scarred by sin, redeemed in Christ, and destined for the kingdom, which is at the heart of our religious heritage. It is the task of theology to elaborate, explain, and apply this vision in each age.[28]

The general consequences of such an eschatological vision center on the tensions created by it. The believer and the believing community will always experience the tension between the imperfections of the present and the fullness of the eschatological future. The perennial temptation consists in trying to deny or collapse this tension. One can collapse the tension by stressing either pole to the detriment of the other. The one approach expects the fullness of the kingdom to come quickly, readily, and easily, thereby forgetting the struggle and the pilgrim nature of the Christian life. The other extreme forgets the pull of the future and merely accepts the status quo without any impulse to change and transform it.

This eschatological vision also serves as a basis for the tension which exists between the believing community and the culture around it. In the words of H. Richard Niebuhr's model, the Christian and the believing community are always striving to transform the culture or society in which they live.[29]

At times because of the finitude, sinfulness, and lack of eschatological fullness present in our world and culture, the church should oppose what is happening in the contemporary society. Too often in the American ethos there has been the tendency for all churches to be too conforming and not to critique certain aspects of the culture. There are different explanations for the general conforming propensities of the mainline American churches, but the immigrant status of Roman Catholicism helped to frame a mentality which tried to show that one could be both Catholic and American at one and the same time. The mainstream of Roman Catholicism from the last part of the nineteenth century adopted such a posture, and this characterized most of the Roman Catholic Church until recent times.[30]

Not only do finitude, sin, and incompleteness mark our contemporary world and ethos, but the goodness of creation, the destiny of the incarnation, and the grace of the resurrection are also present. The Christian believer and the believing communities work with all other individuals and groups within society to try to bring about a greater peace and justice in our world. The relationship of the believing community to the world will always be complex. At times Christians must strongly criticize. At other times Christians can and will learn from the society. However, at all times the believing community must work with all other human beings to achieve a greater but always imperfect peace and justice in our world.

Eschatology's relationship to social ethics takes on a number of different forms. The fullness of the eschaton serves as a negative critique of all existing human institutions and structures. However, such an understanding cannot result in a hands off, "plague on both your houses" type of approach. As Karl Barth phrased it, even in the dark of night not all cats are gray.[31] The negative critique should include the positive commitment to change and transform the existing situation.[32]

The eschatological vision also presents the positive values at which we aim — in this specific case the realities of peace and justice. This utopia or vision gives a general sense of direction to what Christians and the Christian community should try to do.

At times the eschatological vision means that the Christian and the Christian community must reluctantly accept or tolerate some nonmoral evils. Sometimes one must make the prudential judgment that half a loaf is better than none. There are many examples of accepting something less than perfect and of toleration in the strict sense in Catholic teaching and theology. Thomas Aquinas' approach to civil law furnishes a good example. According to Aquinas the civil law is based on the natural law. However, the civil law can permit some evils. Laws are imposed on people according to their condition, but the greater part of human beings are not perfect in virtue. Human law, consequently, should not prohibit all vices from which the virtuous are able to abstain but only those more serious vices which the greater part of human beings can avoid.[33] In discussing whether or not the rights of infidels can be tolerated, Aquinas briefly develops his theory about tolerating evil. Human rulers and human governments are derived from divine government and should imitate the divine example. However, the Almighty God permits certain evils to occur in the universe which could be prohibited, lest in prohibiting them greater good would be taken away or greater evil would follow. Thus human government or rulers can tolerate some evils lest certain goods be impeded or worse evils occur.[34] The Thomistic recognition that evil can be tolerated logically coheres with the eschatological vision proposed above. The previous chapter dealt more specifically with the kind of evil that can be tolerated.

Reactions within the Roman Catholic community to the SALT II treaty also illustrate the tension created by the imperfections of the time in which we live. Opponents to the treaty claimed that it failed to really reduce arms and therefore did not merit a positive reception.[35] Proponents of the treaty, including the official position of the United States Catholic Conference, recognized the very significant limitations of the treaty but endorsed it as a step toward continuing negotiations and the reduction of arms. They obviously maintained that half a loaf is better than none.[36]

Another example has recently occurred in the Roman Catholic Church in the United States. The Roman Catholic bishops have been very public and visible in their support for a constitutional amendment to overturn the 1973 ruling of the Supreme Court on abortion. The bishops never said specifically what type of amendment they supported, but their opposition to all direct abortion was well known.[37] In fall 1981 the American bishops officially supported the Hatch Amendment which provides that a right to abortion is not secured by the constitution. Congress and the states have concurrent power to restrict abortion, but a provision of a law of a state which is more restrictive than a conflicting provision of a law of Congress shall govern. Some Catholic bishops and others involved in the right-to-life movement were upset by such support. Were the Catholic bishops backing down from their strong antiabortion position?[38] Without a doubt if the Hatch Amendment were to become law, there would still be a large number of abortions performed in the United States, but the number would be much less than at present. Obviously the bishops based their decision on political expediency — in the best sense of the term. An amendment prohibiting almost all abortions except in very limited circumstances apparently has no chance of becoming law at the present time. According to the thinking of its supporters there is the possibility that the Hatch Amendment can be passed, especially with strong support from the American bishops. (My own position has been opposed to any attempt to change the ruling of the Supreme

Court by a constitutional amendment both for theoretical reasons and for concerns of feasibility and practicality.)

These eschatological considerations show that the Christian believer and the Christian community will always experience the tension between the now and the eschatological future. This same tension is manifest in the church's relationship to society and culture with the result that the church can never be a total opposition movement nor can it be uncritical of the imperfections and evils of the society in which it lives. The eschatological tension means that the church will always try to transform the present reality, but at times the church will have to settle for something less than the perfect good or will have to tolerate some evil in order to avoid greater evils.

The teaching on peace and war found in the official Roman Catholic teaching well illustrates this eschatological tension. The just-war theory itself expresses such a tension by trying to limit both the right to go to war and the ways in which even just wars are fought but at the same time recognizing that in our present world nations still have the right to go to war in self-defense provided such violence is a last resort and is conducted in a just way. The pastoral letter disagrees with American policy by opposing the first use of nuclear weapons. The bishops do not call for unilateral nuclear disarmament but conditionally accept limited counterforce deterrence provided such deterrence exists only to prevent the use of nuclear weapons and is accompanied by meaningful steps toward negotiated reduction in arms and disarmament. While conditionally accepting some limited deterrence, the pastoral letter continues to criticize significant aspects of both Soviet and American deterrence policies.

IV. Ecclesiology

The ecclesiology to be proposed here is in keeping with the traditional Roman Catholic self-understanding, is consistent with the ethical and eschatological concerns already discussed, and is coherent with the teaching on peace, war, and deterrence discussed in the first part of this paper. This section will discuss the church as a community intimately involved in the life of society and will devote most of its space to a consideration of pluralism within the church on specific social issues such as those under discussion.

The church is a community involved in the struggle for justice and peace in the world. At times the church can and must be critical of the society, but it can never find its total identity as a sectarian movement always opposed to and separated from political life and institutions. The history of the Roman Catholic Church illustrates such an approach. The eschatological considerations discussed in the previous section form the basis for such an understanding of the church. The whole tradition of the church's dealing with the issues of peace and war support such an understanding of the church.

Within the church there exists a pluralism of acceptable positions on specific concrete social questions. The Catholic Church is also catholic — with a small "c." There is a universality about it and a willingness to recognize diverse possible options within the church on specific and complex social questions such as war, peace, and deterrence. Obviously there are limitations to this pluralism, but the Catholic Church in respect to social issues is a "big church" with room for diversity. The historical and existential self-understanding of Roman Catholicism recognizes this pluralism. The Catholic Church community has been big enough to include a Francisco Franco and a Julius Nyerere. American Catholicism embraced both a Dorothy Day and a Father Coughlin. The Catholic teaching on peace and war in both its universal and American contexts recognizes such pluralism and diversity. Both pacifism and just-war theories are acceptable. A complete and unlimited bellicism is outside the pale of Catholic options, but there will always be the possibility of pluralism on issues such as arms reduction treaties. The American bishops explicitly recognize a legitimate pluralism within the church on prudential judgments such as no first use of nuclear weapons.

This pluralism of options within the church is grounded in the ethical and eschatological approaches discussed earlier. Ethical theory recognizes the epistemological problem that in the midst of complexity one cannot attain a certitude that excludes the possibility of error. Since Catholic social teaching recognizes the need to mediate the evangelical vision through reason and the human sciences, it also recognizes the lack of absolute certitude in such specific areas. In addition, the eschatological tension also acknowledges a pluralism of approaches. At times some might be willing to tolerate certain evils which others would not. A further justification for pluralism within the church on specific and complex social issues is a theological reason recognizing the legitimate freedom of the believer. Roman Catholic theory has not given much explicit attention to this reality, but concern for such freedom has existed, even when that freedom was narrowly circumscribed. The theory of probabilism, for example, safeguards the freedom of the individual Catholic against a rigoristic tutiorism or probabiliorism. No confessor can take away the freedom of the individual to follow an opinion which is truly probable even though the contrary opinion might be safer or more probable.[39] Cardinal Krol in his testimony before Congress on the SALT II treaty was very careful to recognize implicitly the freedom of the believer within the Catholic Church community. The Roman consultation in January 1983 mentioned respect for the freedom of the Christian as the first reason calling for a distinction among the various levels of teaching authority found in the American bishops' letter.[40]

Pluralism within the church in dealing with complex social issues cannot be merely a flabby pluralism, for there are definite limits to legitimate pluralism within the church even on issues of peace and war. Even within the limits of legitimate pluralism there are important truth claims involved in the positions taken. One should strive to convince others of the truth of one's own position, but one cannot claim that an opposing position places one outside the church. Since there are a number of different legitimate positions within the church, the church itself must often be seen as a community of moral discourse rather than as a provider of answers for its members in all such cases.

One of the most striking illustrations of this pluralism within Roman Catholicism has been the cautious official acceptance of a pacifist position, which appeared for the first time in *Gaudium et Spes*. As noted in the last chapter, the American bishops are even stronger in their acceptance of pacifism as an individual option within the church. In my judgment there must always be in the church a place for the pacifist position, but the whole church cannot be pacifist in our present circumstances. All the aspects mentioned previously—ethical theory, eschatology, and a catholic ecclesiology—argue against the fact that the whole church can be pacifist today. However, before talking about the different positions within the church, one must always recognize and emphasize the common ground which exists between the pacifist and others in the Christian community. All are called to work for peace. Change of heart, nonviolent approaches, and changes of structures to make peace more of a reality in our world can and should be acknowledged by all. War and violence can never be accepted as anything more than a last resort—an *ultima ratio*. Within the pluralism of the believing community the different positions must realize in theory and in practice that they share much in common.

However, the question remains: If the whole church cannot be pacifist, how can there be a place, even an important place, for pacifists within the church? Note that here we are dealing very much on the level of principle and not just the level of prudential judgments. I think that from within the Catholic tradition an analogy can and should be made with the concept of vocation to religious life. It seems, in a way similar to the stance of Reinhold Niebuhr, that there is a place and a need for a vocation to pacifism within the church community.[41] Religious life rests on a commitment to one or other of the basic Christian values and virtues of poverty, chastity, or obedience. Peace is also a very important value in human existence. Just as in the case of religious life, so too there can and should be vocations in the Christian community through the gift of the Spirit for people to bear witness to the value of peace. Commitment to peace and bearing witness to it constitute a very significant vocation for some Christian people today. Also this vocation serves a purpose for the total Christian community by calling to mind the importance of this value and especially the danger of abuses of violence which all too often have occurred.

Is pacifism a higher calling or something closer to the gospel than the reluctant acceptance of violence as a last resort in the quest for justice? The analogy to religious life in the Roman Catholic tradition might lead one to this conclusion. However, I personally disagree with the older Catholic theology that claimed religious life was a higher state of life. Even in accord with aspects of traditional Catholic theology one can maintain that life according to the religious vows is not a higher form or better grade of Christian existence. According to Thomistic theology the goal of the Christian life is charity — love of God and neighbor. The vows concern only means to an end.[42] An older theory wrongly absolutized these means rather than seeing them as mediations of charity. In the practice of religious life absolutized vows were considered in themselves apart from their primary function to be mediations of charity. All Christians have the same goal, and there is no better or higher way to achieve that goal. In other theological terminology, the primary vow of the Christian is the baptismal vow. All other subsequent vows add nothing to this basic commitment but only specify it.

From a more evangelical perspective one might maintain that pacifism is closer to the gospel ideal of peace and hence something higher and better. However, the Scriptures also need a hermeneutic and must be interpreted in the light of the eschatological tension and signs of the time. Here again I do not think one can talk in terms of a better or higher way. Paul Ramsey, from his perspective on Christian ethics, has tried to indicate that one and the same agape can justify both pacifism and the acceptance of violence as a last resort in protecting the neighbor in need. Agape can take either fork in the road, but one way cannot be necessarily better than the other.[43] My understanding of pluralism thus recognizes an important place for a vocation to pacifism within the church, even though the whole church today cannot be pacifist and pacifism is not necessarily a higher calling.

A final consideration involves the understanding of the prophetic role in the church. This prophetic role stresses the leadership of the church in speaking God's judgment against injustices and evils in the world, often in a very concrete and specific manner. What is the relationship between a church recognizing the pluralism of different options in the area of peace, war, and disarmament and a prophetic church? There can be no doubt that my view of the church in its relationship to the particular questions under discussion and to social teaching in general is much less prophetic than many approaches to church today. Sectarian understandings and an emphasis on a small elite church result in a more prophetic church. At times I have the feeling that some Roman Catholics calling for a more prophetic church still suffer from the genetic disease that constantly threatens all Roman Catholics — triumphalism. This newer form of triumphalism maintains that the church must be the leader in all things and must be there as the "firstest with the mostest." On the other hand, I do not want to leave the impression that the church does not have a prophetic function.

The prophetic function of the church is nuanced and contextualized in the light of the other considerations already developed. The ethical perspective calls to mind the complexity of specific social issues and the difficulty of achieving certitude in these areas. This lack of certitude is bound to temper the prophetic aspect of the church in dealing with specific moral problems. From an eschatological viewpoint the church will always experience the tension between the imperfection of the now and the fullness of the eschaton. The acceptance of a lesser good or the toleration of evil is at times necessary and required. An ecclesiology which stresses a "big church" is also going to limit the prophetic aspect of the church. A big church is comprised of both saints and sinners. In a sense the church itself is always *simul justus et peccator*. The church can never be reduced to an elite of any type. The big church has many functions—the prophetic, the reconciling, the healing, the forgiving, the challenging.

Prophetic is a word which everyone wants to claim for one's self in these days. For that reason I think theologians should be very careful in using the word. It is very interesting to me that in the contemporary life of the Roman Catholic Church the word prophetic often appears in two very different contexts. Some people urge the church to be prophetic and come out in favor of unilateral nuclear disarmament. Anything short of that is seen as being unprophetic and not living up to the fullness of the gospel.[44] The other context in which the word is frequently used is in the defense of the teaching of *Humanae Vitae* on artificial contraception. The proponents of this teaching have frequently referred to it in the last few years as prophetic.[45] From my perspective the prophetic can never be in opposition to what is reasonable. The Catholic tradition has insisted that morality in general and social morality in particular must be in accord with reason.

The prophetic, nonetheless, remains a significant function and reality in the church, but there are different ways in which the truly prophetic aspect can and should become real in the church. In terms of the preaching and acting of the whole church a prophetic criticism of existing structures in the light of the gospel is always called for. Also in words, symbols, and acts the whole community must stress the goal commandments of Christian existence. However, on specific complex issues such as those under consideration one must always recognize the legitimate diversity and pluralism within the church even though one should be strongly committed to one's own position.

Smaller groups and individuals within the church can have a prophetic witness (with emphasis on witness) to one or other important values or aspects of the Christian life even though the total church cannot act in this way. This function has been carried out well in the church by small groups such as the Catholic Worker movement in the United States.[46]

Conclusion

The Roman Catholic teaching on peace, war, and disarmament in the documents of both the universal and the American Church has been studied not primarily in terms of an in-depth analysis of the teaching itself but rather in terms of the relationship of this teaching to broader aspects of moral theology.

The ethical, eschatological, and ecclesiological implications of the official teachings on peace and war are consistent with the general Catholic understanding of these realities. The just-war approach used in these documents, together with the recognition of a vocation to pacifism for some, is thus firmly grounded in Catholic moral theology in general. This just-war theory continues to serve its purpose of both justifying some wars and condemning others while at the same time placing significant limits on the way in which even a just war can be waged.

Obviously, within the parameters of these ethical, eschatological, and ecclesiological dimensions there is room for different approaches to specific questions and to prudential judgments. One, for example, with the same theological perspectives could oppose a bilateral nuclear freeze. Since the theory involved and the general outlines of the approach taken to peace and war in these official Catholic documents are so intimately connected with a broader Catholic theological self-understanding, one can conclude that the same general approach will continue to direct Roman Catholic teaching in the future.

NOTES

1. *Gaudium et Spes*, n. 80. For an English translation of the Vatical II documents see Walter M. Abbott, ed., *The Documents of*

Vatican II (New York: Guild Press, 1966). In subsequent references n. will refer to the paragraph in the document, and page references to Abbott will also be given.

2. Ibid., n. 82; Abbott, p. 295.

3. Ibid., n. 80; Abbott, p. 293.

4. For a defense of this interpretation see Paul Ramsey, *The Just War: Force and Political Responsibility* (New York: Charles Scribner's Sons, 1968), pp. 192-197.

5. *Gaudium et Spes*, n. 78; Abbott, p. 291.

6. Ibid., n. 79; Abbott, p. 293.

7. Ibid., n. 80; Abbott, p. 294.

8. Ibid., n. 81; Abbott, pp. 294-295.

9. Ibid., n. 82; Abbott, p. 296.

10. J. Bryan Hehir, "War and Peace: Reflections on Recent Teachings," *New Catholic World* 226 (March/April 1982): 60-64.

11. Archbishop Joseph Bernardin, "Studying War and Peace," *Origins* 11 (1981): 403-404.

12. "Human Life in our Day," in *Quest for Justice: A Compendium of Statements of the United States Catholic Bishops on the Political and Social Order 1966-1980*, ed. J. Brian Benestad and Francis J. Butler (Washington, DC: United States Catholic Conference, 1981), pp. 57-69. Subsequent references to American episcopal documents will be made to this compendium as *Quest for Justice.*

13. *Quest for Justice*, pp. 43-45.

14. Cardinal John Krol, "Salt II: A Statement of Support," *Origins* 9 (1979): 195-199.

15. From a Catholic perspective see Hans Urs von Balthasar, *The Theology of Karl Barth* (New York: Holt, Rinehart and Winston, 1971), pp. 40-41.

16. John A. Ryan, *A Living Wage* (New York: Macmillan, 1906); Walter Rauschenbusch, *Christianity and the Social Crisis* (New York: Harper Torchbook, 1964).

17. John A. Ryan, "Some Ethical Aspects of Speculation," (S.T.L. dissertation, The Catholic University of America, 1906), p. 1.

18. Joseph Fahey, "Pax Christi," in *War or Peace: The Search for New Answers*, ed. Thomas A. Shannon (Maryknoll, NY: Orbis Books, 1980), pp. 59-71; Patricia F. McNeal, *The American Catholic Peace Movement, 1928-1972* (New York: Arno Press, 1978), pp. 123-299.

19. E.g., Gordon C. Zahn, "The Berrigans: Radical Activism

Personified," in *The Berrigans*, ed. William Van Etten Casey and Philip Nobile (New York: Avon Books, 1971), pp. 97-112.

20. Charles A. Meconis, *With Clumsy Grace: The American Catholic Left, 1961-75* (New York: Seabury Press, 1979).

21. For readings on this debate, see eds., Richard A. McCormick and Paul Ramsey, *Doing Evil to Achieve Good: Moral Choice in Conflict Situations* (Chicago: Loyola University Press, 1978); eds., Charles E. Curran and Richard A. McCormick, *Readings in Moral Theology No. 1: Moral Norms and Catholic Tradition* (New York: Paulist Press, 1979).

22. See, for example, McCormick in McCormick and Ramsey, *Doing Evil to Achieve Good*, pp. 259-261; Curran in Curran and McCormick, *Readings in Moral Theology*, pp. 345ff.

23. Charles E. Curran, *New Perspectives in Moral Theology* (Notre Dame, IN: University of Notre Dame Press, 1976), pp. 47-86.

24. H. Richard Niebuhr, *Christ and Culture* (New York: Harper Torchbook, 1956).

25. *Gaudium et Spes*, nn. 77-90; Abbott, pp. 289-305.

26. "First Draft: Pastoral Letter on War and Peace," *National Catholic Reporter* 18 (July 2, 1982): 11, 12. Note that for the sake of consistency the pastoral letter and its drafts will be referred to in this manner.

27. "Second Draft: Pastoral Letter on War and Peace," *Origins* 12 (1982): 309-311.

28. Ibid., p. 307; "Pastoral Letter on War and Peace," *Origins* 13 (1983): 3.

29. Niebuhr, *Christ and Culture*, pp. 190-229.

30. David J. O'Brien, *American Catholics and Social Reform* (New York: Oxford University Press, 1968), pp. 212-227; O'Brien, *The Renewal of American Catholicism* (New York: Oxford University Press, 1972), pp. 138-162

31. Karl Barth, *Community, State, and Church* (Garden City, NY: Doubleday Anchor Books, 1960), p. 119.

32. Joseph Jankowiak, *Critical Negativity and Political Ethics* (Rome: Pontifical Gregorian University Press, 1975).

33. Thomas Aquinas, *Summa Theologiae* (Turin and Rome: Marietti, 1952), *I^a II^{ae}*, q. 96, a. 2.

34. Ibid., *II^{a}II^{ae}*, q. 10, a. 11.

35. Thomas J. Gumbleton, "Chaplain Blessing the Bombers: Is SALT Worth Supporting? No!" *Commonweal* 106 (1979): 105-106.

36. Krol, "Salt II," *Origins* 9 (1979): 195-199.

37. James T. McHugh, *The Relationship of Moral Principles to Civil Laws with Special Application to Abortion Legislation in the United States of America, 1968-78* (Rome: Pontifical University of St. Thomas, 1981), pp. 109-148.

38. James Castelli, "Hatch Amendment Still Splits Pro-Life Camp," *Our Sunday Visitor* 70 (January 17, 1982): 6.

39. Th. Deman, "Probabilisme," in *Dictionnaire de théologie catholique* XIII, col. 417-619.

40. "Rome Consultation on Peace and Disarmament," *Origins* 12 (1983): 693.

41. John C. Bennett, "Reinhold Niebuhr's Social Ethics," in *Reinhold Niebuhr: His Religious, Social, and Political Thought*, ed. Charles W. Kegley and Robert W. Bretall (New York: Macmillan, 1956), pp. 67ff.

42. Aquinas, *Summa Theologiae*, II^aII^{ae}, q. 184, a. 3.

43. Ramsey, *The Just War*, p. 501.

44. Joan Chittester, "Between Prophetism and Nationalism," *Commonweal* 109 (1982): 429.

45. Pope John Paul II, *Familiaris Consortio: The Role of the Christian Family in the Modern World* (Boston: St. Paul Editions, 1981), n. 29, p. 47.

46. William D. Miller, *A Harsh and Dreadful Love: Dorothy Day and the Catholic Worker Movement* (Garden City, NY: Doubleday Image Book, 1973).

7: Saul D. Alinsky, Catholic Social Practice, and Catholic Theory

Many contemporary theologians understand theology as reflection on the living of Christian life. Gustavo Gutierrez[1] has described liberation theology as critical reflection on praxis. On the Catholic scene liberation theology has been one of the most distinctive developments in the post-Vatican II period. This theology comes out of the struggle for liberation of the economically, politically, and socially oppressed people of Latin America, just as black liberation theology or feminist theology has developed in North America. There has been much talk about what liberation theology would look like in a North American context, but all recognize that the North American experience is quite different from the South American experience.[2]

The theological literature is silent about any such distinctive movements or approaches in the United States to social justice with the exception of the Catholic peace movement in the 1960s and early 1970s.[3] However, as a matter of fact, there has been something new and distinctive in the practical approach to social justice in North American Catholicism which has surfaced since the Second Vatican Council. I refer to the community organization approaches developed by Saul D. Alinsky. Unfortunately, the theological and the ethical communities in Roman Catholicism have not reflected on this phenomenon. I say Catholic theological literature purposely, because there was a significant discussion about Alinsky's approach to community organization in Protestant literature in the late 1950s and the 1960s.[4]

Catholic theological, ethical, and pastoral disciplines are

not the only ones which have neglected to reflect on the Alinsky approach to community organization. A recent sociological article is entitled "Saul D. Alinsky: A Neglected Source
but Promising Resource."[5] The authors maintain that the
sociological literature has failed to deal with the organizing
methods of Alinsky, who in the turbulent sixties was one of
the best-known community organizers in the country and
whose approach offers great promise for the future, especially in the light of reduced federal support.

I

The first step is to prove that support of Alinsky-style
community organizations is the most distinctive practical
approach taken to social justice by the Catholic Church in
the United States. At first sight this fact seems to be quite
implausible. Alinsky was an agnostic Jew who in his own
person illustrated the importance he attached to irreverence
as a primary virtue in the organizer. Alinsky, who gloried
in calling himself a radical, often tweaked the nose of all
establishments, including the Roman Catholic Church.
Alinsky was born in Chicago in 1909 and did graduate work
in criminology at The University of Chicago. Later he
worked with prisoners and released prisoners at Joliet State
Prison. He was attracted by the labor union organizers of
the CIO and later even wrote a biography of John L. Lewis.
In the late 1930s he organized the Back of the Yards area in
Chicago which had been the scene of Upton Sinclair's *Jungle*.
This launched his lifelong work in community organization
which was carried out through the Industrial Areas Foundation which he began in 1940. Alinsky and his staff of trained
organizers worked quite frequently in Chicago areas, but
now their work touches all parts of the country. Alinsky
himself died in 1972, but the Industrial Areas Foundation is
continuing his work of training community organizers.[6] As
implausible as it might seem, this man and the organization
he founded, the Industrial Areas Foundation, have had

more impact on grass-roots Catholic work for social justice than any other person or group in the United States in the last few decades.

In May 1969 the American Catholic bishops passed a resolution that led to the creation of the Campaign for Human Development. The Catholic bishops recognized the great work that had been done in the past by the human services provided under church auspices, but something new was needed in the light of the problems of urban America in the late 60s. The whole purpose of the campaign was to make funds available for organized groups of white and minority poor to develop economic strength and political power in their own communities. A collection has been taken up in all Catholic churches in the United States for the campaign which has averaged over 7 million dollars a year since its inception in 1970. In addition to funding community organizations the Campaign for Human Development also has an educational campaign aimed at making Catholics and others more aware of the problems of poverty. The vast majority of the funding goes to self-help projects involving community organizations using conflictual means in an attempt to bring about substantive changes within the social, economic, and political system. The conflictual character of these community organizations indicate that they are based on the Alinsky model of community organization.[7]

For anyone with a slight understanding of Alinsky's history the fact that the Catholic Church would officially support his approach to community organizations is not totally surprising. The Catholic Church has in many ways been a source of strong financial and moral support for Alinsky over the years. Alinsky's first work as an organizer was in bringing together the Back of the Yards Council in Chicago in the late 1930s. Since the neighborhood was heavily Catholic, he had to work with the Catholic pastors and churches. In this work he was helped and supported by Bishop Bernard Sheil, the auxiliary bishop of Chicago.[8] Chicago remained a strong base for Alinsky's work. There are at least four Alinsky-style community organizations in

Chicago — the Northwest Community Organization (NCO), the Southwest Community Congress (SCC), Organization for a Better Austin (OBA), and The Woodlawn Organization (TWO).[9] Much of Alinsky's funding in the Chicago area in the 40s and 50s came from the Catholic Church. The archbishop of Chicago supported Alinsky's projects and even had him on the diocesan payroll for some time.

In the early 40s Alinsky began a rather close and lasting relationship with Monsignor John O'Grady, the secretary of the National Conference of Catholic Charities. O'Grady invited Alinsky to give an address at the 1942 annual meeting of the National Conference of Catholic Charities. The two collaborated on a number of organizing projects. So close was the relationship that Alinsky, who had previously written a biography of John L. Lewis, wanted to write a biography of John O'Grady. A draft was apparently written, but the project was abandoned.[10]

Although the Catholic theological, ethical, and pastoral literature has persistently ignored Alinsky, the Protestant literature in the late 50s and early-to-mid 60s followed his work with great attention. In general, the editors and writers in the *Christian Century* strongly disagreed with Alinsky, whereas *Christianity and Crisis* supported him.[11] One of the most significant aspects discussed in the Protestant debate was the Catholic Church's support for Alinsky. Charles Silberman, in his popular *Crisis in Black and White*, strongly supported Alinsky and his organizational tactics but pointed out that Alinsky was attacked as "a dupe of the Catholic Church, the mastermind of a Catholic conspiracy."[12]

Alinsky's most ardent Protestant opponents, Harold Fey, the editor of the *Christian Century*, and Walter Kloetzli constantly emphasized Catholic support for Alinsky.[13] Stephen Rose writing in *Christianity and Crisis* supported Alinsky, but the first charge he attempted to refute was that the IAF was dominated by Roman Catholic interests.[14] Thus Catholic support for Alinsky was well recognized. However, in the 1960s in Chicago, Rochester, and throughout the country Protestants also gave very significant moral and financial support to Alinsky's organizing approaches.

There can be no doubt that many people might be surprised by the thesis that Alinsky-style people's organizations are the most distinctive approach to social justice involvement by the Catholic Church in the United States in the last few decades. There are a number of reasons contributing to this lack of awareness. Very little attention has been given by Catholic theologians and ethicists to what has occurred on the American Catholic scene in general. The Campaign for Human Development itself is concerned that the struggle for social justice by means of community organizations using conflict approaches might alienate some church members. The continued financial backing for CHD indicates that the average Catholic still supports the program. However, CHD obviously does not want to call undue attention to the conflictual aspects that are by definition a part of its organizing the poor and powerless.[15] Perhaps the greatest reason for the lack of awareness of Catholic Church involvement in supporting Alinsky-style community organizations comes from ignorance. Even professionals in the church are really not aware of what has been happening. Fortunately, in the near future a new book by P. David Finks, which has been painstakingly researched over a good number of years, will help in making people more aware of the contribution Alinsky has made to new approaches to social justice in the Catholic Church in the United States.[16]

II

The next step is to explain very briefly the Alinsky approach to community organization. Saul Alinsky wrote two books about his approach — *Reveille for Radicals*, first published in 1946 and republished in 1969 with a new introduction and afterword, and *Rules for Radicals: A Practical Primer for Realistic Radicals*, published in 1971.[17] Alinsky referred to himself as a radical in his earlier writings, but in the early 1960s his self-description as a realistic radical was used to distinguish himself from the radicals of the new left.

Our author, in response to his own question, defines a radical as a person to whom the common good is the greatest personal value. The radical wants a world in which the worth of the individual is recognized. All human beings should be economically, politically, and socially free. According to Alinsky a political radical is passionately devoted to democracy. Tocqueville is frequently cited in his writings. Democracy, however, is much more than just voting once a year. The whole purpose of community organization is to enable the powerless and the have-nots to participate in determining their lives.[18]

Alinsky's radicalism can better be understood in the light of his strong opposition to three other groups—liberals, social workers, and the new left of the sixties. From the beginning of his organization of local communities our author contrasted his own approach to that of liberals. As in much of his writing and speaking, Alinsky in this discussion often shows his own irreverence, his tendency to polarize issues, and some hyperbole which can only infuriate his opponents. Liberals like people with their heads, but radicals like people with both their heads and their hearts. Liberals are well-balanced, impartial, and objective; whereas radicals are passionate partisans for the poor and the victims of injustice. The issue of power constitutes a fundamental difference between radicals and liberals. Liberals fear power; they often agree with goals but will never use conflict and power tactics to achieve these goals. Radicals use power and conflict and actually precipitate the social crisis by their actions. There are as many clear lines of distinction between radicals and liberals as there are between liberals and conservatives.[19] It is obvious that Alinsky often found himself at odds with liberals, who agreed with him at least in theory about the existence of the problems and the goals to be achieved, but who strongly disagreed with his tactics.

From the very beginning of his organizing work Saul Alinsky differed with social-work theoreticians and practitioners whom he accused of welfare colonialism. Their approach involves handouts and band-aids but brings about no real structural change. The have-nots still remain powerless. Mass community organizations want to change the system so that the people govern themselves. The establishment is always threatened by such an approach because they must ultimately give up and share some of their power. Fundamental, structural, and truly democratic changes are not going to be brought about by committees and councils composed of professionals and by centralized bureaucracies.[20]

After the mid-60s a new group of opponents appeared on the scene—the radicals of the new left. Pragmatic radicals, unlike the new left, begin with the existing system because there is no other place to begin. A true political revolution (a true democracy) will occur only if there is the supporting base of a popular reformation. To build a popular mass organization is tedious and takes time, but there is no real alternative to working within the system. The new left offers only a mess of rhetorical garbage and meaningless slogans. The American system might have its problems and difficulties, but at least there exist some freedom and the possibility to bring about change.[21]

In a democratic society the people are the motor, and the organizations of people are the gears. The power of the people is transmitted to the gears of their own organizations, and democracy thus moves forward. Democracy is truly a warfare and involves conflict between different power groups. Most of the conflict takes place in orderly and conventionally approved legal procedures. But the building and development of a new power group—a people's organization—is a threat to the existing establishment and power structure.[22]

The purpose of a people's organization is to enable the people to participate in governing themselves and thus to make democracy truly work. Alinsky's people's organization is composed of representatives from smaller organizations or institutions in the neighborhood—clubs, churches, etc. Every year there is a convention at which policy is set in a democratic way. The organized community thus is able to obtain power for itself and its members who heretofore were powerless. The radical organizer frequently mentions that a people's organization must be broad enough to include all the issues facing the neighborhood. Single-issue community organizations cannot last. A people's organization must be broad, deep, and all inclusive.[23]

Alinsky is primarily an organizer and trainer of organizers. The organizer gradually withdraws from the organization as it becomes a vital and living reality. The most controversial aspects about Alinsky are the tactics and approaches he recommends for the organizer and the organization. In building up a mass community organization with indigenous leadership our radical appeals to power, conflict, self-interest, ego, and compromise.[24]

The organizer recognizes that the people in a particular neighborhood are powerless; apathy, resignation, hopelessness, resentment, and despair are the characteristics that mark the people. These are the have-nots or the have-too-littles of our society who truly are excluded from the power structure of political, social, and economic life. At best the professionals, the school boards, and the planning commissions service these people in the name of welfare colonialism, but the people are unable to truly participate. There is no structural change occurring.[25]

The organizer is an outsider coming into such a local neighborhood situation and trying to build ultimately a truly participative community based on the real needs of the community and involving indigenous leadership. The organizer must overcome the suspicion that he or she is an outsider. In the very beginning the organizer wants to manipulate and provoke the establishment into attacking the organizer. This tactic makes the local people sympathize with and identify with the organizer against the establishment. In the early stages it is important also to bring about a victory for the have-nots which will show that they can achieve their goals through the power of the organization.[26]

The first step in community organization is community disorganization — the disruption of the present organization of power. The organizer "must first rub raw the resentment of the people of the community; fan the latent hostilities of many of the people to the point of overt expression." The organizer searches out issues and conflicts, stirs up discontent and dissatisfaction, and provides a channel into which people can angrily pour their frustration. The organizer is an agitator.[27]

In selecting issues Alinsky gives succinct advice: "Pick the target, freeze it, personalize it, and polarize it." In reality nothing is 100 percent good or bad, but in organizing one must act as if the issue is 100 percent. Through such tactics the organizer goads the enemy into a response. The response often involves a tactical blunder on the part of the establishment which helps both the organizer and the incipient community organization.[28]

As might be expected, Alinsky spends much time concentrating on explaining tactics. Tactics are nonviolent but conflictual and imaginative. Ridicule, irony, and forcing the enemy to live up to the enemy's reputed value systems are important. The threat is often more significant than the reality itself, especially if the tactic is consonant with the experience of the have-nots but goes outside the experience of the establishment.[29]

One example illustrates some of the rules for tactics given by Alinsky. Alinsky's organizers brought together a black ghetto community in Rochester, New York. Alinsky polarized the target as Eastman Kodak Company and the local power establishment. One suggested tactic was to buy one hundred tickets to the opening performance of the Rochester Symphony Orchestra, a cultural jewel highly prized in the city. The tickets would be given to one hundred ghetto blacks, who would first be entertained at a dinner party lasting three hours, served in the ghetto and consisting solely of baked beans. In the end Alinsky never carried through on the tactic, but the threat alone accomplished much. One can see here the importance of threats, ridicule, polarization, and targeting the opposition. Above all such a tactic illustrates a very important Alinsky rule — a good tactic is one your people enjoy.[30]

Alinsky was in the business of training organizers but was always afraid that people would merely copy some of the tactics that had been used in the past. There are a number of qualities that are essential for a good organizer — curiosity, with the attendant approach of asking questions, a fair and open mind, an organized personality, a blurred vision of a better world, imagination, irreverence, and a sense of humor. The organizer must come to know the local community; understand the basic issues; spot and support the indigenous leaders; use all one's skill to put together an effective organization with broad-based support from all the different groups in the community; and be willing to play a behind-the-scenes role that is ulitmately to be phased out in favor of the organization once it comes into being.[31]

The most significant attribute in the organizer is a deep faith in the people. The whole purpose of community organizations is to enable the people truly to participate in governing themselves. Never forget that democracy is one of the greatest revolutions in human history. The fire, the energy, and the life of democracy is popular pressure. A people's organization is the machinery through which the people can achieve their program. An all-inclusive organization overcomes all artificial barriers, sectarian interests, as well as religious, national, and racial distinctions. The task of building such organizations is dirty, tedious, and heartbreaking, but only through such organizations can the revolution of democracy survive and prosper. It is only in such a truly democratic atmosphere that the values we cherish can flourish.[32]

III

This section will develop a theological and ethical evaluation of the Alinsky approach to community organization. First, a comparison will be made between the South American liberation theology and Alinsky's approach. Second, Alinsky's theory and practice will be judged in the light of the traditional Catholic understanding of political and social ethics.

There are many similarities between Alinsky's community organization approach and liberation theology, but there are also significant differences. An important similarity concerns the basic understanding of sociology and epistemology. Liberation theology rightly reacts against a value-free sociology with its claim of arriving at totally objective truth and its emphasis on quantitative analysis. A value-free approach by its very nature tends to identify with and reinforce the *status quo*. Knowledge is not as objective and independent of human involvement as a classical understanding once thought. The sociology of knowledge reminds us that all knowledge is situated and subject to prejudice. One must approach all existing realities and thought patterns with some ideological suspicion.[33]

Saul Alinsky is not primarily interested in writing for the academic community, but he stresses in his own way a hermeneutic of suspicion and opposes the myth of knowledge as objective and value free. All of life is partisan. There is no dispassionate objectivity.[34] Rationalization is an important human reality with which any organizer must come to grips. Rationalization not only affects the establishment and those who are committed to the *status quo* but also the have-nots in society. The have-nots need rationalization to explain away and justify the fact that they have not tried to do anything to change their situation.[35]

On the basis of its gospel values liberation theology opts for the poor. Such a partisan approach is in keeping with the understanding of sociology and of epistemology mentioned above. The option for the poor has become very central in both the praxis and theory of liberation theology.[36]

This same option for the poor, especially understood in terms of the powerless, characterizes the Alinsky method of community organization. Alinsky definitely sides with the powerless — the have-nots — in their struggle. Objectivity, like the claim that one is nonpartisan or reasonable, is usually a rationalization used to defend the *status quo*.[37] Alinsky also emphasizes the need to work with the middle class. The great danger is that once the have-nots begin to achieve something, they become counterrevolutionary. Our realistic radical frequently points out that organized labor in the United States has lost its reforming zeal and has become self-defensive and protective.[38] His lifelong commitment was to work to empower the powerless.

Liberation theology gives great importance to Paulo Friere's pedagogy of the oppressed. In the process called "conscientization," through an unalienating and liberating cultural action, the oppressed person perceives and modifies one's relationship to the world. The person thus moves from a naive awareness to a critical awareness.[39]

Although Alinsky does not use the word "conscientization," there is no doubt that such a process is the cornerstone of his method. The powerless must have their consciousness raised. The first step in the process is to become aware of their situation of powerlessness. The organizer must break through the people's own rationalizations of accepting their condition so that they can truly confront their own problems. In the beginning it is very important that the people acquire a sense that the can change things if only they come together to use their power. The organizer must astutely arrange a confrontation with the establishment which can easily be won by the people so that their organizing momentum can continue. An early defeat would cripple further development of a people's organization. The people must learn that through their power they can bring about change.[40]

Raising consciousness is a part of Alinsky's overarching commitment to popular education. "In the last analysis the objective for which any democratic movement must stand is the ultimate objective implicit within democracy — popular education." Our agnostic radical is a romantic Jeffersonian in his praise for popular education. All the teachers, libraries, and buildings will not help if the people do not have a desire for eduction. A people's organization is constantly searching for approaches to create an ethos receptive to learning and education. Alinsky the optimist puts his faith in people and education.[41]

Liberation theology accepts a conflictual model of social analysis and praxis. The option for the poor means that the true Christian is partisan in the struggle against systematic oppression and injustice. So too Alinsky uses a conflictual approach and emphasizes the conflictual nature of the tactics to be employed by a successful people's organization. The use of conflict and conflictual tactics distinguishes the radical from the liberal. Very often in his writings Alinsky describes the strategy of a people's organization in terms of warfare and uses metaphors derived from war. However, this constant conflict will be nonviolent and usually occur within the parameters of the law.[42]

The whole purpose of a people's organization is to bring about change through the use of power. Those in the establishment who have power will naturally resist very strongly any attempt to change the power structure. The very first step in community organization is community disorganization. The organizer is immediately confronted with the need to stir up dissatisfaction and discontent — to first rub raw the resentment of the people of the community.[43]

In describing rules for tactics our organizer constantly refers to "the other" as the enemy. The first rule, for example, states: "Power is not only what you have but what the enemy thinks you have." Perhaps the most famous and distinctive rule is the thirteenth: "Pick the target, freeze it, personalize it, and polarize it." The author of this rule recognizes that in reality no issue is 100 percent good or bad! Conflict requires such an all-or-nothing attitude. In all the theorizing about tactics never forget that the real action is the enemy's reaction. Provoking the enemy into a costly mistake will ultimately play into your own hand.[44] There can be no doubt that power and conflict are fundamental aspects of Alinsky's practice.

Although there are strong similarities between South American liberation theology and the community organization approach used by Saul D. Alinsky in the United States, there are also significant differences. Some liberation theologians adopt a Marxist sociological analysis to understand what is happening in society. One must be careful to note here the different levels of expression of Marxism. Liberation theologians do not accept all the theological and philosophical aspects of Marxism, but many, like Juan Luis Segundo, do use a Marxist analysis and make an option for a type of socialism.[45] Alinsky, on the other hand, defines his radicalism in terms of its commitment to true democracy.

In describing the ideal organizer Alinsky really describes himself as having "one all consuming conviction, one belief, one article of faith — a belief in people." If people have the power and the opportunity to act, in the long run and most of the time they will make the right decision. There are no other alternatives to democracy because all the other alternatives entail rule by one elite or another over other human beings.[46] The people have not only been the strength of the democratic ideal but also its weakness. Alinsky is greatly concerned about the vast masses of our people who because of lack of interest or of opportunity do not truly participate in their life as citizens. Alinsky eloquently maintains that there can be no darker or more devastating tragedy than the death of a human being's faith in oneself and in one's power to chart one's own future. Citizens who cannot or do not participate in their role of being the government sink further into apathy, anonymity, and depersonalization.[47]

The realistic radical's later writings are very clear and vocal in their denunciation of the ideology of the new-left radicals. There is no alternative to working within the system to change it. Alinsky employs all his ridicule and sarcasm against the rhetorical garbage of the new left. One must start with the system and the people, for there is no other place to start except political lunacy. Since democracy must be from the bottom up, Alinsky not only opposes totaltitarianism but also rejects any planning from the top down.[48]

An organizer operating in an open society is a political relativist who realizes that everything is relative. The organizer's most frequent question is "Why?" The primary virtue is irreverence, which never ceases to ask questions and poke fun at all those realities that are absolutized by people. Insistence on constant questioning goes against any fixed ideology. However, Alinsky himself recognizes that he has his own absolutes or his own basic commitment even if he does not want to call it an ideology. The radical has ultimate faith in the people and is committed to true democracy, which is literally and truly of, by, and for all the people. Alinsky, however, recognizes that democracy itself is only a means and not an end. It is the best means of achieving the values proposed by the Judeo-Christian and the democratic political traditions — equality, justice, freedom, peace, and the preciousness of human life with its basic rights.[49]

Alinsky's commitment to these basic values and to true democracy as the means to achieve them colors and influences many other aspects of his thought and differentiates some of these aspects from the approach taken by liberation theology. At times there can be in some liberation theologies a danger of emphasizing just one issue or aspect to the detriment of others. No one can doubt that race or sex or economic structures are the most important aspects for certain people, but there is a danger of so absolutizing one aspect that other aspects of oppression or issues are not given sufficient importance.

In both his books our pragmatic radical insists that single-issue community organizations are doomed to failure. There are both practical and theoretical reasons against a single- or limited-issue(s) organization. Practically, such an approach limits one to a small organization, and recent history shows that such organizations will not last. Problems such as crime, health, unemployment, and poverty cannot be isolated because they have the same basic cause. The underlying cause of all these problems must be overcome. In addition, individuals within the community have a number of different loyalties to diverse organizations and causes — churches, athletic groups, nationality associations, benevolent societies, recreational groups, fraternal lodges, political parties, business and labor organizations. The multiple interests of the individual must be recognized in any successful community organization. But more important than all these reasons is the fact that a democratic community organization must deal with all the concerns of a broad-based membership.[50]

The commitment to democracy and the values it protects also nuances Alinsky's approach to power. On the one hand, Alinsky constantly insists on the importance of power. It is impossible to conceive of a world without power. Life without power is death; a world without power would be a ghostly wasteland.[51] However, the radical organizer had to come to grips with the abuse of power even in his own organizations. The Back of the Yards community organization which he began in the late 1930s had become segregationist in the 50s.[52] So from personal experience with his own community organizations and from observing other institutions and organizations Alinsky knew the abuses of power.

Power must always be limited and controlled. The guiding star for the organizer is the dignity of the individual. Any program or organization that opposes people because of religion, race, creed, or economic status must be opposed. People must come to learn and appreciate the basic values of democracy. Without such a learning process the building of an organization becomes merely the substitution of one power group for another.[53] Power is not an absolute but is in the service of the other values and must be controlled by them.

The realistic North American radical shares with South American liberation theology an emphasis on conflict. Both have been accused of positions incompatible with Christianity with its stress on love and reconciliation. At the minimum Christians would generally have to agree that conflict cannot be an absolute or an ultimate. Catholic moral theology in its traditional approach to just war and strikes has always recognized that conflict can be an acceptable and legitimate tactic for Christians even though the Christian is committed ultimately to love and reconciliation.

Alinsky's dedication to democracy is what justifies the role of conflict but also at the same time limits conflict to a tactic and prevents its ever becoming an ultimate. Democracy by its very nature is going to involve the struggle among different groups and interests in society. The radical organizer refers to democracy as a warfare. We should not criticize lobbies and pressure groups but rather build our own pressure groups. There is no true democracy without conflict. There can be no doubt that the irreverent Alinsky takes personal glee in stressing the conflictual approaches used by a community organization.[54] However, the very nature of democracy keeps conflict from being absolutized and limits it to the role of a tactic. Alinsky recognizes that conflictual tactics will be more prominent in building up the people's organization. However, even in the beginning of a community organization there are limits on conflict. Recall that Alinsky recognizes that most issues are not 100 percent good or bad. Since a community organization must always be broad-based, multi-issued, and truly democratic, there must be room for compromise within the organization. Later on and in dealing with the broader society there will even be more need for compromise.

Saul Alinsky's fundamental commitment to democracy grounds the need for compromise. In dialogue with the new left in the 1960s our author gives even more attention to compromise. Compromise is now linked with power, self-interest, and conflict as the central concepts in our author's approach even though these words and the realities behind them are often looked upon as evil and wrong by many in society. To some, compromise has connotations of weakness, vacillation, and betrayal of ideals and principles. But to the organizer compromise is a key and beautiful word. A democratic society is truly an ongoing conflict interrupted periodically by compromises. A society devoid of compromise is totalitarian. In the light of this dialectic and rhythm of conflict and compromise the organizer must be a well-integrated political schizoid. On the one hand, the organizer polarizes the issue 100 percent to zero and leads the forces into conflict, all the while knowing that when the time comes for negotiations, there is probably only a 10 percent difference with the opposition.[55]

There is a second very profound difference between the Alinsky approach and that of liberation theology. Alinsky does not base his theory on explicitly religious warrants even though he occasionally mentions them. Liberation theologies have emerged in a South American context which is predominantly Christian and Catholic and in which the Catholic Church is the only force in society large enough to challenge the political and economic structures. The United States is a pluralistic society in religion and in many other ways. An effective organization attempting to embrace all cannot have a narrow or sectarian grounding. Catholic acceptance of Alinsky-style community organization involves a commitment to working with all others in the society for the common good. The theory and practice of such an approach must be ecumenical in the broadest sense of the term.

Traditional Catholic social teaching provides another perspective from which one can analyze and evaluate Alinsky's approach. Catholic theory has always seen the state and the political order as based on human nature itself. Human beings are called by their very nature to come together in political society so that they can achieve through their common political efforts what they cannot achieve as individuals for themselves. The goal of society is the common good which flows back on all the individuals who are part of the social whole. The limited end of the common good grounds social ethics and distinguishes social from individual ethics. Intimately connected with this understanding is the recognition that human beings are called to their own fulfillment. The Catholic tradition has never looked upon love of self as something bad or opposed to love of God and of neighbor. The Catholic theological tradition has tried to harmonize and bring into a unity the proper love of God, neighbor, and self.

By appealing both to the common good and to self-interest Saul Alinsky shows himself to be in line with the traditional Catholic understanding even though he does not develop his theory in any depth. The radical "is that person to whom the common good is the greatest personal value." The challenge for our society is to build people's organizations which are all-inclusive of both the people and their many organizations and institutions. The organizer aims to unite all the different people with their different organizations through a common interest that far transcends individual differences.[56] The common good can call for sacrifices on the part of some individuals in order to guarantee ultimately their own freedom and the freedom of all.[57]

The strong appeal to self-interest is constantly stressed but with the recognition that true self-interest must be seen in terms of the common good. Recall that *Rules for Radicals* devotes one chapter to the words prevalent in the language of politics, such as power, self-interest, compromise, and conflict. Many people reject the morality of self-interest by making it synonymous with self-centeredness and opposed to altruism and love. Alinsky firmly believes that self-interest is a very important factor in political life, but it is also a morally good factor. In no way should one condemn acting out of self-interest in the political order, but at the same time there is no incompatibility among morality, the common good, and self-interest properly understood. For this reason Machiavelli's understanding of self-interest as divorced from morality cannot be accepted.[58]

In his typical irreverent and hyperbolic way our author refers to his approach as the low road to morality — but there is no other way. It is not our better nature but our self-interest that demands that we be our brothers' and sisters' keeper. In our world no one can have a loaf of bread when one's neighbor does not. Alinsky the pragmatist maintains that the more practical life is the moral life and that the moral life is the only road to survival.[59]

Even though our pragmatic radical was an agnostic Jew,

he had some understanding of both Catholic and Protestant theology. In addition, at least into the mid-60s, he had been most often supported by the Catholics and attacked by some Protestants. There can be no doubt that he saw his approach as being in conformity with Catholic self-understanding and opposed to some Protestant positions. "The myth of altruism as a motivating factor in our behavior could arise and survive only in a society bundled in the sterile gauze of New England puritanism and Protestant morality and tied together with the ribbons of Madison Avenue public relations. It is one of the classic American fairy tales."[60]

The difference between some Protestant approaches to social ethics and one based on a theory of the common good with its acceptance of self-fulfillment and self-interest properly understood was briefly noted by Alinsky. Writing about the same time, John Courtney Murray from his perspective as a Catholic theologian developed the same point at great length. Murray describes Protestant ethical thought as vacillating between an idealistic approach (the Social Gospel, although he does not use the name) and a realistic or ambiguous approach which admits complexity (Christian Realism, but again he does not use the name). Both of these approaches assume a need to overcome any differences between individual and social morality, reject the pursuit of self-interest in social ethics, and have difficulty seeing power as anything but evil. On the basis of the natural-law tradition Murray sharply disagrees with the way in which both forms of Protestant ethics handle these three issues which he calls pseudoproblems. Civil society and the state are natural societies with limited functions and are not coextensive with the ends of the human person as such. With this limited understanding of the nature of the state one should not attempt to see its morality as univocally the morality of personal life. Self-interest is a very legitimate concern of the state, but in foreign affairs the national interest must always be seen in terms of the needs of the universal world community. There is no dichotomy because national unity is achieved only interior to and as a part of the growing international order. Murray also maintains that there is no politics without power to promote it. All politics is power politics — up to a point. Thus Murray substantiates in the light of the Catholic tradition the point that Alinsky was making against the approach of some Protestants. Political action based on self-interest properly understood is morally good, and politics and power cannot be separated.[61]

Catholic social ethics has always tried to hold on to both the dignity of the individual and to the social nature of the person. The Catholic position historically tried to find a middle ground or a third way between the extremes of individualistic capitalism and totalitarian socialism. Capitalism so stresses the individual that it forgets the social nature of all human beings and denies that to live in political society is natural for all human beings. Socialism so stresses the society that it downplays the natural rights and dignity of the individual person. In Catholic thought the principle of subsidiarity mediates this tension between the individual and the social aspects of human existence. In the political order the smaller groupings should be allowed to do all they can, while the state should step in only when this is necessary to do what smaller groups and organizations cannot accomplish.

There can be no doubt that Alinsky's thinking is totally in accord with that of the Catholic tradition on these points. Our pragmatic radical is deeply committed to the basic rights of individuals but recognizes the significant role of the state in working for the common good. The term "the principle of subsidiarity" does not appear in *Reveille* or in *Rules*, but the reality is ever present. The basic need is for all to participate in self-rule. Today our country and our cities lack citizen participation on the local level. Self-government will perish unless individual citizens are regularly involved. Democracy must be built from the bottom up and not from the top down. In spelling out what a radical stands for, *Reveille* clearly describes significant applications of the principle of subsidiarity. Human rights are more important than property rights. Free universal public education should be available to all. The radical opposes federal control of education in favor of local control, but national governmental authority must be able to eradicate abuses that can occur on the local level. In general the radical fights to defend local rights against usurpations by the centralized federal bureaucracy, but recognition of the use of local or states' rights by Tory reactionaries makes the radical constantly shift now from one side to the other in the controversy over local versus federal power.[62]

In developing his theory Alinsky incessantly underscores the importance of the freedom, equality, and participation of all citizens. The Catholic tradition historically did not emphasize these aspects, but lately special attention has been paid to them. In *Octogesima Adveniens* in 1971 Pope Paul VI describes two aspirations that have come to characterize human beings in our contemporary situation — the aspiration to equality and the aspiration to participation, two forms of human dignity and freedom.[63] Thus the papal tradition has come to accept and articulate human dignity in a way which was defended earlier by Saul David Alinsky.

Intrinsic evidence thus shows that Alinsky's basic theory is in accord with the Catholic understanding of the political order. In addition, what might be called external evidence also supports this basic compatibility. I refer here above all to the relationship between Alinsky and Jacques Maritain, the most famous Catholic philosopher in the Thomistic tradition in the twentieth century. Available sources occasionally refer to this relationship. The first blurb on the back cover of the Vintage book edition of *Reveille* comes from Jacques Maritain: "I consider him [Alinsky] to be one of the few really great men of our century." Stephen Rose, a Protestant who was generally supportive of Alinsky, refers to this friendship between Maritain and Alinsky and relates how, through Maritain, Alinsky spent a week talking with Archbishop Montini of Milan about the social problems of the archdiocese before Montini became Pope Paul VI.[64] P. David Finks' study documents in great detail the friendship and personal involvement between the two. Obviously this friendship also included the sharing of a basic vision about the political life.

Maritain's 1951 book *Man and the State* twice quotes *Reveille for Radicals*.[65] Even more significant is the fact that Maritain's approach to the question is very similar to Alinsky's and gives theoretical support for what Alinsky tried to do in his people's organizations without, however, explicitly saying so. One might even go further and suggest that perhaps Alinsky had even influenced Maritain's understanding and approach.

The themes stressed by Alinsky are also emphasized throughout Maritain's book—democracy is the best form of government; education and trust in people are necessary to make democracy truly work; democracy must be built from the bottom up. In describing morality and means in political life the French Thomist insists on the need to avoid the extremes of hypermoralism and Machiavellianism. There is a political ethics, but political ethics is not the same as individual ethics. Political ethics is concerned with a limited end in a given order—the terrestrial common good. This end is more limited and restricted than the end governing individual morality. The order of means must correspond to the order of ends. Given the end of politics as the terrestrial common good, then realities such as power, force, self-assertion, some distrust and suspicion, the recognition of the principle of the lesser evil, and other realities are ethically grounded.[66]

Maritain recognizes that for a democracy to exist it is necessary for the people to control and participate in the state. The first means for such control by the people is through the right to vote. In the second place the people also use the means of communication to express public opinion and thereby influence the state. The third means involves pressure groups that agitate and act upon the government and the state. The Catholic philosopher refers to these groups and their means as the "flesh and bone means of political warfare."[67] Immediately after this statement Maritain cites Alinsky and takes from him a long quote by Tocqueville. Later on *Man and the State* devotes a section to "prophetic shock minorities" which are absolutely necessary for democracy to truly function.[68] There can be no doubt that Alinsky's people's organizations fit under what Maritain calls the third way by which the people can control government and also fit under the category of prophetic shock minorities. One can only speculate if Maritian would have written about these things if there had been no personal and intellectual relationship with Alinsky.

Without a doubt the most questioned aspect of Alinsky's theory and practice has been the area of means. However, Maritain cites Alinsky precisely in his chapter on means and thereby seems to give implicit approval, at least in general, to Alinsky's approach in this area. On the very second page of the long chapter "Of Means and Ends" in *Rules* Alinsky himself quotes Maritain as saying: "The fear of soiling ourselves by entering the context of history is not virtue but a way of escaping virtue."[69] Alinsky gives no exact citation to Maritain's quote, but it comes from the chapter in *Man and the State* on "The Problem of Means."[70]

I for one would not agree with all that Alinsky writes in his chapter on means and ends in *Rules*, but the disagreements are few. Again one must remember that Alinsky is not writing primarily for ethicists or philosophers; in fact, he chides the intellectual who sits back and condemns the means used by pragmatic radicals who are getting their hands dirty. However, Alinsky does recognize that there are limits in the means to be employed. Means are related to values, and the realistic radical insists on a commitment to the complex of high values that a democracy serves. Even in discussing warfare Alinsky recognizes some, but in my judgment not enough, limits — in war the end justifies almost any means."[71] Thus I would nuance some of Alinsky's seemingly absolute utilitarian statements on means and ends and also disagree with a few of his examples, especially on limits of war. However, in general, and following in the footsteps of the best-known Catholic Thomistic scholar in this century, I find myself in basic agreement with Alinsky's practice and theory about people's organizations and the means they use.

IV

Many other questions can be asked about Alinsky-type community organizations. Studies have pointed up some problems and weaknesses in his approach.[72] The approach has been most successful in middle-class neighborhoods. Alinsky talks about the need for coalitions with other organizations and groups on a broader level, but how effective have they been in practice? Other questions include the practical one of making sure that both conflict and compromise are able to coexist in such democratic organizations. Once the community organization is built and conflictual tactics are less prominent, how can one insure that the continued participation in the democratic process does not wane? The ongoing life of any community or organization is never as dramatic or as interesting as its beginning.

I think there is also a danger in exaggerating what such community organizations can do. They are themselves only a means to a further end which is a truly participative democratic society. Even the democratic ideal itself is only a means to deal with content problems and issues facing society. There are substantive issues involving such important topics as equitable distribution of goods, taxation, health care, education, rights of the poor, military defense, etc. that must be addressed. Not all people in even the most true democracy are going to agree on all these issues. There are also questions of political and economic structures that must be resolved more equitably. Community organizations are limited in what they can do. Substantive and structural questions cannot be ignored. However, Alinsky-style people's organizations are one very important way of trying to make our present system truly more democratic.

The purpose of this study has been twofold. First, this essay has called attention to the fact that Alinsky-style community organizations have been the most distinctive contribution to Catholic social action in the United States in the last few decades. Second, such an approach commends itself to Catholic theology and ethics. Hopefully in the future more discussion will take place on this very important but neglected development in American Catholic social practice.

NOTES

1. Gustavo Gutierrez, *A Theology of Liberation* (Maryknoll, NY: Orbis Books, 1973), pp. 6ff.
2. See, for example, Sergio Torres and John Eagleson, eds., *Theology in the Americas* (Maryknoll, NY: Orbis Books, 1976); Brian Mahan and L. Dale Richesin, eds, *The Challenge of Liberation Theology: A First World Response* (Maryknoll, NY: Orbis Books, 1981).
3. See Charles A. Meconis, *With Clumsy Grace: The American Catholic Left, 1961-1975* (New York: Seabury Press, 1979).
4. For a Protestant view which claims to be "objective" and which reviews much of the Protestant debate about Alinsky, see Lyle E. Schaller, *Community Organization: Conflict and Reconciliation* (New York: Abingdon Press, 1966). For essays on both sides of the debate in American Protestantism see John R. Fry, ed., *The Church and Community Organization* (New York: National Council of Churches, 1965).
5. Donald G. Reitzes and Dietrich C. Reitzes, "Saul D. Alinsky: A Neglected Source But Promising Resource," *The American Sociologist* 17 (February 1982): 47-56.
6. At the present time there is no biography of Alinsky. The data mentioned here can be found throughout his own writings and in the other bibliography mentioned in the notes. Fortunately, Paulist Press will soon publish a very significant biography and study of Alinsky by P. David Finks. I am personally most grateful to Finks for first making me aware of Alinsky's work and for keeping me abreast of his own research on Alinsky.
7. Bernard F. Evans, "Campaign for Human Development: Church Involvement in Social Change," *Review of Religious Research* 20 (1979): 266, 267.
8. Alinsky frequently refers to his work with the Back of the Yards Council in his two books: Saul D. Alinsky, *Reveille for Radicals* (Chicago: University of Chicago Press, 1946); Saul D. Alinsky, *Rules for Radicals: A Practical Primer for Realistic Radicals* (New York: Vintage Books, 1972). References in this chapter to

Reveille will use the Vintage Book edition of 1969 which includes a new "Introduction" and a new "Afterword."

9. For a favorable study of Alinsky's work in Chicago with special emphasis on the Organization for a Better Austin, see Robert Bailey, Jr., *Radicals in Urban Politics: The Alinsky Approach* (Chicago: University of Chicago Press, 1974). For a popularly written and very sympathetic account of Alinsky's work with The Woodlawn Organization, see Charles E. Silberman, *Crisis in Black and White* (New York: Vintage Books, 1964).

10. Thomas W. Tift, "Toward a More Humane Social Policy: The Work and Influence of Monsignor John O'Grady" (Ph.D. diss., The Catholic University of America, 1980), pp. 6, 32, 667, 675.

11. For a summary of this debate see Schaller.

12. Silberman, *Crisis in Black and White*, p. 322.

13. Harold Fey, "Editorials," *The Christian Century* 78 (1961): 579, 580; 79 (1962): 879, 880; 81 (1964): 195-197; 82 (1965): 827, 828; Walter Kloetzli, *The Church and the Urban Challenge* (Philadelphia: Fortress Press, 1961).

14. Stephen C. Rose, "Saul Alinsky and His Critics," *Christianity and Crisis* 24 (July 20, 1964): 143-152.

15. Evans, "Campaign for Human Development," pp. 277, 278.

16. See note 6.

17. See note 8.

18. *Reveille*, pp. 15ff.

19. *Reveille*, pp. 18-23.

20. *Reveille*, pp. 64-69, 174-180.

21. *Rules*, pp. xvi-xxii; *Reveille*, "Afterword to the Vintage Edition," pp. 223-235.

22. *Reveille*, pp. 46-48, 132ff.

23. *Reveille*, pp. 53-63.

24. *Rules*, pp. 48-80.

25. *Reveille*, pp. 38-50, 225ff.

26. *Rules*, pp. 98-104.

27. *Rules*, pp. 116, 117.

28. *Rules*, pp. 130ff.

29. *Reveille*, pp. 89-154; *Rules*, pp. 126-164.

30. *Rules*, pp. 136-140.

31. *Rules*, pp. 63-80.

32. *Reveille*, pp. 190-204.

33. Juan Luis Segundo, *The Liberation of Theology* (Maryknoll, NY: Orbis Books, 1976), pp. 7-68.

34. *Rules*, p. 10.

35. *Rules*, p. 116.

36. Matthew L. Lamb, *Solidarity with Victims: Toward a Theology of Social Transformation* (New York: Crossroad, 1982).

37. *Reveille*, p. ix.

38. *Rules*, pp. 194-196; *Reveille*, p. 200, 234-235.

39. Paulo Freire, *Pedagogy of the Oppressed* (New York: Herder and Herder, 1970); Gutierrez, *A Theology of Liberation*, pp. 91-92, 113-117, 269-270.

40. *Rules*, pp. 109-115.

41. *Reveille*, pp. 155-173. The citation is the very first sentence in his chapter "Popular Education."

42. *Reveille*, pp. 132-135.

43. *Rules*, pp. 115-119.

44. *Rules*, pp. 126-138.

45. Alfred T. Hennelly, *Theologies in Conflict: The Challenge of Juan Luis Segundo* (Maryknoll, NY: Orbis Books, 1979), pp. 157-175.

46. *Reveille*, p. xiv.

47. *Rules*, pp. xxv, xxvi.

48. *Rules*, pp. xx, xxi.

49. *Rules*, pp. 10-12; *Reveille*, pp. 1-23.

50. *Reveille*, pp. 56-63; *Rules*, pp. 76-78.

51. E.g., *Rules*, pp. 49-53.

52. *Reveille*, pp. xi-xiii.

53. *Rules*, pp. 122, 123.

54. *Reveille*, pp. 190-204.

55. *Rules*, pp. 48-62, 78, 79; *Reveille*, p. 225.

56. *Reveille*, pp. 15, 205.

57. *Rules*, p. xxv.

58. *Rules*, pp. 53-59.

59. *Rules*, p. 23.

60. *Rules*, p. 53.

61. John Courtney Murray, *We Hold These Truths: Catholic Reflections on the American Proposition* (New York: Sheed and Ward, 1960), pp. 275-294.

62. *Reveille*, pp. xxv, xxvi, 16, 17; *Rules*, pp. xxii-xxvi.

63. Pope Paul VI, *Octogesima Adveniens*, par. 22, found in *Renewing the Earth: Catholic Documents on Peace, Justice, and Liberation,*

ed. David J. O'Brien and Thomas A. Shannon (Garden City, NY: Doubleday Image Books, 1977), p. 364.

64. Rose, *Christianity and Crisis* 24 (July 20, 1964): 143-152.

65. Jacques Maritain, *Man and the State* (Chicago: University of Chicago Press, 1951), pp. 66, 68. References here will be to the Phoenix edition of 1956 of the University of Chicago Press.

66. Ibid., pp. 62, 63.

67. Ibid., p. 66.

68. Ibid., pp. 139-146.

69. *Rules*, pp. 26, 27.

70. Maritain, *Man and the State*, p. 63.

71. *Rules*, p. 29.

72. For a summary of some questions and evaluations see Reitzes and Reitzes, "Saul D. Alinsky," pp. 52-55.

PART FOUR

Pastoral Practice

8: Theory and Practice;
Faith and Reason:
A Case Study of John R. Cavanagh

Christian existence in general has always insisted on the need for congruity between belief and life. Our Christian existence must live out and put into practice the faith in which we believe. Contemporary theology with its emphasis on praxis and orthopraxis puts even greater emphasis on the need for congruence between faith and daily life. Roman Catholic theology in particular has insisted on the basic compatibility between faith and reason. Chapter four has already discussed this relationship and indicated some of the historical tensions that have existed as the church has tried, sometimes not too successfully, to live out its commitment to both faith and reason.

In addition, Roman Catholic moral theology has always seen an intimate relationship between moral theology and pastoral practice. The manuals of moral theology which came into existence after the Council of Trent were an adaptation to the pastoral needs of the times to train confessors for the sacrament of penance, but unfortunately such a narrow focus had a deleterious effect on the discipline of moral theology as a whole. Throughout history there can be no doubt that pastoral practice has had a great effect on moral theology. As an example, St. Alphonsus Liguori (+1787), a doctor of the church and the declared patron of moral theologians, admitted that his own pastoral experience changed his theology. He was trained as a probabiliorist but in the light of his work in pastoral missions he espoused what he called the more benign position of moderate probabilism.[1]

Catholic moral theology will always experience the ten-

sions of trying to live out its commitment to the basic com-
patibilities between belief and life, faith and reason, and
theory and practice. This chapter will deal with these
various tensions not primarily in a systematic way but
through a case study of the contributions of John R.
Cavanagh. John R. Cavanagh, who died in 1981 at age 76,
was not a moral theologian as such but rather a practicing
psychiatrist who was quite familiar with Catholic moral
theology and tried to show in theory and in practice that
there were no incompatibilities between psychiatry and
Catholic faith, between human experience and moral theology.

Cavanagh's life activities centered on his role as a practicing psychiatrist, a university lecturer for over thirty years,
and an author of many publications.[2] He was an early president of the Guild of Catholic Psychiatrists, the editor of the
Bulletin of the Guild of Catholic Psychiatrists for over twelve
years, and without a doubt the heart and soul of that particular organization. Any impartial judgment recognizes
that the *Bulletin* achieved its greatest success under his
editorship. He was president of the National Federation of
Catholic Physicians' Guilds and a frequent contributor to
and guest editor of the journal of this federation — *The Linacre
Quarterly*. He served on national Catholic committees dealing
with family life, health affairs, and medical morality. The
pope appointed him to the Papal Commission on Population
and Birth Control which studied the question of artificial
contraception in the middle 1960s. He was awarded three
different papal honors (Benemerenti Medal, Knight of St.
Gregory the Great, and Knight Commander of St. Gregory
the Great), but he also signed a statement of dissent from the
condemnation of artificial contraception in the encyclical
Humanae Vitae.

Cavanagh might best be described as a bridge builder —
and the bridges he tried to construct were many. First, he
tried to span the gap between theory and practice. He was
a practicing psychiatrist with his patients and his daily
rounds in hospitals, but he also was a widely published
author with six books and over one hundred articles. Dr.

Cavanagh as a committed believer and a dedicated physician and psychiatrist spent his whole life showing that faith and medicine, especially psychiatry, are not enemies but can and should be brought together in harmonious collaboration. The corollary of this relationship led him to point out and live out the basic congruence between moral theology and the techniques and principles of psychiatry and medicine. For him pastoral counseling was the bridge the pastor used in dealing with the daily problems of people. Perhaps all of these attempts by Cavanagh to bring together aspects that are so often kept apart can best be understood in the light of his lifelong dedication to the task of showing there is no incompatibility between faith and reason.

His many published articles and books show Cavanagh the bridge builder at work. An article, "Mental Nervous Disorders," published in *The Ecclesiastical Review* in 1943 indicates what would be the general direction of much of his future work. One can only conjecture that this two-part article was based on the lectures he gave on pastoral medicine and counseling to the seminarians in the School of Theology at The Catholic University of America. The article aims at helping the priest distinguish between the psychotic and neurotic. The psychotic definitely needs the help of the psychiatrist, but the priest can be of assistance to the neurotic. The priest must keep in mind that the moral responsibility of neurotics is diminished in about a direct ratio to the severity of their symptoms. The various types of psychoses and neuroses are discussed in this article in the light of the above context.[3]

In analyzing Cavanagh's writings there is a logical division between what I will call his basic trilogy and his publications on specific issues. The first major section of this chapter will discuss the basic trilogy: *Fundamental Psychiatry* (1953), *Fundamental Marriage Counseling* (1958), and *Fundamental Pastoral Counseling* (1962). These works explain our author's approach to the three important realities mentioned in the titles. No attempt will be made to examine all the issues and problems he discussed in his writings. The second section of our evaluation will focus on the three issues of death and dying, responsible parenthood, and homosexuality which, in my judgment, are the most significant questions addressed and/or the ones given the most extensive treatment.

I. Cavanagh's Trilogy

Fundamental Psychiatry

In 1953 Cavanagh and James D. McGoldrick, S.J., professor and head of the Department of Psychology at Seattle University, published *Fundamental Psychiatry*. This 582-page text tried to present the psychiatric science within the framework of a material-spiritual philosophy.[4]

Throughout his life Cavanagh insisted on the basic compatibility between religion in general, and his Catholic faith in particular, and psychiatry. When he first entered the field of psychiatry, there was a widespread feeling that irreconcilable differences existed between the Catholic faith and psychiatric principles and techniques. Cavanagh later recalled that the dean of the Georgetown University Medical School counseled Catholics not to go into psychiatry because to do so might result in the loss of their souls.[5] In 1950 he responded to an article in *Sign* magazine, a popular Catholic monthly, which accused the Group for the Advancement of Psychiatry of being the shock troops of Sigmund Freud, atheists, and anti-Christian in their ordered attack upon the human mind and soul. Cavanagh then developed his basic assertion, "There is no conflict between psychiatry and religion. A competent psychiatrist can be a good Catholic without conflict (at least on that score)."[6]

Our author saw the relationship between psychiatry and religion (specifically Catholicism) not only in the more abstract terms of these two realities but also in the personal terms of the collaboration between psychotherapists and clergy. This collaboration requires some mutual understanding. The psychiatrist not only should be trained in the best of the profession but should also be well versed in one's own religion. On the other hand, in addition to theological knowledge the clergy should have some knowledge of psychodynamic principles.[7]

The first book, *Fundamental Psychiatry*, is primarily addressed to psychiatrists and students to show that the science of psychiatry can and should be understood in the context of a Catholic and scholastic philosophical view of the human person. Unfortunately, some people propose a science of psychiatry without recognizing the existence of the "psyche" — the soul. Many texts in psychiatry do not propose an adequate view of human nature, and too often a purely materialistic view of humanity is expounded. The two authors present a brief and somewhat stereotypical Catholic refutation of materialism which denies the existence of God, the soul, the mind, the will, natural law, immutable morality, and the social nature of human beings.[8] *Fundamental Psychiatry* adopts an Aristotelian-Thomistic anthropology, which avoids the two opposite dangers of materialism on the one hand and a Neoplatonic scorning of matter on the other hand. The Scholastic vision brings together matter and spirit into one complete, bewildering, complex, dynamic reality which we know as the human person. In this light a Catholic can accept aspects of Freud's technique without approving his materialistic and deterministic philosophy.[9]

On the basis of this philosophical and theological vision the book gives an introduction to psychiatry, considers the etiology of psychiatric disorders, outlines a clinical approach to psychiatry, discusses psychoneuroses and psychoses, and concludes with a section on the borderlands of psychiatry. A final chapter summarizes the religious and philosophical views of God, humanity, and the world which should govern the work of psychiatry.

The book itself stands as a unique and pioneering contribution — apparently the first attempt to give an organized presentation of psychiatry based on a full and adequate picture of human nature as understood in the

Catholic, Scholastic tradition.[10] However, from the perspective of the relationship between religion or theology and psychiatry there are aspects that can and should be criticized. Especially from a contemporary theological viewpoint one can disagree with the book's use of conformity to God's will as the best way of understanding the moral and spiritual life of Christians. Also, many theologians, even at the time when the book was written, could not accept the statement that God always wills the crosses that come into our lives. God permits but does not directly will evil. However, even apart from a somewhat inadequate theology, the relationship between the spiritual and the mental life is treated much too quickly and one-sidedly. In the last chapter the authors maintain that conformity to God's will removes the basis for psychic depression, excludes fear, anxiety, and inferiority problems, and begets true wisdom, peace, and calm.[11]

Elsewhere, writing at about the same time, Cavanagh himself presents a much more differentiated picture of the relationship between the spiritual and the psychic or mental. Spiritual and mental health are not identical; the soul in the state of sin is not necessarily mentally ill. The confessor deals with objective guilt, whereas the psychiatrist is concerned with neurotic guilt. Real guilt arises from objective deeds; neurotic guilt is based on unconscious conflicts. The treatment given by the psychiatrist does not of itself restore the soul to spiritual well-being.[12] These differences lead one to suspect that perhaps McGoldrick and not Cavanagh was the principal author of the final chapter on psychiatry, philosophy, and religion. In addition, it would seem natural for Cavanagh to defer to McGoldrick on this matter because of the Jesuit's training in philosophy and theology. *Fundamental Psychiatry* could have profited from more nuanced understandings of the relationship between spiritual and mental health and from an in-depth exploration of this topic.

A revised edition of *Fundamental Psychiatry* in 1966 attested to the popularity and importance of the book. The authors note the many changes which have occurred since the volume was originally pubished in 1953. The relationship between religion and psychiatry has shifted from open hostility to peaceful coexistence and even active cooperation. Both the American Medical Association and the American Psychiatric Association have sections discussing religion and medicine, while the Guild of Catholic psychiatrists and the American Catholic Psychological Association have grown and developed.[13] This edition has been greatly changed in some areas, but the concluding chapter on psychiatry and religion merely repeats the second half of the original chapter with its development of twenty-two religious concepts, including the emphasis throughout on the will of God.[14]

Fundamental Marriage Counseling

In 1958 Cavanagh, with the help of a few other contributors who wrote individual chapters, published *Fundamental Marriage Counseling: A Catholic Viewpoint.*[15] The 602-page volume is encyclopedic in its breadth and scope. The author recognizes that no one is likely to sit down and read the book from cover to cover. The volume supplies the marriage counselor with all the information and data necessary for carrying out that role. The book appeals to all specialties without being complete in any one specialty.[16] Ironically, the discussion of counseling, pastoral counseling, and marriage counseling takes up only the first comparatively short chapter of the book.[17] Perhaps the author was already intending to devote a subsequent volume to this subject. The book is written for Catholic marriage counselors, but non-Catholics will also find it of help and interest. The author bemoans the fact that there is little or no preparation and training for the vocation of marriage. This book is to help counselors with premarital training and to assist them in helping couples with marital adjustments. However, prevention is much more significant than cure. Unfortunately, the problems and difficulties confronting married couples today have become even greater in the light of some contemporary social developments.[18]

The book is divided into five sections dealing with the biological aspects of marriage (Cavanagh defends himself against the charge that he has given too great an importance to the biological and medical), the sexual aspects of marriage, fertility in marriage, social aspects of marriage, and religious aspects of marriage. Seven of the thirty-three chapters are written by other contributors.

As one would expect, Cavanagh follows the official teaching of the Catholic Church in the condemnation of artificial contraception and of divorce. The author gives the standard Catholic arguments against contraception but also explains the medical and moral aspects of the rhythm system. He believes, on the basis both of the literature and of his own observations, that the rhythm system is extensively used. If employed intelligently, the method is more effective than the 65 percent effectiveness reported in one study. The Catholic psychiatrist challenges those who complain about having their sex life determined by the calendar. Cavanagh points out the good effects of the rhythm method, including the gaining of self-control which contributes to emotional maturity and the lack of guilt. No ill effects of rhythm are mentioned.[19]

On the morality of rhythm Cavanagh cites at great length the 1951 address of Pope Pius XII. The primary obligation of marriage is the begetting of children, but serious reasons of a medical, eugenic, economic, and social nature can justify the use of the rhythm method. As was his custom, Cavanagh then cited a number of commentaries by theologians trying to make more specific the papal teaching. He quotes at some length the position of Fr. Gerald Kelly, S.J. According to Kelly the positive duty to procreate is considered in the light of, and directed by, the couple's obligation to society. Each couple is morally bound to make an average contribution in terms of the population needs, which Kelly spells out to be perhaps four or five children if possible. To use rhythm to limit the family to four or five children is permissible even without one of the justifying reasons mentioned by the Pope. Cavanagh cannot accept

Kelly's position and favors the more strict opinion of Francis Connell, according to which the divinely imposed obligation to procreation remains substantially unmodified even after a couple has had seven or eight children, providing they have no serious reason for not having more children. Cavanagh then spells out what two theological authorities (Connell and Griese) propose as sufficient causes for the use of rhythm on the basis of the indications proposed by Pope Pius XII.[20]

Fundamental Marriage Counseling does not pretend to be a creative or ground-breaking study. The fact that within a period of eight years this book went through six printings proves how well the author accomplished his goal. *Fundamental Marriage Counseling* was a must for Catholic marriage counselors and found a place on the bookshelves of most priests. The presentation by Cavanagh was clear, precise, up-to-date, and most helpful in supplying the marriage counselor with the relevant medical, psychological, legal, theological, and canonical data.

Looking back on the book more than twenty years later, one can see that it reflects the times in which it was written. Cavanagh insisted that the husband should be the leader and the head of the family not only because of his physical and psychological makeup but also because of the divine injunction. However, Cavanagh also criticized some of the popular understandings of his day and thereby seems quite contemporary. Traditionally in marital love the male is considered the aggressor, the hunter, and the one who takes the initiative, while the female is the hunted, the charmer, and the one who waits to be loved. Our author, however, believes that in marriage the wife who is sexually interested should be just as free as the husband to suggest sexual relations.[21] It is easy but unfair to critique Cavanagh merely from the perspective of our contemporary times.

Yes, *Fundamental Marriage Counseling* does resemble an encyclopedia in its length, layout, and style, but occasionally one sees flashes of the Cavanagh who, as his friends knew, delighted in debunking some traditional understandings. In the midst of a chapter on the marital act dealing with biological and medical data our author in two paragraphs ridicules the American emphasis on the honeymoon. Honeymoons are not only expensive but frequently a fatiguing, boring, and disappointing experience. The best advice for most couples is to spend their honeymoon at home.[22]

Fundamental Pastoral Counseling

The third book of Cavanagh's basic trilogy, *Fundamental Pastoral Counseling: Technic and Psychology*, was published in 1962.[23] Throughout the book Cavanagh insists on the proper descriptions and definitions. Psychiatry is the branch of medical science which deals with persons afflicted with mental disorders. Psychoanalysis aims at eliciting unconscious conflicts and interpreting them to patients by means such as the use of free association, dream interpretation, and the manipulation of the transference phenomena. Psychoanalysis is a specific form of psychotherapy suited only to certain types of diseases. Most psychiatrists are not psychoanalysts and tend to be eclectic in the therapy they use with their patients. The psychologist, unlike the psychiatrist, is not a medical doctor and should not be dealing with the diagnosis and treatment of disease.[24]

In this book, unlike *Fundamental Psychiatry*, Cavanagh gives a brief but important description of the differences between spiritual well-being and mental health, or, as he phrases it, the relationship between the priest and the psychiatrist. Spiritual well-being and mental health are not the same realities. Objective guilt and neurotic guilt are not the same. As the ministrations of the priest do not have for their prime purpose the restoration of mental health, so the treatment given by the psychiatrist does not of itself help the soul's spiritual well-being. The roles played by the pastor and the psychiatrist are complementary, not in opposition but also not interchangeable. [25] Spiritual health and mental health, priest and psychiatrist, like faith and reason, are neither opposed nor identical but are compatible and complementary.

While psychotherapy deals with illness and disease, counseling is concerned with procedures employed with relatively normal people who have personal problems which they feel are beyond self-solution. Cavanagh also accepts further distinctions between education, guidance, and counseling.

Pastoral counseling differs from what our author calls secular counseling because, in addition to the relationship between the counselor and the client, there is also a relationship with God as a third party. The counseling activities of the pastor always bring in this relationship to God and are subordinate to the primary spiritual functioning of the pastor. This special aspect of pastoral counseling gives specific direction to the aims, methods, and techniques of pastoral counseling. The pastoral counselor at times must be directive primarily because of his special role and hence cannot totally accept the exclusively client-centered therapy of Carl Rogers. Cavanagh, in fact, has some problems with client-centered therapy even for the secular therapist. Pastoral counseling should be eclectic and employ a number of different methods. Our author describes the counseling situation and interview stressing the qualities of the pastoral counselor as an empathetic listener.[26]

The pastor as counselor can make his greatest contribution in those areas of conflict which arise out of the frustrations of certain basic human needs such as the need to be loved, to feel secure, and such. To assist the pastoral counselor, *Fundamental Pastoral Counseling* describes the various contemporary schools of psychology and discusses personality development with special emphasis on children, teenagers, and the differences between the sexes.

Cavanagh's primary aim in the book is to describe pastoral counseling and to help equip priests to carry out this function. In a concluding section on personal responsibility the author shows that his mediating role goes in both directions by disagreeing with some psychiatrists who contend that there are no sinners or criminals but only sick people. Specifically, Cavanagh criticizes a statement of the Group for the Advancement of Psychiatry, which is the same group which he staunchly defended in 1950 against the attacks of some Catholics who called this group atheistic and anti-

Christian. In the normal person, our author maintains, the unconscious influences but does not coerce. The normal individual and most neurotic individuals are responsible for their conduct. Free will remains free as long as the person maintains good contact with reality. Responsibility decreases when contact with reality decreases.[27]

Fundamental Pastoral Counseling completes Cavanagh's trilogy of basic books. Here he fills out and develops what had appeared in seminal form in the very short first chapter of *Fundamental Marriage Counseling*.[28] The style is vintage Cavanagh—frequently citing contemporary authors and then drawing his own approach on the basis of and in relation to these others. Cavanagh had been one of the first (if not *the* first) psychiatrist to teach regularly in a Catholic seminary context. Priests needed more than their scriptural, theological, and canonical knowledge. *Fundamental Pastoral Counseling* met a very basic need. The last decades have seen tremendous developments in the pastoral programs existing in Catholic seminaries, but John Cavanagh deserves great credit for being a pioneer in a very important aspect of priestly ministry.

II. Specific Issues

In addition to his three books dealing with the fundamental aspects of psychiatry, marriage counseling, and pastoral counseling, our author dealt with many significant issues which were on the cutting edge of the complex relationship between moral theology and contemporary medicine and psychiatry. In my judgment the most significant issues he considered in his other writings were dying, responsible parenthood, and homosexuality.

Death and Dying

Perhaps the most significant single article written by Cavanagh was "Bene Mori: The Right of the Patient to Die

With Dignity," which originally appeared in the May 1963 issue of *The Linacre Quarterly* and was reprinted in the August 1975 issue of the same journal. This article illustrates our bridge builder at work—this time confronting the medical profession with the Catholic Church's teaching about the right to die with dignity.[29] Cavanagh begins with his own experience as an intern when called to go to the sisters' infirmary to pronounce the death of a nun. The article builds on the theory that the death agony, which many people talk about, is actually a myth. There might be some physical signs of a death agony, but the state of mind of most patients is peaceful when they know that death is near. Death is easy for the dying because the anxiety of not knowing is now overcome. Cavanagh seems willing to admit some of us might challenge this view of the reality of death as peaceful, but all would admit that death ought to be peaceful. The psychiatrist then raises some challenges to the medical profession in terms of questions of death. How many patients has a doctor actually seen die? Too often the physician removes oneself from the dying patient. Why? Is it because of our failure or because our competence is attacked by the very thought of death? The physician should be there when the patient is dying to give help to both the patient and the family.

The biggest problem is the tendency of the medical profession and others not to allow the patient to die in peace but rather to use all possible means and techniques to prolong human existence. Our author defends the thesis that when the dying process (i.e., the time in the course of an irreversible illness when treatment will no longer influence it and death is inevitable) is beyond doubt, the patient should be allowed to die with dignity unencumbered by useless apparatus. Cavanagh is here applying the historically accepted distinction in the Catholic tradition between ordinary and extraordinary means. Only ordinary means of medical care need be employed. In defining the term Cavanagh would have been better to follow the definition of Gerald Kelly whom he does cite elsewhere in this section. Kelly puts into the definition the aspect of the need for a hope of success.

Cavanagh here makes the mistake of many medical people who tend to define extraordinary means on the basis of what is not ordinarily available. Our author recognizes that the concept of extraordinary means does include the condition of the patient and the hope of success, not simply the availability of the means, but he fails to incorporate these important aspects into his definition.

While rejecting euthanasia, the article calls upon the medical profession to promote the idea of *bene mori* — to allow the patient to die peaceably and in dignity. Cavanagh also points out that the primary decision-making here is to be done by the patient and then by the next of kin, but the doctor can offer the proper advice. The article represents Cavanagh at his best, addressing the practices of his medical colleagues on the basis of his theological understandings. Long before death and death with dignity became popular subjects even in the more scientific literature, Cavanagh had considered the question with clarity and compassion.

Responsible Parenthood

Perhaps the most significant theoretical and practical problem in the life of the Catholic Church in the last few decades has been the matter of responsible parenthood and the control of conception. In view of Cavanagh's background and interests he naturally was in the center of this discussion. As already mentioned, *Fundamental Marriage Counseling*, published in 1958, accepted the Catholic moral teaching rejecting contraception and justifying the use of rhythm if there was a sufficient reason to limit the size of one's family. The method can be somewhat effective if used intelligently and even has some advantages, including the building up of self-control and the lack of guilt which comes from the use of artificial contraception.[30]

In the light of Cavanagh's book an article published in the popular Catholic magazine *Marriage*, in September 1960, is most puzzling.[31] As would be expected, the author points out that contraception, sterilization, and abortion cause serious negative psychological effects coming from the same basic causes—frustration and guilt. Our author's approach is entirely a priori and philosophical. The sex act is designed by nature primarily for the procreation of offspring and the needs of the species. On this basis the Catholic tradition has condemned artificial contraception and sterilization as going against the plan of nature.

Cavanagh surprisingly goes further and includes the use of periodic continence or rhythm as frustrating a natural need. After including periodic continence as frustrating a natural end, Cavanagh claims all methods of contraception control make the sex act a purely physical reaction, make sexual pleasure an end in itself, and destroy the "oneness" and "we" of marriage. Even if repressed, the effects of frustration persist. This frustration is especially true when rhythm is used because rhythm forbids sexual relations at the time that the woman's sexual drive is at its greatest— during the period of ovulation. Also there is stress in the long delay waiting for the sterile period. Frustration causes hostility, which in its extreme degree aims at the destruction of the source toward which it is directed. This reaction can lead to feelings of guilt even though no actual guilt is present. At other times in the article Cavanagh limits his discussion to artificial contraception, but he definitely makes the point that even rhythm produces harmful psychological effects.

The article raises a number of questions. He is obviously changing his position on the psychological effect of rhythm. He never explicitly says that rhythm is morally wrong, but he describes rhythm as a frustration of the natural end. It does not seem consistent with his own principles to accept as morally good what is psychologically harmful. Our author maintains that the only psychologically safe method of spacing children is the use of abstinence for limited periods of time. But if rhythm interferes with human desire and therefore produces a psychological disharmony, what about the harmful effects of abstinence? One could conclude that this article represents a very conservative Catholic approach which even raises questions about the use of rhythm.

A 1962 article in *Marriage* discussed the reliability of rhythm in commenting on a recent book of J.G.H. Holt of Holland.[32] Cavanagh first heard about this book in a newspaper article which claimed that the rhythm method gave an unqualified guarantee of safety. Our author strenuously objected to that, but after meeting personally with the Dutch physician, he concluded that Holt's method is quite satisfactory and easy even though it does shorten the safe period in which sexual and marital relations can be had. What is still needed is a very accurate way of determining exactly when ovulation occurs.

Dr. Cavanagh's interest in the issue of responsible parenthood and the church led him to write in 1964, and to publish in 1965, *The Popes, the Pill, and the People: A Documentary Study*.[33] His purpose is merely to explain the facts about the Pill (our author always capitalized Pill), its history, and its present moral status. The teaching of the popes and statements of hierarchies and of some bishops from the 1958 address of Pope Pius XII to 1964 are given. The official teaching and all the theologians maintain that artificial contraception is intrinsically evil. The Pill affects the ovarian function and prevents ovulation, thus making conception impossible. By its very nature the Pill can also have beneficial therapeutic effects on the ovary and the female reproductive system. The moral principle is clear. Direct, temporary sterilization (the Pill ethically speaking is a type of temporary sterilization and not of contraception because it affects the sexual faculty and not the sexual act itself) is wrong. Indirect sterilization can be permitted for a sufficient reason. The treatment of certain menstrual disorders with the Pill is an indirect and permitted sterilization.[34] After summarizing the scientific and medical literature, our author concludes that the Pill is an effective contraceptive with some unpleasant side effects, most of which are not necessarily harmful. After eight years of use no adverse long-term results have been noted.[35]

The book then reports the casuistry which was then current in the theological literature about the ways in which the principle of double effect might justify the use of the Pill. The book cites the opinions of the various theologians, and then in summary conclusions the author generally expresses his opinion. The Pill can morally be used by a married woman to correct an irregular menstrual cycle so that she can more effectively use the rhythm method. He also concludes that the moral consensus does not seem to accept the position of Canon Janssens of Louvain that the nursing mother may use the Pill to guarantee that the normal condition of anovulation during lactation will truly be present. The book concludes with a survey of the papal natural-law arguments condemning artificial contraception. Pope Paul VI has announced that the Pill as a means to control conception is now under study. Further definitive comment on this must come from the pope or from the Second Vatican Council which was then in progress.[36] Throughout the book Cavanagh did not even try to make an argument in favor of using the Pill as a contraceptive.

Cavanagh himself was to play a part in this papal study. On November 20, 1964, he was appointed by a letter from Cardinal Cicognani, the papal secretary of state, to the special papal commission studying problems of population and birth control. At this time many new members were added to the commission to bring its number to 58 members. Cavanagh then participated in the two subsequent meetings of the commission held on March 25-28, 1965, and in the period of April 18 – June 28, 1966.[37]

In the meantime Dr. Cavanagh continued to write and published two articles on the subject in late 1965. A short *Jubilee* article was entitled "The Church Will Not Change."[38] Despite polls showing a majority of Catholics in favor of a change in the teaching of the church against artificial contraception, the American psychiatrist insists that the possibility of change to a large extent exists only in the wishful fantasies of many Catholics and can only be supported by emotional arguments. It is very important for the church leadership in this country, whether clerical or lay, to bring this message of no change to the people; otherwise, the disappointment of many will be great.

An article in *Marriage* again indicates that no change is to be expected.[39] Rhythm can be an effective and satisfactory way of exercising responsible parenthood. Unfortunately rhythm has received a bad press in this country and has been downgraded by priests, physicians, and couples. Now the author wants to hear from successful users about how good rhythm is. His readers can help others to share their success if they will now tell their experience for the benefit of others. The successful users are asked to fill out a questionnaire or to respond in a narrative form to Dr. Cavanagh.

These articles were published after Cavanagh had participated in the papal birth control commission meeting of March 1965. Here he had heard reports from Pat and Patty Crowley, the leaders of the Catholic Family Movement, who were overwhelmed by the strong consensus of the people they contacted from their membership in favor of a change in the church's teaching. At that same meeting other voices were also raised in favor of change.[40]

In spring of 1966 Cavanagh was present at what proved to be the final meeting of the commission and was also reviewing replies from his *Marriage* article request to hear from successful users of rhythm. In the course of the final meeting it became evident that a vast majority of the commissioners were now in favor of change. At the time of their appointment most of the members probably upheld the official teaching, but through common discussion the minds of many had changed.[41] John R. Cavanagh was one of those who changed his position. In a June 20, 1966, letter to Cardinal Heenan of England our author expressed his opinion:

When I ask myself why I changed, it seems that up to three years ago I accepted this teaching without question. Now having studied it, I find it is no longer acceptable. I am in no position to discuss the theological aspects of the problem. The position taken by the majority of the theologians of the commission is very convincing. I would tend to disregard the few negative opinions, because they are held by very rigid individuals in whom change is unlikely.[42]

The response from his questionnaire also had a great effect on Cavanagh. The August 1966 issue of *Marriage* carried his first reaction to the returns sought from successful users of rhythm.[43] The strongly negative response to his questionnaire and the many stories told by his respondents made him wonder if God expected Catholics to suffer so much. (Seven months earlier he had rejected such arguments as emotional.) The responses showed him two things. First, most of the returns, instead of supporting rhythm, strongly opposed it as a satisfactory and effective means of practicing responsible parenthood. Second, the responses showed that the peak of sexual desire in the woman is at the time of ovulation and just before and after menses. The rhythm becomes very frustrating to the woman and her sexual desires and interest. As a clinician Cavanagh concludes, in large part on the basis of this study, that rhythm is productive of serious psychological harm.

Although Cavanagh claims that in large part the response to his article in *Marriage* magazine changed his mind on rhythm and artificial contraception , one assumes there were other factors, especially his participation in the papal commission, as was mentioned in his letter to Cardinal Heenan, and his frequent discussions with many people about this question. Cavanagh appears rightly defensive about the survey, since it was not truly scientific. There neither was a carefully selected sample nor were there any controls.[44] One can only surmise about the influence of his own psychiatric and counseling experience with married Catholics.

In his report on the *Marriage* survey he highlighted just two items — the complaint about rhythm and the time of sexual desire in the female. Of 580 narrative responses to his article 73 percent said that the woman's greatest sexual desire was at the time of ovulation (the unsafe period for rhythm users), and 57 percent of the total found this to be a source of frustration. This frustration aspect was pursued further by Cavanagh in subsequent articles. In addition to the data from the *Marriage* survey he also studied the sexual cycles of thirty married and single women in psychotherapy. Cavanagh in his articles surveys the literature which indicates some diversity about the time of peak sexual desire in the human female. He concludes on the basis of his survey and his studies that there is a consistent rise in the sexual desire of women before and after the menses and in the preovulatory period. Women who practice rhythm in the strict way are deprived of sexual relations until the twenty-first to the twenty-third day of the cycle, which means many are frustrated because of the strong peak of sexual desire in the postmenstrual and preovulatory period. Cavanagh in discussing the peak of sexual desire refers back to his 1960 article about the frustrations involved in the use of rhythm. However in the 1960 article he grounded this frustration both in his philosophical understanding of the nature of the act and in the reality of the sexual desire as experienced by women. In concluding his 1967 article Cavanagh gives six reasons to prove that the rhythm method is more psychologically harmful than other methods of conception control.[45]

On July 29, 1968, Pope Paul VI made public his encyclical *Humanae Vitae* condemning artificial contraception. On August 1 Cavanagh joined with the other American lay members of the papal birth control commission in agreeing in substance, from the viewpoint of their respective competencies, with the statement of those theologians who maintained that one could disagree in theory and in practice with the papal teaching and still be a loyal Roman Catholic. Cavanagh was one of twenty professors from Catholic University who signed that statement of the theologians. These twenty were subsequently subjects of an inquiry mandated by the Board of Trustees of Catholic University to determine if by their actions and declarations they had violated their responsibilities. The inquiry lasted for almost the whole academic year, with the final result that the inquiry board found that the subject professors had acted responsibly.[46]

After *Humanae Vitae* was issued, Cavanagh used his editorials and comments in subsequent issues of the *Bulletin of the Guild of Catholic Psychiatrists* to express his opinions on the encyclical. He cited the dissenting statement by theologians and affirmed that he too had signed the statement and was now "on trial" at Catholic University because of it. An editorial called for the widest possible dialogue in the church and objected to a policy of repression by church authorities. Cavanagh criticized the "bulldozing tactics" of Cardinal O'Boyle; the "ecclesiastical gobbledegook" of the American bishops who lacked the courage to make a clear concise statement; and "attempts at brain washing by the Pope or Hierarchy." It was psychologically unsound for the pope to attempt to reassert his authority on this issue at this time.[47] The strong language obviously reflects the strong feelings of a person who, within a period of three years, had moved away from his position that the church cannot change on artificial contraception.

A 1969 article in *The Linacre Quarterly* does not talk about dissent from the encyclical but rather maintains that the Pill or other contraceptives may be used to prevent a neurosis in a woman who has fear of pregnancy or abnormal anxiety about a future pregnancy. In this case the sterilization is only indirect, since the Pill or the contraceptive is used as a necessary remedy because of the condition of the woman's organism understood in terms of the mental health of the woman. The Pill or contraceptive directly intends to deal with the problem of mental health and not to prevent conception. Thus Cavanagh sees this as an acceptable use of the Pill or contraceptives even in the light of the teaching of the papal encyclical.[48]

This article is curious. Cavanagh here cites Canon Paul Anciaux as favoring this particular use of the Pill to prevent neurosis. In *The Popes, the Pill, and the People* our author had mentioned Anciaux's opinion but then followed it with a refutation from the American Jesuit theologian Joseph Farraher.[49] The basic principles espoused by Cavanagh in his earlier book would have to condemn the use of the Pill in this case. The use is a direct sterilization because here the contraceptive aspect is a necessary means in order to accomplish the good effect of overcoming the abnormal anxiety or fear. Cavanagh never even responds to this objection in his 1969 article. In addition, our author makes two interesting expansions. First, he permits the use of any contraceptive, and not just the Pill, for this purpose. Second, in one case he allows the woman to use an IUD because of the psychiatric needs of her husband. One can safely say that theologians working on the basis of the official papal teaching after *Humanae Vitae* would not allow the use of the Pill or of other contraceptives in these cases.

Why does this article differ so much in tone and substance from his comments in the *Bulletin of the Guild of Catholic Psychiatrists?* The reader can only speculate. One important reason is that Cavanagh was not the editor of *The Linacre Quarterly* and, consequently, did not have the editorial freedom he had in his own journal. An editorial comment after Cavanagh's *Linacre* article indicates that the editor did have a problem with some of Cavanagh's content. Perhaps our author, who had been criticized for his opposition to *Humanae Vitae*, was attempting to provide another way to make sure that troubled people (those whom he had served throughout his professional life) would not be unnecessarily burdened by the problem of artificial contraception.

Cavanagh's discussions over the years on the question of rhythm and of the Catholic teaching on responsible parenthood show not only dramatic changes but also some apparent inconsistencies. At the very minimum these writings indicate the struggle in Cavanagh's own mind over this entire question. Our author experienced the tensions of trying to live out his commitment to bring together faith and reason, and theory and practice.

Homosexuality

A third issue which Cavanagh frequently discussed was homosexuality, but here there is no discernible change or development in his thinking. *Fundamental Psychiatry* (1953) contained a short chapter dealing with the definition, etiology, and treatment of homosexuality.[50] *Fundamental Marriage Counseling* (1958) included a chapter on "Marriage and the Homosexual."[51] Homosexuality is mentioned parenthetically in *Fundamental Pastoral Counseling.*[52] However, in 1966 Cavanagh wrote *Counseling the Invert*, and in 1976 he published a revised edition under the title *Counseling the Homosexual.*[53]

The title of the newer edition is changed from "Invert" to "Homosexual," but Cavanagh gives no explanation for the change. Both editions agree that homosexuals are not perverts because perversion refers to external acts. Homosexuality is a condition of the person, an inversion but not necessarily a perversion.[54] For all practical purposes the material found in the first edition is repeated in the same form in the second edition except for the addition of two chapters written by Father John Harvey and the elimination of one chapter from the second edition. Cavanagh maintains that homosexuality is not a disease *per se* but rather represents a defective development of the personality with a fixation of the libido at an early stage of development.[55] The basic cause of homosexuality is psychological, not physical or genetic.[56] Our author accepts Kinsey's scale of sexuality which poses a scale of 0 to 6 going from exclusive heterosexuality to exclusive homosexuality.[57]

A number of practical problems are discussed in individual chapters. Cavanagh believes that there should be no law against homosexual acts between consenting adults in private.[58] There is no evidence that homosexuals are security risks. A change in the present law would solve the general objections against employing homosexuals in government jobs and even in security-related jobs. However, because of the nature of their sexual drive there is no place for homosexuals in the armed forces.[59] As for the entry of the homosexual into religious life there are no hard and fast rules, but some suggested guidelines to prove the ability of the person to observe chastity and celibacy are proposed.[60] As for marriage, when homosexuality is present in its true form, the couple should be urged not to become married.

Ecclesiastical authorities should give thought to making homosexuality an impediment to marriage.[61]

As for the morality of homosexual acts, the earlier edition merely accepts and briefly relates the officially proposed and traditionally accepted position that homosexual acts are objectively immoral.[62] The newer edition contains a chapter by John Harvey defending this position and disagreeing with newer positions put forth by John McNeill, Gregory Baum, and Charles Curran. Harvey also contributes here a new chapter on the change in the nomenclature by the American Psychiatric Association.[63]

The new edition leaves out only one chapter which appeared in the original, but this chapter on moral responsibility is, in my judgment, very significant. In this chapter Cavanagh made some important distinctions. The genuine homosexual is not responsible for the origin of one's inversion. The state of being a homosexual has no more responsibility about it than the state of being a heterosexual. Our author then proposes a nuanced judgment about subjective moral responsibility for individual acts. The psychotic ordinarily is not responsible for one's acts. In some other cases responsibility is diminished, and this is probably true far more often than was admitted in the past. Much depends on all the variables in the situation.[64] The important distinction between the homosexual orientation and homosexual acts and the nuanced understanding of responsibility for individual acts were subsequently incorporated in the "Principles to Guide Confessors in Questions of Homosexuality" issued by the American Bishops' Committee on Pastoral Research and Practices in 1973. These guidelines are appended to the end of the last chapter in the second edition of Cavanagh's book.[65] However, the reader of the second edition does not see how closely in these respects they follow what Cavanagh himself had proposed earlier.

The treatment of homosexuality is the work of psychotherapy. Cavanagh is cautious about the outcome of treatment and never says what are the percentages and possibil-

ities of changing the homosexual to a heterosexual orientation. Sometimes the aim of therapy should not even be such
a change but only an acceptance of one's condition. The age
and willingness of the person, the nature of the inversion,
and even the financial cost of the therapy are important factors. The chapter then discusses the different kinds of treatment, including both physical and psychological methods.[66]

The pastoral counseling of homosexuals by its very nature
is not geared to the reorientation of the homosexual. The
counselor should be content to have as an ultimate aim the
adjustment of the homosexual to a life of chastity. In the
case of deep psychological disorders the pastor should urge
the homosexual to seek psychiatric help and should collab-
orate with the psychiatrist. Specific guidelines are proposed
for the pastoral counseling of the homosexual. The individual must be urged to admit one's homosexual orientation
and also to recognize that one is not completely determined
and controlled by this condition. All homosexual activity
must stop and previous homosexual companions should be
avoided. The counselor must try to give the homosexual
an insight into his/her homosexual condition and to stress
the role of the will. The homosexual should be urged to
keep silent about the homosexual condition. The counselor is
also called upon to supply a socially and morally acceptable
sublimation.[67]

Cavanagh never tried to run away from the difficult
questions. He was convinced by his own practice, by other
psychiatric evidence, and by the teaching of the church and
of moral theology that homosexual acts are always objectively wrong. On this issue he disagreed with some newer
and somewhat different positions proposed in both the psychiatric and theological literature. I have developed my own
approach to this question in chapter three. However, his
discussion of homosexuality in all its ramifications was
nuanced as illustrated in his distinctions between homosexual orientation and homosexual acts and between morality
and legality. Many of his ideas were accepted by and incor-

porated into the "Principles to Guide Confessors in Questions of Homosexuality" issued by a committee of the American Bishops' Conference.

Conclusion

This assessment of Cavanagh's work and writings has made no claim to be final or complete. By its very nature the evaluation has been limited primarily to a theological perspective. One could and should discuss Cavanagh's work from the perspectives of psychiatry and of counseling. Perhaps there is no one individual who is competent to make such a complete evaluation. This fact in itself is a tribute to the wide-ranging interests of our author.

In his day there can be no doubt that Cavanagh's work was most significant and important. The fact that his books went through so many editions proves how successful he was. There was no one else on the Catholic scene in the United States who wrote more on bringing together psychiatry and religion, moral theology and counseling. He dealt with the important areas of interaction between theory and practice. The topics that interested him were the most significant issues of the day. It is no wonder that Cavanagh's work was so influential and so popular.

What about Cavanagh's impact on the future? I do not think that many people will read Cavanagh in the future. Such is the fate of anyone whose work is primarily that of building bridges for the present. Cavanagh was quite successful in bringing together the disparate areas of theology and of psychiatry, of moral theology and of counseling, of theory and of practice. By definition such people are dealing with the issues of the present but do not pretend to make original or long-lasting contributions.

Dr. Cavanagh was not a professional theologian and made no pretense to be one. However, he was very well read in, and concerned with, the moral theology of his time. On many matters he opted for the middle of the road theological opinions—but not always. He knew well the moral theology of the manuals and the pre-Vatican II approaches, but he was obviously less at home with the changes which began to occur in Catholic theology at the time of the Second Vatican Council.

But in a very true sense the many volumes and publications of John R. Cavanagh transcend the time in which they were written and have important significance for the future. What Cavanagh did in his life and writings the church as a whole and its individual believers should try to do at all times—to show the basic complementarity between faith and reason. Cavanagh, like the Catholic tradition, committed himself to this goal, experienced the tensions of this vocation, but resolutely continued to struggle with such a mission. The number, significance, and intent of his writings constitute a memorable legacy and a great challenge to all of us.

NOTES

1. Bernard Häring, *Free and Faithful in Christ I: General Moral Theology* (New York: Seabury Press, 1978), pp. 45-51.

2. Warren T. Reich, "John R. Cavanagh—Eulogy Delivered at His Funeral," *Linacre Quarterly* 48 (1981): 212-214.

3. John R. Cavanagh, "Mental Nervous Disorders," *The Ecclesiastical Review* 109 (1943): 170-189, 257-271.

4. John R. Cavanagh and James B. McGoldrick, *Fundamental Psychiatry* (Milwaukee: Bruce, 1953); 2nd ed. (Milwaukee: Bruce, 1966).

5. John R. Cavanagh, "The Guild of Catholic Psychiatrists, 1948-1964," *The Bulletin of the Guild of Catholic Psychiatrists* II (1964): 139.

6. John R. Cavanagh, "Psychiatry, Catholic Plan," *The Sign* 30 (November 1950): 19.

7. John R. Cavanagh, "Religion and Psychiatry," *The Bulletin: Georgetown University Medical Center* 6 (May 1953): 137-139.

8. *Fundamental Psychiatry*, pp. 534-538.

9. *Fundamental Psychiatry*, pp. v, vi, 88-93.

10. *Fundamental Psychiatry*, 2nd ed., p. viii.

11. *Fundamental Psychiatry*, pp. 545-547.

12. "Religion and Psychiatry," pp. 137-139.

13. *Fundamental Psychiatry*, 2nd ed., pp. vii, viii.

14. *Fundamental Psychiatry*, 2nd ed., pp. 514-522.

15. John R. Cavanagh, *Fundamental Marriage Counseling: A Catholic Viewpoint* (Milwaukee: Bruce, 1958).

16. *Fundamental Marriage Counseling*, preface, p. vii.

17. *Fundamental Marriage Counseling*, pp. 3-19.

18. *Fundamental Marriage Counseling*, introduction, pp. xi-xxii.

19. *Fundamental Marriage Counseling*, pp. 271-283.

20. *Fundamental Marriage Counseling*, pp. 283-289.

21. *Fundamental Marriage Counseling*, pp. 89-99.

22. *Fundamental Marriage Counseling*, pp. 172, 173.

23. John R. Cavanagh, *Fundamental Pastoral Counseling: Technic and Psychology* (Milwaukee: Bruce, 1962).

24. *Fundamental Pastoral Counseling*, pp. 188-94.

25. *Fundamental Pastoral Counseling*, pp. 183-203.

26. *Fundamental Pastoral Counseling*, pp. 3-93.

27. *Fundamental Pastoral Counseling*, pp. 121-236.

28. *Fundamental Pastoral Counseling*, pp. 239-271.

29. John R. Cavanagh, "Bene Mori: The Right of the Patient to Die with Dignity," *The Linacre Quarterly* 30 (1963): 60-68; reprinted in 42 (1975): 157-167.

30. *Fundamental Marriage Counseling*, p. 283.

31. John R. Cavanagh, "The Psychological Effects of Birth Prevention," *Marriage* 42 (September 1960): 6-12.

32. John R. Cavanagh, "How Reliable is Rhythm?" *Marriage* 44 (November 1962): 10-16.

33. John R. Cavanagh, *The Popes, the Pill and the People: A Documentary Study* (Milwaukee: Bruce, 1965).

34. *The Popes, the Pill and the People*, pp. 1-27, 38-45.

35. *The Popes, the Pill and the People*, pp. 28-37, 46-59.

36. *The Popes, the Pill and the People*, pp. 60-113.

37. William H. Shannon, *The Lively Debate: Response to Humanae Vitae* (New York: Sheed and Ward, 1970), pp. 78-104. In preparing his book Shannon consulted Dr. Cavanagh's files on the commission. Our study of Cavanagh is limited to his published works, but his personal files might be of great importance, especially on this topic of responsible parenthood.

38. John R. Cavanagh, "The Church Will Not Change," *Jubilee* 13 (December 1965): 40, 41.

39. John R. Cavanagh, "Is Rhythm Better Than We Think?" *Marriage* 47 (November 1965): 1-4.

40. John H. Kotre, *Simple Gifts: The Lives of Pat and Patty Crowley* (Kansas City: Andrews and McMeel, 1979), p. 93.

41. Ibid., pp. 89-104; Shannon, *The Lively Debate*, pp. 76-104.

42. Cited in Shannon, *The Lively Debate*, p. 89.

43. John R. Cavanagh, "Special Marriage Report on Rhythm," *Marriage* 48 (August 1966): 36c-36h.

44. John R. Cavanagh, "Rhythm of Sexual Desire in Women," *Aspects of Human Sexuality* 3 (February 1969): 35.

45. John R. Cavanagh, "The Rhythm of Sexual Desire in the Human Female," *The Bulletin of the Guild of Catholic Psychiatrists* 14 (1967): 87-100; *Medical Aspects of Human Sexuality* 3 (February 1969): 29-39.

46. Charles E. Curran, Robert E. Hunt, et al., *Dissent in and for the Church: Theologians and Humanae Vitae* (New York: Sheed and Ward, 1969), especially pp. 8-9.

47. John R. Cavanagh, *The Bulletin of the Guild of Catholic Psychiatrists* 15 (1968): 200-202. 205, 206; 16 (1969): 10, 11, 36, 37. These were his last editorials and comments in *The Bulletin*, for he had previously announced that he would retire as editor with the May 1969 issue.

48. John R. Cavanagh, "Psychiatric Indications for the Use of Contraceptives," *The Linacre Quarterly* 36 (May 1969): 92-99.

49. *The Popes, the Pill and the People*, pp. 62-64.

50. *Fundamental Psychiatry*, pp. 521-529.

51. *Fundamental Marriage Counseling*, pp. 194-208.

52. *Fundamental Pastoral Counseling*, p. 289.

53. John R. Cavanagh, *Counseling the Invert* (Milwaukee: Bruce, 1966); John R. Cavanagh, *Counseling the Homosexual* (Huntington, IN: Our Sunday Visitor, 1977).

54. *Counseling the Invert*, pp. 17-27; *Counseling the Homosexual*, pp. 37-48. In the future, references will be just to the later work, although the material is also found in the earlier, and now out-of-print, edition.

55. *Counseling the Homosexual*, p. 49.

56. *Counseling the Homosexual*, p. 69.

57. *Counseling the Homosexual*, p. 111.

58. *Counseling the Homosexual*, pp. 165-182.

59. *Counseling the Homosexual*, pp. 83-103.

60. *Counseling the Homosexual*, pp. 155-164.

61. *Counseling the Homosexual*, pp. 146-154.

62. *Counseling the Invert*, pp. 255-256.

63. *Counseling the Homosexual*, pp. 222-238; 30-36. It should be noted that Dr. Cavanagh and Fr. Harvey were friends who had worked together for many years.

64. *Counseling the Invert*, pp. 225-250.

65. *Counseling the Homosexual*, pp. 268-281.

66. *Counseling the Homosexual*, pp. 239-251.

67. *Counseling the Homosexual*, pp. 252-268.

9: The Pastoral Minister, the Moral Demands of Discipleship, and the Conscience of the Believer

The question of dissent, diversity, and pluralism within Roman Catholicism has come to the fore in the last fifteen years. Sociological studies have proved the existence of such diversity. Archbishop John R. Quinn of San Francisco, for example, in addressing the International Synod of Bishops in 1980 cited without comment one study of fertile married couples which "concluded that 76.5 percent of American Catholic women (as compared with 79.9 percent of all U.S. women) were using some form of birth regulation, and that 94 percent of these Catholic women were using methods condemned by the encyclical."[1] Especially in the Western world there are many divorced and remarried Catholics who still consider themselves good Catholics and frequent the sacraments of the church. The report of the 1980 National Pastoral Congress of England and Wales recognized this reality and asked the bishops to consider with compassion the desires of such divorced and remarried people to establish unity with the church through the sacraments.[2] In Africa there is much discussion about polygamy and the relationship of polygamists to the eucharist and the church.[3] In many third-world nations there is the question of the relationship of the Christian to the Marxist and revolutionary groups.[4] These are only some of the many practical issues highlighting the fundamental question of the problem of unity and diversity in the church. In addition there are many other questions of a more doctrinal nature, but this chapter will concentrate primarily on questions in the realm of morality and practice.

In many ways there already exists a somewhat abundant literature both on the fundamental problem of unity and diversity in the church and on the particular issues under discussion. The basic problem is often addressed in terms of the question of authority in the church, the role of the hierarchical magisterium, the role of theologians, and the possibility of dissent. Despite this abundant literature in general there has been little or nothing written or discussed about the role of the pastoral minister in the midst of this problem. How does the minister, baptized and/or ordained, in counseling, sacramental preparation, teaching, and sacramental celebration deal with the question of unity and diversity in the church, especially as it affects the conscience of the person the minister is dealing with? No one can deny the tensions which the theoretical issue also creates for the pastoral minister. How does one minister to the divorced and remarried in the parish? How does the minister react to the couple preparing for marriage who casually mention that they have been and are living together now? What does one say to a homosexual couple who want to join the parish? How does one counsel a married man thinking about a vasectomy?

In addition to these issues in the area of sexual ethics problems also arise in the area of social and political ethics. Many Roman Catholics in the United States have expressed their dissatisfaction with some aspects of the American bishops' letter on nuclear weapons, such as the bishops being against any first use of such weapons or their rejection of a limited nuclear war. In Canada there has been disagreement with the statement from a bishops' committee which includes the insistence that "unemployment rather than inflation should be recognized as the number one problem to be tackled in overcoming the present crisis."[5] Perhaps it is a sign of maturity that the questions about dissent and diversity facing the pastoral minister in the first world are no longer only sexual questions.

The results of one survey bear out the significance of this issue of pluralism and dissent for pastoral ministers. A survey of the pastors in the diocese of Chur, Switzerland, reveals that "in the opinion of the pastors, it was they themselves who suffered the most from the publication of the encyclical [*Humanae Vitae*]."[6] In some ways the problem for the pastoral minister is much more difficult than for others because the pastoral minister cannot avoid the issues. One in pastoral ministry necessarily deals with questions of this type every single day. Theologians and others living more in the theoretical realm have the luxury of not dealing with these issues if they do not choose to. The editorial staff of *Le Supplément*, a French journal dealing explicitly with issues in moral theology and associated with the French Association of Moral Theologians, planned their last issue of 1979 to deal with the subject of contemporary Christian sexuality. The editor was quite surprised by the number of authors who turned down requests to write articles on this subject. In the end the journal appeared with only two articles on sexuality and five other articles dealing with different subjects in moral theology. The editor attributes the unwillingness of authors to contribute articles on this subject to the significant cleavage between the official teaching of the church and pastoral practice, between the traditional rules of the church and the actual behavior of Christians.[7] Even if the theologians and others might avoid dealing with the thorny issues involving possible dissent and diversity, the pastoral minister does not have the luxury of being able to ignore them.

I. Understanding the Problem

What precisely is the basic problem and how should one understand it? Often the issue for the pastoral minister is experienced in terms of the tension between the authoritative teaching of the church and the conscience of the individual. Throughout this chapter the discussion will be confined to what is technically called authoritative, noninfallible teaching. The pastoral minister is not merely a private individual, but in the various functions of counseling, teaching, preparing and celebrating the sacraments the pastoral minister truly is a representative of the church and must act and teach in accord with the church. The pastor must be true to the church and at the same time respectful of the conscience of the individual. This experience of the problem is certainly true, but one must understand this experience in a broader perspective.

The Christian is called to be and to live as a disciple of the Lord, to change one's heart and be converted. Christian life involves the living out of this converted existence. The subjective reality of the Christian as a disciple of Christ in the community of the disciples of the church is strongly underscored in all objective sources of theology. The Scriptures call for a fundamental change of heart and the need to produce the fruits of the Spirit. Christianity in the very beginning was often called "the Way." The Didache, one of the oldest and most revered pieces in the patristic literature, talks about the two ways—the way to life and the way to death. Throughout history belonging to the church has meant that the baptized disciples are to act in a special way in accord with their union through the Spirit with Jesus and with one another. The Christian life is the reality which the church proclaims, celebrates in its liturgy, and strives to live in its daily life. Truth is not merely something to be contemplated but something to be done. Praxis has become very important in much of contemporary theology. Too often in the past the emphasis has been only on orthodoxy, but now theology emphasizes also the need for orthopraxis. The individual believer belongs to the church, or community of the disciples of the Lord, and is committed to being truly converted and living in accord with the meaning of discipleship.

There is no doubt that the pastor often experiences the problem in terms of the tension between church teaching and the conscience of the individual. However, a third term must be considered which in a true sense is superior to both the authoritative teaching of the church and the conscience of the individual. This term is the truth and practice of the Christian faith. The Christian conscience is committed to seeking the Christian truth and practice. The hierarchical teaching office in the church exists in the service of Christian truth and practice.

Yves Congar has pointed out a significant development in the understanding of the rule of faith in Catholic history. In modern times the rule of faith as the *quod* (that which is handed down) has been replaced by the *quo* (that by which it has been handed down; namely, the teaching authority of the church). Such an approach gives too much independent weight to the teaching authority in the church and does not see that this teaching office is always in the service of Christian truth and praxis. My understanding of the problem experienced by the pastoral minister is analogous to and based on Congar's understanding of the relationship between the hierarchical teaching office and theologians. Congar insists that the problem of hierarchical magisterium and theologians should not be limited to these two terms but must include a very important third term to which both the others are related and subordinate. "We must think in three terms: above, the truth, the transmitted apostolic faith, confessed, preached, and celebrated. Beneath this, at its service, the 'magisterium' of the apostolic ministry, and the work or the teaching of the theologians, as well as the faith of the faithful."[8]

In an analogous manner in the question we are discussing, the most important reality is the transmitted apostolic faith, confessed, preached, celebrated, and lived. Beneath this, at its service, and committed to it, are both the hierarchical teaching authority of the church and the conscience of the individual believer. Such an understanding in no way calls for a perfect equality between the hierarchical teaching authority and the individual conscience, for the teaching office is a special gift of the Spirit. Traditional Roman Catholic theology has recognized this point by speaking of a presumption in favor of the teaching office. One cannot deny that on a pastoral level the problem is often experienced in terms of the tension between the teaching authority and the conscience of the individual, but both in theory and in practice these two realities are at the service of Christian truth and practice.

Is this really a new problem? The answer is both yes and no. There can be no doubt that to some extent there have always been tensions in the church between church moral teaching and the conscience of the individual members. Individual believers have often had difficulties in living up to the meaning of discipleship. The whole penitential practice in the church attests to some gap between Christian commitment and Christian living. But there are new dimensions today. In many areas some individuals in the church are contesting a particular teaching and disagreeing with it. They will not accept the proposed teaching as a moral norm whether it might be the ban on artificial contraception or the ban on first use of nuclear weapons. In addition the frequency of the tension is much more apparent today.

How can the pastoral minister deal with this underlying tension and the many specific issues which are aspects of it? In some situations the individual person is morally bound to separate oneself from the community of the church. Think, for example, of a young couple who really have no faith but feel they should be married in the church for the sake of their parents. Here the pastoral minister can offer to help them to see the contradiction in their situation and perhaps even explain their situation to their parents, so that they too will understand and accept the decision of the couple not to be married in the church. However, there are other cases in which the individual can and should continue to belong to the community of the church. In all these situations the minister above all needs the great pastoral virtue of prudence.

The purpose of this chapter is not to discuss all these various instances or problems, but rather to supply the pastoral minister with two important tools that might help one deal with the questions. These two tools are the distinction between the realm of pastoral counseling and the realm of moral theology, on the one hand, and the possibility of dissent in the church, on the other hand. The following two sections will develop these two approaches.

II. Pastoral Counseling As Distinct from Moral Theology

The perspective of pastoral counseling is not the same as that of moral theology. Moral theology looks at the objective morality of particular actions. Pastoral counseling must include the data of moral theology but also looks at the subjective culpability, responsibility, and possibilities of the subject.

The distinction between the realm of pastoral counseling and of moral theology is rooted in the complexity of the human act and in the traditional distinction between the objective morality of the act and the subjective responsibility or culpability of the person performing the act. Traditional Catholic moral theology recognized that many factors might reduce, diminish, or even take away subjective culpability. Take the case of drunkenness. All agree that drunkenness is morally wrong, but the alcoholic is not necessarily subjectively culpable and responsible.[9] This traditional distinction in Catholic moral theology is recognized by many others. Philosophy speaks of the causes that justify an act as distinguished from the causes that excuse an act. The justifying causes make the act morally good; the excusing causes diminish or take away subjective culpability and responsibility. Our legal system recognizes the same distinction, since punishments are less when culpability is diminished for any number of reasons.

The prudent confessor has always recognized and employed this distinction. As a result, in practice one could deal with some difficult cases even though one still maintained the objective wrongness of a particular act. In this light the differences between some proposals of situation ethics and traditional Catholic morality are not as great in practice as they might seem at first sight. Joseph Fletcher, the Protestant situation ethicist, made famous in the 1960s the case of Mrs. Bergmeier. Mrs. Bergmeier was imprisoned in Russia after the war while her husband and three children were finally together in postwar Germany, desperately hoping to be reunited with her. She learned that if she became seriously ill or pregnant, she would be released from the prison camp as a liability and sent home. After much thought and prayer she asked a friendly guard to impregnate her. Mrs. Bergmeier became pregnant, was released and reunited with her family, and gave birth to a son, whom they loved more than all the rest with the view that little Dietrich had done more for them than anybody.[10] What would a confessor say to Mrs. Bergmeier? Even the most rigid Jansenistic confessor would probably do no more than assign a nominal penance and tell her not to do it again! But pastoral counseling comes into play before the act. What should Mrs. Bergmeier do? How should a pastoral minister counsel her?

The exact distinction between the level of pastoral counseling and the level of moral theology has really been proposed only briefly and in contemporary times by the noted German moral theologian Bernard Häring. However, this distinction is basically rooted in the subjective and objective aspects of the human act. One very important development in the tradition of moral theology which is especially relevant for this contemporary understanding of the realm of pastoral counseling is the discussion about invincible ignorance even of the natural law. In the eighteenth century the more rigorous and objectivist position maintained there could be no invincible ignorance of even the more remote conclusions of the natural law. The natural law is given, and the individual cannot be invincibly ignorant of its demands. St. Alphonsus, who subsequently became the patron of confessors and of moral theology, defended the possibility of such invincible ignorance by insisting that the law is not promulgated unless the person has certain knowledge of that law. But such certain knowledge of the remote aspects of the moral law can be lacking without any fault.[11]

For Alphonsus an act done in invincible ignorance even against the remote principles of the natural law is formally a good and meritorious act. His reason is that the goodness of an act is determined by the goodness apprehended by the intellect to which the will consents and not by the mere material object of the act. Alphonsus' theological opponents such as Patuzzi and Concina disagree both with his position on this matter and with his invoking the authority of Thomas Aquinas for his position. According to their interpretation of Aquinas whatever is against the law is always bad and is not excused by the fact that it is in accord with conscience. Alphonsus attributes great importance to the human person's apprehension of the law and to the distinction between formal adherence to the divine law and material adherence. A person acting in invincible ignorance is materially violating the law but is formally in accord with it. Since the formal aspect is what determines the moral goodness or badness of an act, such an act for Alphonsus is thus morally good.[12]

On the contemporary theological scene Bernard Häring, a true spiritual son of St. Alphonsus, has made the distinction between the realm of pastoral counseling and the realm of moral theology. In developing his position Häring builds on Alphonsus' concept of invincible ignorance. Alphonsus in the light of his own times understood ignorance in a rather abstract and intellectual sense, but Häring wants to understand invincible ignorance in a more existential sense that embraces the total person. In accord with such an understanding, invincible ignorance is expanded to mean the existential inability of the person to realize a moral obligation.[13]

Bernard Häring understands the modern distinction between pastoral counseling and moral theology in the light of his heavy emphasis on the law of growth in Christian life. The call to conversion and to continual conversion has always been the central part of Häring's moral theology. The dynamism of the Christian life cannot be dealt with by an ethics based only on static external norms. The Christian is called to grow in the change of heart and in one's union of love with God, neighbor, and the world. All the followers of Jesus are called to holiness and to be perfect even as the heavenly Father is perfect. This emphasis on growth will logically call people to go on beyond the minimal requirements of universal law, but at the same time the principle of growth can and should be applied to those who are unable to realize concretely the objective moral good in a particular situation. The German Redemptorist theologian sees this situation in the light of the way Jesus dealt with his disciples. There are many other things I could say to you, but the burden is too great for you to bear at the present time.[14]

Häring not only explains theoretically the difference between pastoral counseling and moral theology but also gives an example or application. In a symposium on abortion James M. Gustafson, the American Protestant ethicist, brought up the case of a pregnant woman in her late twenties. This woman, a lapsed and divorced Catholic, was raped by her former husband and some of his friends. She had experienced perduring emotional problems and now was without a steady job or source of income. Gustafson uses the case to argue against what he describes as the traditional Catholic approach which views the situation as an external judge and does not seem to consider the person and all the other aspects of the case. The Protestant ethicist wants to consider all these aspects — the medical, the legal, the spiritual, and the emotional. Gustafson is opposed to abortion in most cases, but here he concludes with an analogy to killing in war. The conscientious soldier is convinced that he may kill the enemy if necessary in a just war, but such a killing is always mournful. In this abortion case Gustafson is convinced that the life of the defenseless fetus may be taken less justly but more mournfully.[15]

In response to Gustafson's treatment Häring appeals to the different levels of moral discourse which Gustafson himself developed in an earlier article. Following Henry D.

Aiken, Gustafson distinguishes four levels of moral discourse — the expressive-evocative level, the moral level, the ethical level, and the postmoral level. The moral level answers the question: What ought I to do in the situation? The third level, or ethical level, raises the question about the rules or other considerations that justify a particular moral judgment. Most Catholic treatments of the rules governing abortion are on the third or ethical level, but most of Gustafson's consideration in the particular article is on the second or the moral level. Häring sees these different levels as corresponding to the level of pastoral counseling and the level of moral theology.

The Redemptorist theologian claims that on the level of pastoral counseling a Catholic moralist might come to almost the same conclusions and even to almost the same way of friendly discourse as Gustafson. Häring explicitly refers to Alphonsus' teaching that the confessor can leave the penitent in good faith when confronted with an invincible error if pastoral prudence suggests that one's admonition would do more harm than good for the penitent. If owing to the psychological effects of her traumatic experience, this woman cannot accept the moral teaching not to abort, it is possible to leave her in invincible ignorance. While refraining from any rigid judgments, Häring would not advise the person to abort and would not say this is the right decision if the person has made up her mind to abort.[16]

It seems to me that perhaps Häring's closing remarks are not totally in keeping with what he said earlier. He maintains there can be no formal sin in this particular case and quotes his patron to show that God punishes only formal sin. It seems, then, if he is convinced in this case there is no formal sin, he should be willing to say at least this to the person involved.

In my judgment Häring has creatively developed the Catholic tradition in his insistence on the distinction between the level of pastoral counseling and the level of moral theology. Unfortunately, other theologians have not paid much attention to this very significant question, especially for the pastoral minister.[17] However, the hierarchical magisterium has recognized and even employed a distinction of sorts between the moral level and the pastoral level. The occasion for this consideration and distinction by the hierarchical magisterium was the teaching of the papal encyclical *Humanae Vitae* issued by Pope Paul VI in 1968. In this context I am not primarily concerned with what the encyclical says about the specific issue of the morality of contraception, but rather with the emphasis the encyclical gives to the difference between the moral and the pastoral level. This distinction which is found in the encyclical and exists even to a greater degree in the later commentaries by different national groups of bishops can be applied in many other areas by the prudent pastoral minister today.

The distinction between the moral level and the pastoral level is made by the encyclical itself. Section II is entitled "Doctrinal Principles" and discusses the moral teaching, while Section III, "Pastoral Directives," considers the many different pastoral aspects. Among these pastoral aspects is the recognition that the teaching itself will appear to many as difficult or even impossible to follow. The pastoral section directly addresses different people — public authorities, scientists, doctors, bishops, priests, and Christian couples themselves. Couples are reminded of the serious difficulties that they face in trying to live up to God's law. Even if sin should still keep its hold over them, they should not be discouraged but have recourse with humble perseverance to the mercy of God which is poured forth in the sacrament of penance. Priests are advised to proclaim the full Catholic teaching but also to show the patience and goodness the Lord himself showed to people in need. The Lord came not to condemn but to save; he was intransigent with evil but merciful toward individuals.[18]

The encyclical differs from its predecessor *Casti Connubii* issued by Pope Pius XI in 1930 precisely because of its heavy emphasis on the pastoral aspect. Even more than the en-

cyclical itself, the subsequent commentaries by different national conferences of bishops give even more attention to the
pastoral level and definitely go beyond, although not necessarily against, what was said in the pastoral section of the encyclical itself. Since our purpose is not a thoroughgoing
treatment of the encyclical and its aftermath, our discussion
will be limited to examining the statements of two different
bishops' conferences insofar as they deal with the pastoral
aspects of the question.[19]

The commentary issued by the Italian bishops follows the
two parts of *Humanae Vitae*—doctrinal reflection and spiritual and pastoral directives. The document accepts and
praises the papal teaching and then in the second or pastoral
section addresses a number of different groups—theologians, priests, and married couples. Couples who experience
difficulty in living up to the teaching of the church should
not become discouraged. The church, whose function it is to
declare the total and perfect good, does not ignore the fact
that there are laws of growth in doing the good. In striving
for the ideal one will go through imperfect steps and stages.[20]
Note that this position follows Häring's insistence on the law
of growth in the Christian life. One can conclude, although
the Italian bishops do not explicitly draw the conclusion,
that such imperfect acts, while falling short of the ideal and
perfect good and not in material conformity with the moral
norm, can still be formally good acts.

The response of the French bishops to *Humanae Vitae* addresses in a pastoral way both those who accept the encyclical but find themselves unable to respond to its demands and
those who are unable to accept the teaching. In speaking to
the first group the French bishops maintain that contraception can never be a good. It is always a disorder, but this
disorder is not always culpable. The document explains that
the spouses consider themselves confronted by a true conflict
of duties. When one faces a dilemma of duties where one
cannot avoid any evil no matter what is done, traditional
wisdom requires the individual to pursue the greater duty.[21]

There has been much discussion about the exact meaning of this part of the French bishops' statement. Some understand this approach as going beyond the traditional subjective-objective distinction as applied to ignorance and lack of freedom. Josef Fuchs sees here a moral theory according to which the sin of the world as concupiscence in the acting subject brings it about that the choice of evil (not the evil itself) does not count as morally wrong and in the proper sense sinful.[22] I am not too sure if Fuchs' interpretation differs that much from the distinction between the orders of pastoral counseling and of moral theology developed above. However, at the very minimum one can legitimately understand the approach of the French bishops in the light of the pastoral counseling–moral theology distinction.

One resolution of the 1980 Synod of Bishops reminds pastoral ministers to keep in mind the law of gradualness in dealing with married couples. However, there can be no false dichotomy between Catholic teaching and pastoral practice.[23] Pope John Paul II in his homily at the close of the synod and in his apostolic exhortation *Familiaris Consortio* recognizes the pastoral significance of the law of gradualness but also warns against confusing "the law of gradualness" with "the gradualness of the law."[24] In other words, the Pope does not want this pastoral approach to affect the objective order of morality.

At the present time within Roman Catholicism there exists a recognition even by the hierarchical magisterium that there are differences between the moral order and the pastoral order. Bernard Häring has made a most creative and satisfying distinction between the order of pastoral counseling and the order of moral theology. This section has tried to develop this distinction and show its roots in traditional and official Catholic teaching. Even if an act is objectively morally wrong, the formal act or choice of the individual who is existentially unable to realize the moral obligation is morally good. The dangers of abuse of such a distinction are obvious, but abuse does not take away use. The prudent pastor thus has a very significant tool to use in dealing with many of the tensions arising in ministry.

III. Dissent

A second tool that a prudent pastoral minister can use in some situations is the legitimate possibility of dissent within the church. The question centers on the authoritative, noninfallible hierarchical teaching. All would admit that much of the church's moral teaching on specific moral norms (e.g., masturbation is always wrong; the direct killing of the innocent is always wrong) falls into this category. With others I maintain that there has never been and never can be an infallible church teaching on a specific moral issue. However, the difference between these two positions is not all that great in practice.

Much has been written about dissent in the church.[25] This discussion will not attempt to break any new ground from a theoretical perspective but rather will relate the question of dissent to the work of the pastoral minister. The first part will consider the possibility of such dissent in general, and then the second part will briefly discuss the feasibility of dissent in particular situations.

In discussing the possibility of dissent, again it is important to understand the question properly and not merely in terms of opposition between the authoritative church teaching and the conscience of the individual believer. Here too there is the all-important third term—the Christian moral truth to which both the hierarchical teaching role and the individual conscience are subordinated. However, such an understanding does not mean that the teaching of the hierarchical magisterium and the conscience of the individual believer are on exactly the same level. Traditionally Catholic theology has talked about a presumption in favor of the teaching of the hierarchical magisterium on noninfallible issues precisely because of the gift of the Spirit given to the hierarchical office of the church. This presumption itself, however, always cedes to the truth.

There are both theological and ecclesiological reasons grounding the possibility of dissent from authoritative, noninfallible teaching on specific moral issues. The theological reason primarily concerns the area of epistemology. The more specific and complex the problem, the more difficult it is to claim a certitude that excludes the possibility of error. There can be and should be certitude and unanimity in talking about general values and goals such as the right to life. However, the solution of difficult cases by invoking the principle of double effect necessarily involves complex philosophical notions which by their nature are open to development, discussion, and error. It is a basic principle of logic that the more specific and complex the reality, the greater the difficulty in being able to claim certitude.

The ecclesiological grounding of dissent comes from the fact that the hierarchical magisterium itself is the servant of the saving moral truth of the gospel. Recall that we are dealing here only with what has since the nineteenth century been called authoritative or authentic, noninfallible church teaching. The word infallible should make one pause. What is the opposite of infallible? The most obvious response is fallible. By definition this type of teaching has always recognized its fallible nature.

Within recent Catholic theology the Second Vatican Council has insisted on recognizing the hierarchy of truths.[26] An older Catholic theology emphasized the importance of theological notes which in a certain sense tried to indicate how a particular truth related to the core of faith.[27] Specific moral norms by their very nature are not that core and central to the Christian belief within the Roman Catholic community. Thus, one can disagree with such a specific moral norm and not deny the faith. The Canadian bishops specifically mention that those who disagree with some of the conclusions of *Humanae Vitae* are not denying a point of divine and Catholic faith and should not be considered nor consider themselves cut off from the body of the faithful.[28]

The very nature of the hierarchical teaching office in the church and of authoritative, noninfallible teaching together with a recognition that such specific moral norms are not central to divine and Catholic faith grounds the possibility of dissent.

One important point needs to be mentioned. Too often the whole discussion about dissent seems to imply that those in favor of dissent are "liberals" in the church, whereas the "conservatives" are opposed to all dissent. All realize the problems and difficulties with labels such as those of "conservative" and "liberal," but also pastoral ministers are very aware of a reality corresponding somewhat to these terms. There can be no doubt that especially in the areas of sexual morality it has been a case of the "liberals" in the church dissenting from the official hierarchical church teaching. However, now that there has been so much more discussion about social issues, it is interesting to see that the "conservatives" are now talking about dissent from church teaching.

In the United States the first case of public dissent from official, noninfallible hierarchical church teaching was from a "conservative" point of view. In the July 29, 1961, issue of *The National Review* the editor, Mr. William Buckley, criticized the teaching of the encyclical *Mater et Magistra.* Two weeks later the magazine reported the epigrammatic response of some Catholic conservatives to the encyclical: "Mater, si; magistra, no."[29] Buckley's comments touched off some debate within the church about dissent, although the debate quickly subsided. One important contribution to the debate was the book published in 1964 by Gary Wills, *Politics and Catholic Freedom,* which reviewed the controversy over *Mater et Magistra* and ultimately supported the position about the possibility of dissent for Roman Catholics in social and political matters. It is very interesting to note that at that time what might be called the "liberal" position demanded that there be no such thing as dissent from the papal encyclical.[30] In this whole issue of the possibility of dissent the issue is unfortunately too often decided on the basis of whose ox is being gored. The possibility of dissent is ultimately not a question of "liberal" versus "conservative" but the recognition by all that one can disagree with such noninfallible teaching on specific moral questions and still belong to the one, true church of Jesus Christ. My whole thrust is to insist on the catholicity of the church—the church by its very nature is catholic and big. It must have room for "conservatives" and "liberals" within it. There must be room for possible dissent on such issues. The unity of the church is very important, but the unity of the church should not be found in the area of specific moral norms or issues. Chapters five and six showed how the pastoral letter of the American bishops on peace and war has recognized a legitimate pluralism in the church on such specific issues.

Can the pastoral minister who represents the church dissent from official church teaching? The minister, even though not always ordained, is not speaking and acting in one's own name but in the name of the church. In addition, in the celebration of sacramental reconciliation the priest receives faculties from the bishop and absolves in the name of the church. The pastoral minister is not just a private person. Some would maintain that the pastoral minister because of one's role must always teach and act in accord with the official teaching. I disagree. The pastoral minister is a representative of the total church with its hierarchical structure, and such a role demands that the pastor be true to one's calling. The pastoral minister must be true to the self-understanding of the church.

If dissent is a legitimate possibility within the church, then the minister must recognize this fact and explain it to the people. The pastor's responsible action must be based on the many aspects of the pastoral role in the church. The teaching of the hierarchical magisterium must always be presented in a clear and objective way. However, the pastor can at times indicate that in this particular area there is some dissent within the total church. The pastoral minister can at times express in the proper manner one's own personal conviction on the matter.

What about the possibility of dissent on the part of the individual believer who is not a trained theologian? Our discussion is dealing with questions in the moral order, but the ordinary Catholic is not a moral theologian and does not seem to have the necessary expertise to dissent. Such an approach unfortunately overemphasizes the role of the theologian and downplays the role of the individual believer. One does not have to be a theologian or an ethicist in order to make good moral decisions. The primary teacher in the church is the Holy Spirit, and the Spirit dwells in the hearts of all the faithful. The expertise of the theologian is more in the theoretical and systematic realms, but in the practical realm the ordinary Catholic is at no disadvantage when compared to the theologian. I often use the analogy with the relationship of the psychiatrist and the ordinary person to understand better the relationship between the theologian and the baptized Christian. One does not have to be a psychiatrist in order to be a balanced, mature human being. (There are even those who would say that being a psychiatrist might make it more difficult!) The psychiatrist, like the theological ethicist, makes a contribution on the level of theory, systematization, and second-order discourse.

To its great credit the Catholic tradition has never claimed that one has to be a theologian in order to get to heaven or to do the right things in this world. Yes, the individual Christian must be aware of one's limitation, finitude, and sinfulness. Yes, there is a presumption in favor of the hierarchical teaching; but in good conscience an individual Catholic can come to the conclusion to act against a specific moral teaching of the hierarchical magisterium. In making such a decision the individual person would often consult the theologian as the prudent person often consults experts before making one's decision. But the final decision rests with the individual. Is this not what is actually happening in the way in which Catholic married couples are deciding about contraception?

Does not dissent and especially frequent dissent go against the unity of the church and cause scandal? Unfortunately, sociological conditions in countries in which

Roman Catholicism existed in a pluralistic religious situation have tended to identify Roman Catholics precisely in terms of specific moral norms or practices—Mass on Sunday, no meat on Friday, and no contraception. However, all must admit these are not truths pertaining to the core of our faith. As mentioned earlier, the unity of the faith should not be found ultimately on these particular specific moral issues.

What about scandal? Many of those who oppose the possibility of dissent frequently bring up the problem of scandal. Yes, some people are scandalized by dissent in the church. The solution to the problem, however, is to explain to them exactly what is involved and why such dissent is a possibility within the church. There has been an unfortunate tendency in the church to exaggerate the scandal of the weak and not to give enough importance to what might be called the scandal of the strong. According to Andrew M. Greeley a one-third decline in American Catholic religious practice between 1963 and 1974 is linked mostly to the encyclical *Humanae Vitae*. Even those who might not agree with this statistic must recognize that many Catholics have been estranged from the church precisely because of the teaching of *Humanae Vitae*.[31] It would indeed be a scandal if these people thought this cut them off from the church. There is a great need to explain to these and to all the possibility of dissent.

Undoubtedly there are many parishioners who are scandalized by such a possibility, but others are scandalized by the unwillingness to recognize and deal with the actual problem. The prudent pastoral minister must come up with ways to deal with all God's people. Such pastoral approaches should be based on the understanding explained above.

The discussion thus far has considered only the possibility of dissent from authoritative, noninfallible church teaching. The more practical question involves the legitimacy of dissent in a given particular case. Since it is impossible to study in depth all the individual issues, the remainder of this section will briefly mention the more general aspects involved in discerning the legitimacy of dissent in a particular issue or case. Here too one must avoid facile and one-sided solutions. The controlling factor must always be the call of the gospel and moral truth. The very fact that something is only a part of the noninfallible church teaching and is not a matter of divine faith does not mean that it can be dismissed. The failure to give great importance to such teachings would also result in a practical denial of the historical and incarnational nature of the church. The contemporary emphasis on praxis reminds us that historical and concrete moral action is an essential dimension of our Christian belief. The legitimacy of dissent must be proved in every case.

The judgment about the acceptance of dissent in a particular case should follow the process and rules involved in any good conscience decision. Since the individual is striving to know and live the moral truth of discipleship, the basic biblical attitude of readiness to hear the call of God should be the most important attitude of the baptized disciple of the Lord. The individual must ultimately take responsibility for one's own decision, but one must also honestly recognize the limitations that beset all of us — our finitude and our sinfulness. The recognition of these limitations means that the person must be ever vigilant to the need to be truly open to the call of God. The discernment process involves giving a privileged place to the official hierarchical teaching. In addition, the praxis of believers in the community and the work of theologians and ethicists as well as the experience of all people of good will can furnish some wisdom to the individual decision-maker. The individual is never alone but exists primarily in and through the church which is called to be a community of disciples of the Lord. My theory of conscience stresses that the peace and joy of a good conscience constitute the ultimate sign of a good decision, but one must recognize the many pitfalls and dangers that exist in the way of arriving at such true peace of conscience.[32]

In conclusion, the pastoral minister today is faced with many difficulties, not least of which is the more frequently occurring experience of dealing with the tension between the conscience of the individual and the official teaching of the church. This study has tried to understand the problem properly and to suggest two approaches which at times might be used. However, these approaches or tools are quite delicate and call for great prudence on the part of the pastoral minister. Such prudence can never be taught in an article, a textbook, or in a classroom but can only be learned by a prayerful and respectful minister of the gospel and the church in and through one's own experience.

There is another aspect which the prudent minister of the church cannot forget. Part of the consideration here has been based on the law of growth in the Christian life. The entire discussion of this study has considered primarily the lower floor of the level of growth. The prudent and prayerful pastor must recognize the full range of the law of growth in the life of the disciples of the Lord. The minister in the name of the gospel and of the church must challenge and urge all the disciples of the Lord to live out the fullness of the gospel message but at the same time never forget the mercy, forgiveness, and compassion which likewise characterize the gospel and the church.

NOTES

1. Archbishop John R. Quinn, "New Context for Contraception Teaching," *Origins* 10 (October 9, 1980): 263.

2. *Congress Report: The Principal Documents of the 1980 National Pastoral Congress of England and Wales* (London: Catholic Truth Society, 1980), p. 22.

3. See, for example, for both sides of the debate Francisco Javier Urrutia, "Can Polygamy Be Compatible with Christianity?" *AFER: African Ecclesial Review* 23 (1981): 275-291; Eugene Hillman, "Reply," *AFER* 23 (1981): 292-307.

4. John Eagleson, ed., *Christians and Socialism: The Christians for Socialism Movement in Latin America* (Maryknoll, NY: Orbis Books, 1975).

5. Canadian Bishops' Commission, "Alternatives to Present Economic Structures," *Origins* 12 (January 27, 1983): 523.

6. Kajetan Kriech, "A Firsthand Report on the Current Crisis in Catholic Sexual Morality," *Concilium* 100 (1976): 43.

7. F. Refoulé, "Liminaire," *Le Supplément* 131 (Novembre 1979): 425-427.

8. Yves Congar, "A Brief History of the Forms of the Magisterium and Its Relations with Scholars," in *Readings in Moral Theology No. 3: The Magisterium and Morality*, eds. Charles E. Curran and Richard A. McCormick (New York: Paulist Press, 1982), p. 328.

9. Marcellino Zalba, *Theologiae Moralis Summa*, vol. 1: *Theologia Moralis Fundamentalis* (Madrid: Biblioteca de Autores Cristianos, 1952), pp. 103-220.

10. Joseph Fletcher, *Situation Ethics: The New Morality* (Philadelphia: Westminster Press, 1966), pp. 164, 165.

11. Charles E. Curran, *Invincible Ignorance of the Natural Law according to St. Alphonsus* (Rome: Academia Alfonsiana, 1961).

12. Ibid; Zalba, *Theologiae Moralis Summa*, pp. 258, 259. Recall that Catholic moral theology also counseled the confessor to leave the invincibly erroneous penitent in good faith if there was no harm to others, no scandal, and if warning the penitent would do more harm than good.

13. Bernard Häring, "A Theological Evaluation," in *The Morality of Abortion: Legal and Historical Perspectives*, ed. John T. Noonan, Jr. (Cambridge, MA: Harvard University Press, 1970), pp. 139, 140.

14. Bernard Häring, *Shalom: Peace — The Sacrament of Reconciliation* (New York: Farrar, Straus and Giroux, 1968), pp. 39-49.

15. James M. Gustafson, "A Protestant Ethical Approach," in Noonan, *The Morality of Abortion*, pp. 101-122.

16. Häring, "A Theological Evaluation," pp. 140-142.

17. One moral theologian who briefly develops the traditional notion of invincible ignorance along the same lines as Häring is Louis Monden, *Sin, Liberty, and Law* (New York: Sheed and Ward, 1965), pp. 136-141.

18. Pope Paul VI, *On the Regulation of Birth: Humanae Vitae* (Washington: United States Catholic Conference, 1968), pp. 12-19.

19. Some bishops' conferences recognized the possibility of dissent in practice, while others asserted that disobedience to the encyclical is morally wrong. A center group often emphasized pastoral sympathy and consideration for those struggling with the decision. For the development of these categories see William H.

Shannon, *The Lively Debate: Responses to Humanae Vitae* (New York: Sheed and Ward, 1970); Joseph A. Selling, "The Reaction to *Humanae Vitae*: A Study in Special and Fundamental Theology" (S.T.D. dissertation, Catholic University of Louvain, 1977).

20. *N.C. News Service,* September 21, 1968; Shannon, *The Lively Debate,* pp. 122-124.

21. *N.C. News Service,* November 22, 1968; Shannon, *The Lively Debate,* pp. 135, 136.

22. Joseph Fuchs, "The 'Sin of the World' and Normative Morality," *Gregorianum* 61 (1980): 62-68.

23. These resolutions were not officially released, but a version was published in *National Catholic Reporter* 16 (December 12, 1980): 22.

24. Pope John Paul II, *The Role of the Christian Family in the Modern World: Familiaris Consortio* (Boston: St. Paul Editions, 1982), n. 34, p. 56.

25. For reactions to *Humanae Vitae* by bishops and theologians, including the recognition of the possibility of dissent on this issue, see Shannon and Selling. For a collection of articles giving different positions see Charles E. Curran and Richard A. McCormick, eds., *Readings in Moral Theology No. 3: The Magisterium and Morality* (New York: Paulist Press, 1982).

26. Decree on Ecumenism, n. 11.

27. Sixtus Cartechini, *De Valore Notarum Theologicarum* (Rome: Gregorian University Press, 1951).

28. *N.C. News Service,* October 11, 1968; Shannon, *The Lively Debate,* pp. 128-130.

29. "The Week," *National Review* 11 (July 29, 1961): 38; "For the Record," *National Review* 11 (August 12, 1961): 77.

30. Gary Wills, *Politics and Catholic Freedom* (Chicago: Henry Regnery, 1964).

31. Andrew M. Greeley, William C. McCready, Kathleen McCourt, *Catholic Schools in a Declining Church* (Kansas City: Sheed and Ward, 1976), pp. 103-154.

32. For a fuller development of my position on discernment and conscience formation see Charles E. Curran, *Themes in Fundamental Moral Theology* (Notre Dame, IN: University of Notre Dame Press, 1977), pp. 191-231.

Index

257